P9-DNR-596

Oct 9

HUNTINGTON LIBRARY PUBLICATIONS

MEXICO

THE CHALLENGE OF
POVERTY AND ILLITERACY

By RAMÓN EDUARDO RUIZ

THE HUNTINGTON LIBRARY
San Marino, California

1963

Copyright 1963
Henry E. Huntington Library and Art Gallery
San Marino, California

Library of Congress Catalog Card Number 63-12523

The publication of this volume has been aided by a grant
from the Ford Foundation.

Designed by Ward Ritchie
Printed in the U.S.A. by Anderson, Ritchie & Simon

A MI PADRE
QUIEN ME ENSEÑÓ A CONOCER MÉXICO

ACKNOWLEDGMENTS

I AM INDEBTED to the Board of Trustees of the Huntington Library for making possible the publication of this book, and to the American Philosophical Society for a grant during the summer of 1958. Whatever value this study may have has been enhanced immeasurably by Karl M. Schmitt, who read and criticized the entire manuscript, and by Arthur Mann, who offered suggestions. To thank the many Mexicans who gave their time and ideas would be an endless task; the book would not have been written without them. I am particularly grateful to Luis Alvarez Barret and Mario Aguilera Dorante, two able and selfless officials of the Ministry of Public Education, and to Angélica Castro, an anthropologist who has dedicated her life to the Indian of Mexico. Special thanks go to Morris Swadesh, who read the language chapter, and to Manuel Gamio, Juan Comas, and Lauro Zavala for their encouragement and advice. Parts of chapters VII and IX are taken from articles originally published in the *Harvard Educational Review* (Spring 1958) and *Social Research* (Autumn 1958). Obviously, I am responsible for all errors.

Northampton, Massachusetts
May 1962

CONTENTS

		PAGE
Introduction		xi
I.	Background and Challenge	3
II.	The Conservative Pioneers	22
III.	The Socialist School	45
IV.	Business in the Saddle	65
V.	Twentieth-Century Missionaries	88
VI.	Schools for Teachers and Farmers	104
VII.	Nationality, the Indian, and the Educator	123
VIII.	The Noble Experiment	142
IX.	The Struggle for a Universal Language	158
X.	Between Dogma and Doctrine	173
XI.	Assets and Liabilities	195
	Bibliography	217
	Index	227

INTRODUCTION

I

THE UNDERDEVELOPED NATIONS of Latin America, Africa, the Middle East, and the Orient cover a vast area in the world of today. These regions share common, if not identical, problems. Most of them are characterized by great rural poverty, unbalanced economies that favor urban minorities, the concentration of land in the hands of the few, ethnic and language divisions, rampant illiteracy, and ancient traditions that make change difficult. There are stirrings of revolt in these regions; millions are demanding a better way of life. Among the reforms advanced in their behalf is rural education.

Mexico, the subject of this study, offers a particularly good picture of the struggles of an underdeveloped nation, with all of the aforementioned problems, to achieve social and economic change through rural education. The present study is divided into two parts. Chapters I through IV lay the groundwork and give the historical picture since 1910. Chapters V through XI are arranged topically, around questions and problems that arose during those years.

II

Mexico's difficulties stem from the Conquest, though some were there before the coming of the European in 1521. Soldiers and priests, adventurers and wanderers, selfless and dedicated men, fortune hunters and mercenaries conquered for Spain, forming an explosive combination of drives and ambitions that survived for three centuries. When the patriots won independence in 1821, the eclectic character of the conqueror was stamped on Mexican society. The Catholic Church, in particular, represented a major challenge, for it was a political and economic institution that controlled nearly all of the intellectual life of the country. Freedom from Spain brought a clash between the powerful and wealthy church and the newly established and impoverished republic. Not until the war of *La Reforma* in the mid-nineteenth century was the separation of church and state achieved, and then only superficially. Questions touching on education lingered on until the twentieth century. The church-state conflict over who is to control the school is a question that is not yet entirely decided today.

Spain won an Indian empire where millions spoke more than 400 local languages and dialects, many of which survived the Conquest and colonial period and remained entrenched in the twentieth century. Today there are still approximately 4 million Mexicans who speak one of 52 languages or dialects. The multiplicity of languages has represented a major barrier to the advance of public education, one that has confronted Mexico's leaders since the advent of the rural school.

Long before the Orient and Africa had stirred, a social revolution swept over the Mexican countryside, upsetting a system nearly four centuries old. From the Revolution of 1910 to 1920, whose ideology is still a factor in Mexican thought, there emerged a social reform program, the first of its kind in Latin America, antedating in certain respects the Soviet experiment. The Constitution of 1917, the most important single achievement in the history of the Revolution, sanctioned major political and economic changes. There were laws covering land ownership, foreign investors, the Catholic Church, and labor. Alongside of these, and equally important, was a law providing public education for the long-forgotten rural masses.

Legislating an educational program was one accomplishment; getting the schools built was another and more arduous task. In 1920, when the program was organized, Mexico had no background of experience with rural education to draw upon and no teachers for the thousands of schools required to satisfy the hunger for learning in the tiny communities that dotted the countryside. Nor were there programs and ideas to adopt from abroad, for Mexico's needs were peculiarly its own. Mexican policy planners had to begin from scratch, building an educational system around local characteristics and needs. By necessity this called for an experimental approach, which vacillated with the prevailing political and economic philosophies of the groups in power. There were never sufficient funds, for Mexico was poor.

The Constitution makers of 1917 believed that the solution to Mexico's ills lay in taking the land away from the *hacendados*, the feudal barons of their day, and giving it to the peasants, the dispossessed. The land would offer them the means to a better way of life and provide them with a cash surplus to exchange for the industrial goods that Mexican industry, also projected by the reformers, would eventually produce. Reflecting native and foreign ideals, the reformers recognized two types of land ownership: the privately owned small farm and the *ejido*, the communal lands of the Indian village, out of which were organized the largest voluntary collective farms in the world. The success of the reform program, however, rested as much on the rural school as on the land itself, for the average peasant was not a farmer. Because of the nature of the hacienda system, he had mastered only one or two operations on the great estates, usually one-crop plantations. Someone had to show him how to use his land; how to cultivate and water it wisely; how to market his harvest. When collectivist ideas found favor in the halls of government, the peasant had to learn about *ejidal* banks and cooperative societies. If he was to live better, someone had to teach him to build decent housing, to accept the need for sanitation and medical advice, and to give up pulque. This was the role of the rural school, the representative of the Revolution in the isolated village. It could not just stress the three R's; it had to concern itself also with the raising of corn and hogs.

Unlike that in the United States, rural education in Mexico is usually the responsibility of the federal government. While the states and municipalities support schools, a majority of them are in the cities and towns. Rural schools are generally federal schools. Since rural education is in federal hands, the direction comes from Mexico City. At the top of the pyramid is the federal Ministry of Public Education, which rules the Republic-wide network of schools through a vast organization extending to the smallest municipality. Local officials are appointed by Mexico City. Each state has a federal officer in charge of the federal schools. The states are divided into districts or zones, corresponding somewhat to counties in the United States, each with its federal inspector.

At the heart of the system is the Ministry in Mexico City. A political appointee, the minister of education is its titular chief and its spokesman in the president's cabinet. He represents the political aspects of the Ministry. His assistant, the undersecretary, a political appointee from the professional ranks of the Ministry, represents the technical side. He plots policy and handles the problems of the teachers. The *Oficial Mayor*, the third of the top officers, represents the administrative phase. The Ministry is subdivided into departments covering specific kinds of education: primary schools, urban schools, teacher-training schools, and others.

The Ministry is the weather vane of Mexican politics. More than any other federal department, it is often disrupted by political turnovers; for education has never been a simple matter of how to teach the three R's, but a question touching upon economic, social, political, and religious problems. The history of rural education, therefore, offers an excellent picture of the political twists and turns that Mexican leaders have taken over the years. Three periods stand out clearly. From the Constitution of 1917 until about 1933, northerners ruled; they had no taste for radical reforms, but accepted moderate change and particularly rural education, which focused on cultural and social conditions in the village. The northerners were followed by radical collectivist reformers from the south, who destroyed the ancient landholding classes and created a militant school, as much concerned with politics and economics as with learning. After 1941 lawyer-politicians, spokesmen for the rising urban middle class and the new industrialists, and bureaucrats in general won power. They have turned away from the agrarian ideas of the thirties, demanding peace and stability in the countryside. Their rural school tends to copy traditional pedagogical methods and to stress literacy.

Mexico has built thousands of rural schools since the Revolution, and much has been done to bring the rural population into the modern world. Yet traditional evils survive, particularly in the countryside, where the poverty of yesteryear is strong. Forced to wage an uphill and often isolated struggle, especially since 1941, the rural school has not yet eliminated illiteracy; there are more Mexicans today who do not know how to read and write than ever before (and more Mexicans who do than ever before). If anything may be learned from the Mexican experience, perhaps it is that education alone is of scant use in combating problems of underdevelopment unless major social and economic reforms are undertaken simultaneously. What this implies is that education, the traditional panacea of the conservatives, will fail in countries like Mexico without the radical reforms, and especially the land reform advocated by the extreme left, anathema to the ruling classes. Good planning, furthermore, apparently does not guarantee success, for the pitfalls encountered in the execution of programs are enormous among masses of illiterate, disorganized, and indifferent people. Leadership at all levels, therefore, is of paramount importance to the success of any kind of reform program. This the rural school must provide in predominantly rural countries but will not without social and economic stimulation from the top.

MEXICO
THE CHALLENGE OF POVERTY AND ILLITERACY

Chapter I

BACKGROUND AND CHALLENGE

I

Mexico's rural school rose out of the Revolution of 1910, a social upheaval that ravaged the country for almost ten years. Ignited by discontented city reformers and northern rancheros, the spark of rebellion blazed brightly in rural Mexico, where three out of four Mexicans lived in poverty-stricken villages whose life had not changed for centuries. Exploited by an elite of landlords and foreigners, denied the lands of their ancestors, and barred from the classrooms of the time, the peasants filled the ranks of the rebel armies and drove their masters from power. Among the reforms they demanded were land and schools.

For the rulers of the old regime 1910 began as a banner year, marking the centenary of Mexican independence and nearly thirty-five years of prosperity. Oblivious to the discontent rampant in rural Mexico, which the restlessness of urban labor and professional groups magnified, they celebrated, feasting and toasting hundreds of foreign dignitaries and diplomats who had come to pay homage to Porfirio Díaz, spokesman for the elite and master of Mexico. Ernest Gruening reports that they drank "twenty carloads of champagne."[1]

The Mexican elite had ample reason to celebrate. Díaz had accomplished miracles. After more than half a century of chaos and turmoil, he had brought peace, unknown since the day that the Spanish conqueror had departed from Mexico. There were visible signs of progress for everyone to see. An industrial economy was only a dream when Díaz came to power; in 1910 it was a reality. There were more than a hundred cotton mills with thousands of employees. Tobacco factories turned out millions of cigarettes and cigars and tons of pipe tobacco. From the sugar mills came 127,000 tons of refined sugar. There were silk and woolen mills, jute factories, iron foundries, smelters, paper mills, soap factories, breweries, and meat-packing plants. The national income had risen from less than 20 mil-

[1] *Mexico and Its Heritage* (New York, 1928), p. 64.

lion pesos a year to nearly 100 million pesos; there was a surplus in the exchequer of 75 million pesos. Mexico was exporting five times what it had in the past. The railways had grown from 400 to 15,000 miles; telegraph lines had more than quadrupled. There were modern harbors at Tampico, Coatzalcoalcos, and Manzanillo. Before Díaz, Mexico had no credit abroad; now it could borrow all the money it wanted.[2]

Mexico's elite lived in the cities, the showplaces of the old regime. The capital was the heart of the Republic. Mexicans likened it to Paris, and the comparison was good, confessed the indefatigable English lady Ethel Tweedie. While "not so bustling as New York," neither was it as "sleepy as London."[3] If Charles Macomb Flandrau, a coffee planter turned writer, had a less exalted opinion of the city, he acknowledged that its "noises and lights were the noises and lights of a metropolis."[4] There were shops catering to European tastes, an opera house, beautiful parks, wide avenues, and majestic homes. These were "simply spendid," recalled Mrs. Tweedie (p. 231), "patio after patio, stabling for twenty or thirty horses downstairs, suites and suites of apartments!" Servants were counted by the dozens, "forty or fifty for one household!" The families of the elite, with imported tapestries and gold service in their homes, claimed Europe as their own. Their sons were educated in England at Stoneyhurst and Belmont, and some even attended the universities. Men of society copied foreign ways. Some, a flattered Ethel Tweedie observed (p. 146), "looked, dressed, and spoke so much in accordance with English ideas, that it seemed impossible to believe that they are . . . Mexicans." Their sisters had gone to convents abroad and spoke French without the trace of an accent. On a smaller scale the Mexicans of Guadalajara, Puebla, San Luis Potosí, and Monterrey aped the ways of capital society.

Outside of the favored enclaves lived rural Mexico, a backward and underdeveloped land even by the standards of the eighteenth century. A quasi feudalism based on local ways, often harsh and indifferent, characterized the scene, wrote Moisés Sáenz, a principal architect of Mexico's rural school. Here ruled the *hacendado*, who had all of the advantages but few of the responsibilities of the feudal lord. His kingdom was the hacienda, a manorial estate built around the master's castle, a massive edifice of giant walls, turrets,

[2]Ibid., p. 62.

[3]*Mexico As I Saw It* (New York, 1901), p. 144.

[4]*Viva Mexico!* (New York, 1917), p. 281.

and ramparts. The *hacendado*'s quarters, which he used on his visits to the plantation, were filled with imported luxuries and not infrequently equipped with billiard rooms, swimming pools, racetracks, and bullrings. Next door were the manager's house, the church, and the storerooms. Beyond the protection of the mighty walls rose the homes of the workers, often tiny hovels of mud and sticks where "women, children, pigs, and dogs lived in promiscuity."[5]

Friendly and courteous to their kind, the *hacendados* controlled the countryside with an iron hand. There was little that did not belong to them by 1910. By the land laws of 1883 and 1894 millions of acres passed into their hands or those of surveying companies and speculators. While some steps were eventually taken to protect the peasant holdings, the *hacendados* encroached upon the lands of the villages until the fall of Díaz, according to Moisés González Navarro, author of the recent *El porfiriato*.[6] A Mexican economist reported that seventeen families inherited 96 million acres—150,000 square miles—approximately a fifth of Mexico's land, an area larger than Finland, Ecuador, Ireland, Italy, New Zealand, Japan, Norway, Rumania, or Poland. Seven prominent concessionaires in Chihuahua received 35 million acres.[7] By 1910 one per cent of the population had 97 per cent of the national territory.[8]

Their land taken from them, the people of the countryside became serfs: peons, they were called in Mexico. These landless men represented nearly nine tenths of the agricultural population in 1910. Of the 70,000 rural communities, 55,000 were on hacienda lands,[9] two thirds of the population. For "all practical purposes," to quote Eyler Simpson, they were "entirely dependent upon the large estates for their means of holding body and soul together."[10] The hours were long and the wages poor, twenty-five centavos a day on the central mesa, to cite the figure computed by Ernest Gruening.[11] A Mexican economist charged that the peon's buying power was "1,400 per cent

[5]Moisés Sáenz and Herbert I. Priestley, *Some Mexican Problems* (Chicago, 1926), p. 34.

[6]*El porfiriato: La vida social*, in *Historia moderna de México*, ed. Daniel Cosío Villegas [Vol. V] (Mexico, 1957), pp. 205-209.

[7]Cited by Carleton Beals, *Porfirio Díaz: Dictator of Mexico* (Philadelphia, 1932), pp. 300-301.

[8]Ramón Beteta, *Pensamiento y dinámica de la revolución mexicana* (Mexico, 1950), p. 239.

[9]Ibid.

[10]*The Ejido: Mexico's Way Out* (Chapel Hill, N. C., 1937), p. 36.

[11]*Mexico and Its Heritage*, p. 136.

less than that of the American farm laborer of the same class and time."[12] Inasmuch as the peasants were unable to live on this income, they borrowed from their masters, who furnished credit through the *tienda de raya*, the company store. The result was debt peonage, for the laborer could not pay his debt and move away, Flandrau pointed out. If he fled, the *hacendado* had him put in jail by the *jefe político*.[13] Since hundreds of peons were employed on the vast haciendas, their indebtedness was correspondingly large. The debt of the peons on a hacienda in San Luis, which employed nearly a thousand, was $120,000, Ethel Tweedie was told. Anyone who purchased a hacienda of this type, she learned, had to buy the peon's debt; for all practical purposes, the peons were sold as slaves.[14]

John Kenneth Turner, whose *Barbarous Mexico* stirred the anger of thousands of American readers, called peonage a slavery more cruel than that of the antebellum South.[15] There was no security for the peon. The public authorities served the *hacendado*, to whom their appointments were usually submitted for approval. When the peon rebelled against his master, he was turned over to the army.[16] If a crime was committed in the neighborhood and the guilty not captured immediately, the *jefe de operaciones* often punished the first person he caught as a warning to all. On the peninsula of Yucatán, where labor on some haciendas began at four in the morning, peons were flogged frequently, writes González Navarro (p. 226), who also states that a number of local *hacendados* branded their Chinese workers.

Rural Mexico was "set apart and kept apart by a *caste* as defined and rigid as divides society to-day in Hindoostan," observed F. Hopkinson Smith, painter and writer.[17] The legacy of the peasant was poverty and suffering, and he expected nothing else of the future. Flandrau's description of a peasant's hut in southern Mexico told the story. "The house," he wrote, was an "inclosure of bamboo . . . the steep, pointed roof covered with rough, hand-made shingles of soft wood that soon rots and leaks." Offering only slight protection from the wind and rain, the dirt floor was damp and muddy near the walls. There was a *bracero* on one side of the shack, "raised from the ground

---

[12]Cited by Simpson, p. 38.

[13]Flandrau, p. 18.

[14]Tweedie, p. 51.

[15](Chicago, 1910), pp. 34-35.

[16]Emilio Portes Gil, *The Mexican Schools and the Peasantry* (Mexico, 1936), p. 10.

[17]*A White Umbrella in Mexico* (Boston, 1889), p. 66.

on rough legs and filled with hard earth." Fire from green wood smoldered day and night, filling the room with an eye-irritating smoke. On the edges of the *bracero* sat three or four earthenware jugs; the top of the *bracero* was used to bake *tortillas*. For sleeping, frayed *petate* mats of woven palm or rushes were on the ground.[18] Food consisted of beans and local foods seasoned with chili. So rancid was the water in some areas that even the natives did not drink it, preferring to quench their thirst with pulque or another beverage.

Had the hacienda been efficient, some justification might have been found for it, but it was not. Countless observers testified that it was a marginal institution relying on cheap labor for survival. Agriculture, Mexico's chief industry, "remained in the state to which the conquerors had raised it by importing draft cattle to the New World," wrote Gruening. After visiting a number of famous haciendas, he concluded that "the Cortésian innovation of oxen, dragging the wooden plow of Egypt, was the last word in Mexican agronomy, while the native often wielded machete in lieu of spade and hoe." Instead of cultivating his land intensively, the *hacendado* preferred to spread out, using "his political power to enlarge his estate rather than to make it productive, to speculate in foodstuffs rather than to grow them, to exploit labor more and the soil less."[19] Andrés Molina Enríquez, whose *Los grandes problemas nacionales* (Mexico, 1909) shook Mexican complacency, charged that most of the haciendas were inefficiently operated, heavily mortgaged, one-crop holdings, victims of antiquated techniques and poor management.

For their *raison d'être*, like their contemporaries in the United States, the *hacendados* picked a theory that best defended and explained their position. Having decided what they wished to believe, they chose a concoction of Positivism and Social Darwinism to justify it, while accepting Gobineau's racist doctrines uncritically. Herbert Spencer had preached the validity of Darwin's laws for human relations. Life was a struggle for existence: the strong survived and the weak fell by the wayside. This conflict among individuals overlapped into a struggle among the different peoples of the world. Those who survived—races, nations, or individuals—were the sturdy and intelligent, those fitted to rule. By the same token, those eliminated were unfit for power or life.

Social Darwinism's impact on Mexico was tragic. Using Spencer's fable as a guide, the rich and powerful judged themselves virile and

[18]Flandrau, p. 117.

[19]Gruening, *Mexico and Its Heritage,* pp. 134, 133.

strong, typing the poverty-stricken rural population weak and expendable. Because the masses were predominantly of Indian ancestry, and the rulers were not, the apostles of the old regime postulated the superiority of the white man, proceeding to contrast his resplendent civilization with the muck and mire of the native peoples. By 1910 the rulers of Mexico looked abroad for inspiration and guidance, deprecating the native traditions. The result was that a Mexico overwhelmingly rural had no place for its people, which prompted some to say that Mexico was the mother of the foreigner and the stepmother of the Mexican.

Since the poor were the stragglers who held back the march of progress, why waste funds and schools on them, the aristocracy reasoned. So their intellectual needs were ignored. Of a total budget of almost 59 million pesos in 1900, the Ministry of Public Instruction and Justice received less than 2.7 million pesos; War and Marine had nearly six times as much. During the banner year of 1910 the Díaz regime spent less than 7 per cent of its income on education. Nearly 85 per cent of the population was illiterate; the percentage in rural areas soared beyond this. Hundreds of villages had no one able to read and write. Only 5 per cent of the population was in school, one fourth of Mexico's school children. Despite Justo Sierra's cherished Ministry of Public Instruction, established late in the dictatorship, Mexico had schools only in the cities and almost none in the country. What few schools were established represented the efforts of local governors, particularly those of Veracruz, Puebla, and Sonora. Few of them outlived their benefactors. Perhaps this was as it should be, Turner philosophized (p. 329), for "can a hungry baby learn to read and write? What promise does study hold out for a youth born to shoulder a debt of his father and carry it to the end of his days?" In the United States by 1900, meanwhile, the child who did not attend school for at least six years had become a rarity in all but a few remote sections of the country.

Ignorance, beggarly diets, and flimsy housing bred a sick land, with one of the highest mortality rates in the world. In Mexico City, where medical facilities were best, the death rate averaged sixty per thousand. Outside of the metropolis, where doctors seldom ventured, only a tiny minority reached the age of fifty. Millions succumbed in their infancy; millions of others suffered from intestinal disorders, malaria, hookworm, tuberculosis, and syphilis. Existing from day to day, their lives barren of hope, countless Mexicans drank themselves to death. If half of the money spent on pulque and other liquors had gone into food and lodging, Mexico would have been a different land. Yet, as matters stood in many regions, pulque was an essential part of the common people's diet. In the case of children, for whom there was not enough milk available, it frequently meant the difference between life and starvation.

Cut off from the world—Díaz built few roads and no highways, and the railroads running between Mexico City and the United States left vast regions railroadless—rural Mexico, victim of poverty and neglect, remained sullen, superstitious, fatalistic, and distrustful of strangers. Faced with the hostility of a Western-trained minority, it came to fear modern ways, seeking safety in isolation and tradition. Later it would frequently oppose reform with the same tenacity with which it had defended itself for centuries.

Despite the substantial achievements of his era, Díaz had failed. By rejecting his people, he had built an artificial world, from the opera house to the gilded palace. Material progress was a sham, for Mexico was "a country without political freedom . . . without political parties, without any of our cherished guarantees of life, liberty and the pursuit of happiness," to cite Turner (p. 9). Nor did Díaz solve any of the deep-seated social, economic, and political ills that he inherited. "On the contrary," wrote Gruening, "he deepened many of the national vices, stifled what vestiges of evolutionary self-development might have grown out of the labors" of earlier reformers and "inculcated deception, hypocrisy, abasement, and the rule of force."[20]

Yet the responsibility was not all Díaz'. Centuries of Mexican history had nourished almost insoluble difficulties. Díaz' mistake was to turn the country back toward a past that offered nothing to a majority of the population. Aside from some surface differences, Gruening concluded, little had changed since the days of the viceroys. Under the exotic trappings of twentieth-century industrialism, Mexico was still a quasi-feudal state, with "a sixteenth century social structure and a corresponding psychology."[21]

II

Behind Díaz lay a centuries-old story, for Mexico's challenge stems partly from a tragic past. Popular customs had taken shape "when Anglo-Saxons were . . . amazing Caesar's legionaries by painting themselves blue and dancing to the Druid's tune," Howard Cline points out.[22] Traditions were not cast off lightly in the countryside.

[20]Ibid., p. 64.

[21]Ibid.

[22]*The United States and Mexico* (Cambridge, Mass., 1953), p. 3.

Ways of life rooted in yesteryear struggled against the currents of modern civilization, leaving behind eddies of human activity isolated from the world around them.

Long before the coming of the European, man was in Mexico. Stone Age man arrived nearly 20,000 years ago. South of Mexico City, just off the highway to Cuernavaca, rises the pyramid of Cuicuilco, the oldest monument to civilization on the American continent. Judging from investigations of the lava flow that partially covered the pyramid, it may have been there when the Greeks built their Parthenon, almost five centuries before the birth of Christ. Some archaeologists believe that Cuicuilco is a contemporary of the one Cheops erected in Egypt. Scholars have established that the ancestors of the builders of Cuicuilco came to America by way of the Bering Strait; the ancient Mexicans, therefore, were of Asiatic descent.

Other civilizations succeeded the people of Cuicuilco. When the Spaniards landed in Mexico in 1520, there were scores of dissimilar groups. More than four hundred languages and dialects, reflecting distinct usages and manners of thought of as many tribes, testified to the heterogeneity of Mexico. Some of the groups, like the Mayas of Yucatán, had passed their apogee of power; others had not reached it. At the head of these groups was the fabled Aztec confederation, an association of tribute-paying towns and villages centered around Tenochtitlán, now Mexico City. South of the Aztecs there were other groups. Oaxaca was a hodgepodge of tribes, clans, and rulers. There were eighteen dynasties among the Mayas. West of Tenochtitlán the Tarascans battled the powerful Aztecs and held their lines. To the north the warlike Chichimecas plundered at will, hated and feared by the sedentary people of central Mexico. "Small areas formulated the limits of thought," Cline points out (pp. 24-25). "No broadly unifying concepts of religion, politics, or common destiny bound aboriginal Mexico together into any sort of unity. Rather the reverse was true."

The core of pre-Hispanic life was the family; then came the clan, a cluster of families; above them was the tribe, a group of twenty clans that often joined together into a confederation. Pre-Hispanic man lived in small villages and towns, raised maize, beans, and vegetables—and often cotton for weaving—on land held in common, and labored as a serf on the estates of his rulers during parts of the year. There was little individual freedom. Everyone conformed to the wishes of the majority and lived and labored for the common welfare. Those who refused to cooperate were compelled to do so; punishment was severe for the nonconformist. There was no freedom of thought or action. As George C. Vaillant concluded, the Aztecs would have been horrified at the naked isolation of the individual's life in the Western world.[23] On all sides the few ruled the many, with religion and war a vital part of everyone's existence.

Folklore and the arts added strength and beauty to ancient Mexico. Unlike today, there was no art for the sake of art; no class had an exclusive monopoly; everyone shared the delights of form, design, and color. Still a place was found for specialists: painters, sculptors, scholars, and craftsmen of every ilk. Without metal tools or the wheel, the Indians fashioned works of stone richly carved and ornamented. When the Spaniards greeted Montezuma's emissaries at Veracruz, they were amazed at the array of gifts offered them. There were shields and helmets covered with gold, bracelets and collars of precious metals, robes the texture of silk, copper birds and animals decorated with pearls, and wagonloads of fine cotton cloth. Not everyone in pre-Conquest Mexico, however, had reached this stage of civilization. Living next door to the advanced cultures of central and southern Mexico were people of lower civilizations. The northern nomads were no better than savages.

Then came the Conquest. Led by the audacious and capable Hernando Cortés, the Spaniards overwhelmed the ancient Mexicans. Old ruling dynasties were wiped out, pagan cults were ostensibly replaced by Christianity, and Mexicans were made part of feudal Spain. Yet countless traditions, ways of life, and institutions survived. Rather than destroy all vestiges of the old, Spain compromised, superimposing its colonial system on the native scene. From this union emerged a life both European and Indian. As before the Conquest, the minority ruled. On top was an elite of Spaniards; the vassals were the Indians, perhaps as many as 13 million at the time of the Conquest. The victors ruled with an iron fist, often with the aid of Indian caciques, chieftains of pre-Columbian Mexico who exchanged their supremacy of yesterday for the privileges granted them by the Spaniards because they kept the masses at work. With the passage of time the caciques became local petty tyrants, spokesmen for the central authority. To this day their successors are the bane of village politics.

Spain had much to offer America. There were scores of foods: citrus fruits, wheat, all sorts of herbs, vegetables, rice, sugar cane, and olives. Animals of all types arrived with the invasion: oxen, mules and horses, and the humble burro that became the inseparable companion of the peasant. For eating there was beef, mutton, pork, and poultry,

[23]*Aztecs of Mexico* (Garden City, N. Y., 1941), p. 122.

and milk to drink. New tools and techniques made their appearance. From the expert craftsmen of Toledo came the ax to replace the dull stone instrument of pre-Columbian days, while Seville contributed fine saws. Two-wheeled carts soon covered the byways of Mexico, carrying weights no Indian porter could hope to handle. In place of the planting stick there was the wooden plow, which revolutionized farming. Before the coming of the Europeans no one wrote books, and no one could read them. Now there was a printing press turning out books for scholars at the universities. Medicine, clothing, and weapons were among the countless other contributions that transformed Mexico.[24]

At the same time not all that Spain brought proved good. Tangible human considerations fell by the wayside, for great was the psychological blow of defeat and subjugation, concedes Cline. By upsetting cherished native traditions, the Conquest produced an individual and group trauma that survives today.[25] By accepting much from the ancient cults, Christianity healed some of the wounds but not all of them. Barring the unselfish efforts of the sixteenth-century friars, little was done to compensate the Indian for his losses. Despite the undeniable advances that Spain brought, he continued to live much as he had before. The rural corn economy dominant before the Conquest lingered on almost intact. Although the Spaniards employed European methods, the Indians labored as their forefathers had. Worse yet, by expanding the pre-Columbian system of large estates, the Conquest aggravated a growing evil. Seeking to reward the conquerors, the crown gave away large tracts of land. Cortés received 25,000 square miles, which included the valleys of Cuernavaca, Oaxaca, and Toluca, the western side of the Isthmus of Tehuantepec, twenty-two towns and their land, and a population of more than 100,000 souls. Guanajuato, a province of 10,000 square miles, became the property of one of Cortés' lieutenants. Another received a grant of vassals larger than that given Cortés.[26] Out of these grants and the lands won by other Spaniards and their descendants emerged the hacienda of Díaz' time. Though the Indians kept much of their land, which the Laws of the Indies guaranteed them, the haciendas had come to dominate rural Mexico by the time of independence.

Above everything else, Spain gave its blood. Most of the conquerors settled in Mexico and raised their families there. Over the

[24]Cline, pp. 31-32.

[25]Ibid., p. 32.

[26]Gruening, *Mexico and Its Heritage*, p. 115.

years a class of Spaniards born in America—the creole—appeared on the scene, whose local birth put them below those born in Spain. More important, the Spaniards took Indian women as mistresses and even as wives; for the Spaniards, unlike the Anglo-Saxons, overlooked racial differences. From this union came the mestizo, offspring of Spanish father and Indian mother, and infrequently the other way around. Out of this racial intermingling, which has continued until today, a heterogeneous population was born. Since only a minority of Spaniards came to Mexico, perhaps as few as 300,000, the mestizo supplanted Indian and Spaniard as the dominant group. Eventually mestizos had children by others of mixed blood; in some of these children the Indian strain predominated, in others the Spanish. So was born the Mexican, a blending of races and cultures that came to include also the Negro along the tropical coasts where the Spaniard imported slaves.

From this babel of races and groups rose a host of ethnic problems, all tied intimately to economic and social questions. There were classes and castes, Spaniards and Indians, and people different from both and from each other. Most Spaniards belonged to the upper classes, but some were poor. A few mestizos, usually more Spaniard than Indian, climbed the echelons; the majority served the Spaniards and creoles. The peasant, linked by close blood bonds to his Indian forebears, served them all. Some Mexicans lived like Europeans; others had not advanced beyond the age of the Conquest, millions of them knowing only one or two simple Spanish words. In no other spot on earth, to paraphrase José Vasconcelos, father of Mexico's public school system, was there such a coexistence of human types, separated by centuries and even epochs of ethnographical development, people differing in blood, traditions, and habit. Nor was the process of Mexican history, he emphasized, one of orderly and regular growth, the "evolving of one period into the other." Instead a "continuous destruction and substitution of cultures" had taken place.[27] After four centuries of this development, Luis Cabrera could write that there was no such thing as a "Mexican people," but various peoples living at different levels of civilization, levels that demanded study and consideration when national programs were formulated.[28]

Independence in 1821 confirmed the patterns established by the Conquest. Where the Spaniard had ruled, now his American-born

[27] José Vasconcelos and Manuel Gamio, *Aspects of Mexican Civilization* (Chicago, 1926), pp. 3-4.

[28] "The Key to the Mexican Chaos," in Hubert C. Herring and Herbert Weinstock, eds. *Renascent Mexico* (New York, 1935), p. 24.

progeny gave the orders. One set of rulers replaced another and left the system intact. Freed from the Laws of the Indies, the rulers of Republican Mexico won greater power. Landlords expanded their holdings, confiscating additional communal lands and forcing their owners into peonage. Spain had offered three centuries of peace; now chaos prevailed as the outs battled the ins for power. Through all of this the peasants suffered, fighting the local wars that raged and dying as their parents had during colonial days. Little had changed. There were flurries of hope under Valentín Gómez Farías in the 1830's and again when Benito Juárez raised the banners of *La Reforma* in the fifties and won recognition for a mestizo professional class. Neither destroyed the injustices inherent in the economic and political system, and *La Reforma* worsened matters by enacting in the Constitution of 1857 principles of private property used by Díaz and his supporters to strip the Indian of more land. When Díaz came to power in 1876, the scene was ready for him. After more than half a century of unrest the people hungered for peace at any cost. Díaz' price was high.

III

What race, history, and Díaz offered, the land complicated. Mexico was a land of extremes, of sierra and lowlands, heat and cold, desert and tropical jungle. Along both coasts lay gigantic mountain ranges, stretching from the borders of the United States south to the Isthmus of Tehuantepec, where they disappeared to rise again in Chiapas in a veritable forest of mountains and hills. Sheltered by the ranges was the central plateau, rising from 3,000 feet at Ciudad Juárez to over 7,000 feet in the south. Towering volcanic peaks—Popocateptl, Iztaccihuatl, Orizaba, Sangangüey, and Colima—hovered dramatically over the coastal ranges and disrupted the land on the plateau. Lesser volcanoes surrounded the major peaks. Giant ravines stretched inland for hundreds of miles from both coasts. Just 8 per cent of the land was level. Much of the flat country lay in Yucatán or in the north. The mountains occupied two thirds of Mexico's total area, which was about one fifth the size of continental United States.

Because of the mountains, altitude and not latitude dominated Mexican life. Mexicans spoke of going up or down, not of traveling south or north. There were three distinct levels. From sea level to 3,000 feet lay the *tierra caliente*, or the hot lands, usually tropical. Above them to 6,000 feet was the *tierra templada*, or temperate zone, much of which was desert. The *tierra fría*, the cold lands, rose still higher, often barren and inhospitable. At the heart of Mexico was the central mesa, favored by nature and thickly populated. The north was an extension of the mesa but arid except for occasional rains. On the west was the Pacific slope, rich but cut off from the mesa by almost unconquerable mountain ranges; on the east lay the Gulf slope, fertile but unhealthy. Michoacán, Guerrero, Oaxaca, and Chiapas formed the mountainous region of the south. Jutting into the Gulf was the peninsula of Yucatán. Completing the geographic picture was the long and arid arm of Lower California, sparsely populated and isolated from the rest of the country by the Gulf of Lower California and the deserts of Sonora.

Outgrowth of this mosaic was a society of villages. Of the approximately 15 million Mexicans in 1910, nearly four out of five lived in communities of less than 4,000 souls. Almost half of rural Mexico had homes in villages of less than 500 inhabitants; 70 per cent lived in villages of fewer than 1,000.[29] Isolated from each other by mountains and deserts and living in a roadless age, countless nearly independent civilizations thrived, having little in common but the Spanish language, and that only among those using it. There was local uniformity but regional diversity. The community on the rain-swept side of the mountain differed from its neighbor on the dry slope across from it, even though both represented identical ethnic stocks and lived at the same altitude. Neither resembled similar villages above and below them. Frank Tannenbaum has written that the physical geography of Mexico isolated it from the family of nations and Mexicans from one another.[30]

From Ciudad Juárez to the Guatemalan border, Tlaloc, the Aztec god of rain, ruled with grim humor. He made the north a desert; rainfall averaged seven and a half inches a year. On the southern and coastal lowlands of the Gulf of Mexico—Veracruz, Campeche, Tabasco, and the Isthmus of Tehuantepec—he dumped four to ten feet of water annually. There the farmers suffered tropical maladies while the rain leached the land of its plant food and turned it into a green desert harboring disease-ridden villages. Only from Aguascalientes to Mexico City did Tlaloc offer his people the water they craved. Even here farming called for irrigation. Translated into meaningful agricultural terms, these were the facts of the water supply. Two thirds of Mexico's arable land suffered from scarce seasonal rainfall;

[29]Simpson, p. 13.

[30]*Mexico: The Struggle for Peace and Bread* (New York, 1950), p. 3.

crops thrived only during the rainy season. A bare 6 per cent of the arable land lay in regions where irrigation was not required.[31]

Millions of Mexicans had lived on this land for centuries, using primitive farming methods to raise their food. Eventually the soil lost its fertility. As it wasted away, the peasants, desperately in need of arable land, moved up the slopes of their mountains and hills, burning the protective forests in order to plant their seeds. Ignorant of good farming methods, they cut their furrows to run vertically up the slopes. Animals followed the peasants and added to the destruction, and then the rain and wind attacked the defenseless earth. When the land no longer nourished their seeds, the peasants moved higher up the mountains, and the process was repeated.

When conservationists took stock of the situation, erosion had wrecked much of the cropland. At the time of the Conquest, 60 per cent of Mexico was covered with forests; four centuries later, two thirds of them were gone. All Mexico had suffered to some degree. Almost all of Tlaxcala was barren land, where wheat, corn, vegetables, and avocados had flourished before. Nearly 80 per cent of Aguascalientes' arable land had disappeared; Oaxaca had lost 70 per cent of its farming soil, Hidalgo and Guanajuato more than half of theirs. More than 800,000 hectares of former cropland in the state of Mexico and 2 million in Jalisco lay idle, useless for crops of any kind. Puebla, Querétaro, San Luis Potosí, Veracruz, Morelos, Guerrero, and nearly all of the north were victims of erosion.[32]

While Germany and France farmed over two fifths of their land, Italy nearly half, and the United States one fifth, Mexico tilled only slightly more than one sixteenth of its land, about two acres per person in 1910.[33] Nor was the arable land gathered together in large clumps, but rather it was scattered patchlike over the northern plains, the central valleys and peninsular flatlands, and the southern highlands. If there was a shortage of arable land in an always sparsely settled territory, here was one answer. Nature and man had made it so.

Over this scene the trinity of corn, beans, and squash held court. Of the three, corn was lord and master. Corn the tyrant, Lesley Byrd Simpson called it. Although corn covered two thirds of the croplands, Mexico had to import it, buying over 12 million pesos' worth in 1909. Despite the imperative need to raise more, corn production lagged on the haciendas. For the Bajío of Guanajuato, part of Mex-

[31]Tom Gill, *Land Hunger in Mexico* (Washington, D. C., 1951), p. 21.
[32]*Excelsior*, July 15, 1959.
[33]George M. McBride, *The Land Systems of Mexico* (New York, 1923), p. 21.

ico's breadbasket, Alexander von Humboldt had estimated yields of 86 bushels per acre at the close of the colonial period. A century later the harvest brought 9 to 12 bushels an acre.[34] As late as 1930 Iowa produced more corn than all of Mexico.[35] This was not for lack of work, for the peon labored from dawn to dusk; but primitive agricultural techniques were no match for the barren soil.

These problems confronted the reformers of the twentieth century. They and the land combined to create another. By ministering to the needs of a people in a country where only a fraction of the land was arable, the reformers upset nature's equilibrium, the land-to-man ratio of economists. As reforms penetrated downward, millions of Mexicans began to live slightly better than before, and out of this slim upturn in the way of life came a population boom, with disastrous implications for the future of Mexico and of rural education.

Between 1900 and 1925 Mexico had an annual population growth of 0.5 per cent; this jumped to 2.1 per cent in the second quarter of the century and to 2.9 per cent by 1950. Not only was the death rate cut in half but the birth rate began to rise slightly. As statistics indicate, the impact on population totals was tremendous. In 1921 there were 14,334,780 Mexicans; 16,552,722 in 1930; 19,653,552 by 1940; and some 35,000,000 in 1960.

Nearly every Mexican and all parts of the economy felt the impact of the population boom. Despite impressive gains in agriculture, for example, food shortages were not eliminated. Since Mexico had only so much arable land, and limited opportunities for irrigation, additional production could be achieved only with improved farming techniques. Yet mechanization limited the number of workers that agriculture could absorb, and there were more workers to be absorbed each year. The new industries in Mexico City and elsewhere employed a fraction of the working force, so there was chronic unemployment. While the diet of the average Mexican improved, daily per capita intake was inadequate. Manufacturing gains were remarkable, but they did not keep pace with the demand for goods; and manufacturing output lagged for want of an internal market with the purchasing power required to keep it rising. By 1959 population growth represented the major threat to a higher standard of living.[36]

[34]Ibid., p. 39.

[35]Chester Lloyd Jones, "The Economic Position of Mexico," in Hubert C. Herring and Katharine Terrill, eds. *The Genius of Mexico* (New York, 1931), p. 168.

[36]Harold L. Geisert, *Population Problems in Mexico and Central America* (Washington, D. C., 1959), p. 28.

Equally significant, the population explosion held enormous implications for the education program. Despite thousands of new schools, Mexico failed to keep pace with the population challenge. By 1960, to illustrate this point, there were more children out of school than ever before, in the face of the greatest enrollments in Mexican history. Millions used books, magazines, and newspapers for the first time, more than in any other era in local history; yet half of the population could not read or write. Before all was well with the Mexican school, someone would have to put an end to the population boom. But in this land where modern birth control methods were unknown to a majority of the population and remained anathema to millions of loyal Catholics, there was no solution to the population question on the horizon.

IV

Porfirio Díaz' Mexico survived until 1910. Everything had gone well for the dictator until the mild protest of a Coahuila *hacendado*, Francisco I. Madero, toppled his regime. Out of the collapse of Díaz, the bankruptcy of his successor, and the discontent rampant in the countryside flared the Revolution, a struggle that dominated Mexican life until 1920 and whose ideology lingered on after that.

With the Revolution came the rediscovery of Mexico. Gradually Mexicans learned that the disciples of Comte and Social Darwinism had erred, that the environment—an environment forged by individuals and subject to change by individuals—and not heredity, determined success or failure. What was wrong with Mexico was not the Mexican, but a system that had enslaved him and delivered his country to a handful of foreign and native exploiters. There was "stamina and pluck" in the Mexican. Give him social justice and the freedom to think and act on his own, and he would correct the faults of his motherland. Rejecting the foreign tutelage of the past, native ideas won recognition. The Constitution of 1917, the Magna Carta of the Revolution, specifically recognized the Indian *ejido*, the village land system of ancient Mexico. Seeking a native rationale for the school in the village, the reformers resurrected local tradition and folklore, casting aside the European-oriented dialecticism so long honored by the masters of Mexico.

Out of this new respect for things Mexican, which often resembled xenophobia, there emerged a blueprint for the rural school. The ambition of the reformers was to give the rural masses a better way of life. This called for change: the destruction of the haciendas, the division of their lands among the landless, the building of dams and irrigation projects, and the linking by road and highway of thousands of isolated villages. If those benefited did not know how to take advantage of these gains, however, they were wasted. This was the job for the rural school: to provide the people in the village with the learning and wisdom required to use the reforms of the Revolution judiciously. If reform floundered without schools, learning was useless in the absence of economic improvement. Hungry stomachs did not encourage healthy ideals. Despite periodic flights away from it, this philosophy has become the core of Mexican educational thought.

The rural school offered something else. Speaking for a Revolution that publicly eulogized native ways, it could say to the forgotten peasants: "You are Mexicans." By bringing millions of peasants together, as Sáenz put it, the rural school began to integrate Mexico, "that is to teach the people of the mountains and far-away valleys, the millions of people that are Mexicans but are not yet Mexican, to teach them the love of Mexico and the meaning of Mexico."[37] If this dream was less tangible than some others, none had greater apostles, for this was the cherished vision of the men who built Mexico's system of rural schools.

Mexico's rural school saw the light of day in a land that had only sporadically known it. Once in the distant past there had been schools for the people, but to find them one had to delve into the pages of the history books that recorded the activities of the Catholic friars of the sixteenth century. Driven by a selfless humanitarianism and a faith that believed the Indians worthy of redemption, the friars had overcome indifference and greed to found schools for the vanquished. Pedro de Gante had one at Texcoco; San Juan de Letrán was a school for foundlings of mixed blood; Bishop Juan de Zumárraga built a school at Tlaltelolco for the sons of Indian chieftains. Such schools as these drilled their pupils in the fundamentals of Catholicism and the Spanish language. Others, those of Bishop Vasco de Quiroga of Michoacán, for example, also schooled the Indians in the vocational arts. Unfortunately for Mexico, the friars lived ahead of their age. Nowhere in Europe were there public schools, and Catholic Spain was heavily illiterate. Since the colonial Spaniards, like their masters across the seas, knew nothing of public education, the schools of the friars did not outlive them. For the colonists did not want to educate Indians; they wanted cheap and docile labor. Once the crusading ardor of the monks had cooled, the vanquished got few schools.

[37]Sáenz and Priestley, *Some Mexican Problems*, p. 73.

The coming of independence did not alter the picture. In the 1830's Gómez Farías, chief executive in the absence of the tyrant Antonio López de Santa Anna, pushed through school reform but neglected the village. After the return of Santa Anna even educational reform was forgotten until Juárez rekindled interest in schools at mid-century. Some say that Juárez looked beyond the needs of urban groups, visualizing schools for the villages. If he did, the conspiracy of the conservatives and the ambitions of Napoleon III shattered his dream. After Juárez, public officials seldom remembered the village.

Not until the twentieth century did a demand arise for rural schools. Pleas for them were voiced by the precursors of the Revolution, particularly by Ricardo Flores Magón and his followers. Later Andrés Molina Enríquez called attention to the appalling illiteracy. Francisco Belmar's *Sociedad Indianista Mexicana* also advocated rural schools. Díaz' immediate successors, interim-president Francisco León de la Barra and Madero, established a number of rudimentary rural schools, later abandoned. Finally a demand for schools rose from the countryside. The *Plan de Ayala*, voice of the agrarian chieftain Emiliano Zapata, rallied the people around the cry for land and schools.

Faced with a Republic-wide plea for schools and convinced of their necessity, scores of revolutionary chieftains made rural education a major plank in their platforms. When the victors assembled at Querétaro to write a new constitution, many of them called for federal school legislation. To them the illiteracy of rural Mexico symbolized a cultural backwardness, an obstacle to the growth of a modern state. Where newspapers, magazines, and books were meaningless to a majority, there could be no enlightened government, which came only through participation in public affairs by articulate citizens. On the basis of education alone, Mexico lacked the foundations for wise rule. For men of this opinion, the sessions on Article 3, which dealt with the school question, represented the climax of their business at Querétaro.[38] Even lukewarm supporters of public education partially accepted this view. Venustiano Carranza, the conservative self-styled First Chief of the Revolution and later president of Mexico, attended the opening debates on the article. While the debates covered the entire complex of education, the issue was rural education, for the states and municipalities had urban schools. Federal school legislation, therefore, pertained almost exclusively to rural education. Whatever else was involved, the fate of the rural school hung in the balance.

[38]Félix F. Palavicini, *Historia de la constitución de 1917* (Mexico, 1938), I, 225-226.

In the face of the importance attached to learning, what came out of Querétaro represented, paradoxically, a setback for rural education and the first of many mistakes in school policy. As finally enacted, Article 3 merely provided that "primary instruction in public institutions shall be gratuitous." Nothing was done to organize a national network of rural schools. Worse yet, Sierra's cherished Ministry of Public Instruction was abolished. Supporting a weird concoction of centralized authority and regional autonomy. Carranza gave his blessing to local pressure groups that feared federal encroachments upon their prerogatives. Unwilling to accept a federal system of public schools, they prevailed upon him to leave to them the implementation of Article 3. Article 73, which empowered Congress "to establish professional schools of scientific and fine arts, vocational agricultural and trade schools . . . and other institutions of higher learning," carefully omitted primary schools.

Leaving rural education to the states and municipalities made no sense whatsoever, for the local bosses were usually its worst enemy. By delivering rural education into local hands, the men of Querétaro had merely engaged in double talk. Mexico had no genuinely independent local political units. Everything flowed from Mexico City, including the funds that were required to organize schools in the villages. Despite the tributes paid to education at Querétaro, therefore, little was accomplished to make it a reality. Not until more sympathetic leaders replaced Carranza was a federal system of rural education established.

Although the decisions of Querétaro were shortsighted, not all was lost. The Constitution of 1917 publicly recognized the importance of public instruction. If federal responsibility was evaded, the principle was acknowledged. By authorizing federal schools in the Federal District and territories, something was accomplished. Local failure to build schools would eventually compel the federal government to step in, which Carranza's successors did in the 1920's. They were not, as it will be made clear later on, less conservative than Carranza. Like the First Chief, they represented the moderate or conservative side of the Revolution, the political officeholders who had to shoulder the job of reconstruction once the armed struggle had subsided. Unlike their old boss, however, they wisely recognized that the reforms demanded by the hordes who had fought under Zapata and other leaders could not be postponed indefinitely. Caught between pleas for land and schools, they chose to grant the latter. The schools they built came at a time when most Mexicans had tired of reformers, and the world around them had no taste for radical programs.

Chapter II

THE CONSERVATIVE PIONEERS

I

LIKE SUCCESSFUL REVOLUTIONARIES the world over, the Mexican leaders who came to power in the 1920's were not radicals, having weathered the political storms of the past by placating bureaucrat, landlord, and foreigner. They were conservatives, spokesmen for a nebulously defined political democracy based on compromise and evolution. Shunning the leftist agrarian promises of the Constitution of 1917, the Northern Dynasty, which was to rule until 1934, embraced the landlord and businessman as partners of the yeoman farmer of the north. Despite declarations of official concern for his plight, the peasant received a minimum of benefits. It was this Northern Dynasty, paradoxically, that gave birth to Mexico's rural school.

Problems of every variety, which would have taxed the potentates of a rich industrial nation, beset the rulers of the twenties. Either on the local or national scene, Mexico had been at war since 1913. Tired of the military strife, of the pillage and destruction that came with it, the people of village and city hungered for peace. With it there would be time to elevate law above banditry and brutality, the opportunity to bring order out of chaos, and the chance to rebuild a shattered economy.

After a decade of turmoil the Republic lay prostrate. Mining, Mexico's chief source of national income, was on the verge of collapse; exports of minerals had fallen off badly. The agricultural picture was equally drab. Ravaged by marauding bands, their fields burned, their equipment destroyed, countless farms and haciendas lay idle, their owners discouraged and fearful of what the future had in store for them. Their inactivity threatened the national food supply, and hungry peasants filled the ranks of the armies of discontent. Something had to be done immediately to remedy the situation, but the problem was complicated a thousandfold by the lack of funds, for the treasury was bare, with a deficit of nearly 50 million pesos by 1924. What funds there were fell victim to peculation and graft, for honesty seemingly had become a virtue rare among public officials.

Every sector of national life, meanwhile, demanded money: funds and bribes for the army, fat, ambitious, and omnipotent; millions for reconstruction, so that life could begin anew; and millions for reform, lest conflict should erupt again. Faced with challenge from every direction, the rulers of the twenties had to placate a powerful northern neighbor, and the nation of Warren G. Harding and Calvin Coolidge had no sympathy for social experiments, particularly if they threatened American investors in Mexico, of whom there were legions. Angered by Mexican claims, Harding withheld recognition for two long years and gave it only after Mexico promised to respect the oil interests; Coolidge alternated between sending grim notes to the Mexican government and threats of intervention. Not until 1927 were relations between the two governments established on a friendly basis.

Practical considerations as well as personal convictions, therefore, led the rulers of the era to compromise, procrastinate, and renege on the promises of the Revolution. Long overdue reforms were postponed, some for want of funds and personnel, others because they lacked the support of men hostile to them. Unwilling to sponsor fundamental reform, yet aware of the public demand for it, the Northern Dynasty searched diligently for a way out of the dilemma that would quiet the popular clamor and leave the *status quo* intact. By sponsoring a modicum of change, by granting limited reform at critical intervals, and by relying on demagoguery and political chicanery when other means failed, the Northern Dynasty "managed to juggle and talk" its way out of the muddle until the Great Depression toppled its structure.[1]

Partial answers and concessions were the prescriptions. Land reform, for which the Revolution was waged, was blessed as a principle but almost abandoned in practice. Great landlords themselves, the masters of the period envisioned a Republic of private property. If there was something Jeffersonian about their agrarian policy, their overall economic and political blueprint followed the gospel of Hamilton. Their idea of property was that of the mid-nineteenth-century *Reforma*, carried out by the *bourgeoisie*, with dire results for the peasants. Their spokesmen confessed publicly that they believed in a small-property class that would support "the existing order of things" so that capital would have guarantees and freedom to develop.[2]

[1]Cline, p. 201.

[2]Plutarco Elías Calles quoted in New York *Times*, Nov. 27, 1927.

As Howard Cline has written, the architects of the Northern Dynasty were ranchero- and even hacienda-minded. Although they accepted what had been done in land reform—which was almost nothing—they never proposed a full-scale attempt to redistribute the land.[3] They rejected the concept of a permanent *ejido*—the common lands of the village—and had no wish to break up private property, almost exclusively in the hands of the *hacendados,* in order to create *ejidos.* As with Madero before them, "it was the disappearance of the [northern] ranchos, not the elimination of the *ejidos* [under Díaz], that disturbed" them.[4] If on paper they accepted the *ejido,* it was only as a temporary measure to encourage individual land ownership.[5] Land reform, based upon the needs of the Indian, was never an integral part of northern plans. To paraphrase Cline (p. 200), the redemption of the Indian, a question tied closely to the land program, meant placating a few Yaquis rather than entering into a full-blown program that would be of benefit almost exclusively to the central zone.

Until 1927 the Northern Dynasty promised change through political reform, but after the *rapprochement* with the United States even this halfhearted policy was shelved. With the coming of Dwight Morrow to Mexico, banker and partner of the House of Morgan and able goodwill ambassador, the conservative tenor of the regime grew stronger. Some lukewarm measures were passed, but little else. By 1929 the rulers of Mexico had branded agrarian reform a mistake and a failure. Having approved local legislation setting a final date for the end of land redistribution, they affixed their signatures to a federal resolution in 1930 sounding the death knell of the national agrarian program.[6]

There was no organized opposition to the new policy. Politicians at the local levels with their ears cocked to the prevailing winds, business groups, the landed aristocracy, and the few industrialists rallied behind the new dictum. As the National Chamber of Commerce declared, the remedy for Mexico's ills lay in calling a halt to the nonsense of agrarianism and in enacting legislation offering protection to domestic and foreign capital.[7]

Without the redistribution of the land, however, rural reform was

[3]Cline, p. 200.

[4]Charles C. Cumberland, *Mexican Revolution, Genesis under Madero* (Austin, Tex., 1952), p. 209.

[5]Calles quoted in *El Demócrata,* April 18, 1924.

[6]Simpson, p. 118.

[7]*Excelsior,* May 27, 1931.

an empty gesture. Nor had the need for land reform disappeared. Despite the activity of a decade, landholdings of more than 1,000 hectares, which were in the hands of 2,700 individuals, represented 50 per cent of rural property. Nearly one fourth of the rural real estate belonged to 114 proprietors. Foreigners, 0.71 per cent of the population, had 20 per cent of the arable land.[8] Although more than three out of four Mexicans tilled the soil for a living, the lion's share of the national income went to a minority of urban residents, foreigners and natives. Unless this picture was altered, there would be no effective reform in rural Mexico.

Nowhere was this more obvious than on the educational scene. Until the great estates were destroyed, education could stress almost nothing touching upon the fundamental questions of rural Mexico, which were economic in nature. It could do little to change the *status quo*, which rested on the land systems of yesterday. The rural school established, therefore, was a conventional one, evolutionary in character, with a philosophy modeled after those of western Europe and the United States, where the economic and social conditions of the workingman were vastly superior. Economic change, which was desperately needed, was minimized by the pedagogy of the era; education dealt primarily with the social and cultural and advocated long-term improvements rather than radical reform.

II

Two men gave their names to this era. Alvaro Obregón (1921-1924), the one-armed hero of the victory over Pancho Villa at Celaya, and Plutarco Elías Calles (1925-1928), taciturn master of puppet presidents until 1935, came from the north. They spoke for the rulers of Sonora—both were Sonorenses—Chihuahua, and sister states. Like Madero and Carranza before him, Obregón was a great landlord, who had parlayed a chick-pea monopoly into millions of pesos. Calles, once a schoolteacher, represented the ranchero class. As spokesman for landlord and ranchero, they were conservatives. At first Calles was less so than Obregón, yet Calles had forsaken reform by 1929. Both accepted capitalism and urged safeguards for foreign investment; hence the scope of their activities was limited. There was nothing radical about the Revolution under their tutelage, "despite all the froth and vituperation that issued from ... newspaper editorial columns" in the United States.[9]

[8] Beteta, *Pensamiento y dinámica de la revolución*, pp. 239-240.
[9] Gruening, "Emerging Mexico," *Nation*, CXX (June 10, 1925), 650.

Both potentates surrounded themselves with men of like stripe. Alberto Pani, a conservative, dictated policy in the treasury, the key spot in the government. Obregón's cabinet, wrote Ernest Gruening, resembled Harding's.[10] Of Calles' puppet presidents, only Emilio Portes Gil (1929-1930), a lawyer-politician from Tamaulipas, favored land reform. His successor, Pascual Ortiz Rubio, symbolized the conservatives of his age; weak and vacillating, he was removed from office by Calles in 1932. Abelardo Rodríguez, a military figure from Sonora and the last of the puppet presidents, had grown rich from the border tourist trade; as president he did nothing to antagonize his benefactor.

Since the rulers of Mexico feared drastic change, they placed education in the hands of men who shared their antipathy for radical action. It is in this light that José Vasconcelos, the architect of the Revolution's system of public education, and José Manuel Puig Casauranc, minister under Calles, may be understood. Both represented views friendly to those of the Northern Dynasty. Despite obvious similarities, however, the two men were quite different.

Puig Casauranc, a practicing physician famous for his proclivity to enjoy life, was a political appointee, with "no particular qualifications for the supremely important task of directing the nation's education, which requires both preparation and an apostolic devotion."[11] A former member of Congress, he supported Calles over Adolfo de la Huerta in the uprising of 1923 and served as Calles' campaign manager. Calles rewarded Puig's loyalty and labor with the Ministry of Education. "A man of personal attractiveness, of courtly manner, kindly, and both intelligent and adaptable," he made up for his lack of preparation by his willingness to accept the advice of others more qualified than he.[12]

Vasconcelos was a man of ideas, which he put down in scores of books and essays on history, philosophy, and education. He liked to think of himself as the Ulises Criollo of Mexico, a Mexican facsimile of the ancient hero of Greek mythology, which he knew and loved so well. A supporter of the martyred Madero, he had been an original member of the *Ateneo de la Juventud*, that famous group of talented thinkers that repudiated the Positivism of the old regime.

A traditionalist at heart, Vasconcelos believed firmly in the ways of the *bourgeoisie;* he tempered this belief with his Catholic faith. His social gospel was democracy, not that of the United States, but

---

[10]*Mexico and Its Heritage*, p. 661.

[11]Ibid., pp. 660-661.

[12]Ibid., p. 660.

that of the Latin world, a society along the lines of that of José Ortega y Gasset, which recognized the superiority of an aristocracy of learning. His idol was Sarmiento, the headstrong, conservative Argentine statesman of the nineteenth century. In Sarmiento's attacks on the gaucho and the peasant, Vasconcelos saw the basis for Argentina's leadership of the Latin-American world. Like Sarmiento, he was essentially a supporter of the doctrine of *laissez faire*, despite his denunciations of it in later years. But as a Catholic humanist who believed firmly in the equality of all races, he rejected Gobineau's racist theories, which had influenced the middle class of the nineteenth century.

Vasconcelos offered two remedies for the ills of Mexico. There was public education, which was slow to show results, and moral pressure in behalf of a democratic government of honest civilian leaders. You could not educate without honorable men in public office; moral authority was the chief weapon of the teacher, and this was not wielded by the agents of despotism. Salvation lay through political propaganda for citizenship. As Vasconcelos declared, "any race may fall into chaos but that action of moral forces, properly organized, is always strong enough to raise any people to the highest standards."[13]

This strange combination of moralist and planner was not a pedagogue, nor had his ideas prepared him for the Mexican reality. To quote Verna Carleton Millán, "he had been nurtured, like some exotic flower, upon the ripe lusciousness of a decadent European culture."[14] His education was a moral crusade, upholding platonic ideas, stressing the three R's, and scorning Deweyites and American pedagogy in general. Distrustful of what was new in education, he found his inspiration in the ancient Greeks and in the friars of the Conquest.

The classics represented the flower of literature; they were not the exclusive property of the well-to-do but belonged to everyone. So Vasconcelos had printed and distributed the works of Dante, Homer, Cervantes, Pérez Galdós, Rolland, and Tolstoy; the last three were his favorites. Pérez Galdós he called the literary genius of the Spanish people; Rolland provided answers to questions of contemporary life; and Tolstoy represented the "most genuine incarnation of the Christian spirit . . . in our times."[15] But the masters had not written for the Mexican peasants, and their message never reached them.

[13]Vasconcelos and Gamio, *Aspects of Mexican Civilization*, p. 71.

[14]*Mexico Reborn* (Boston, 1939), pp. 44-45.

[15]Universidad Nacional de México, *El movimiento educativo en México* (Mexico, 1922), p. 37.

Pérez Galdós and his friends were out of step with reality, a fact that Millán illustrates beautifully. Obregón and his party, among whom was Vasconcelos, had lost their way in a remote region. After riding all day, the party eventually sighted a tiny hut in the distance. When the party rode up, an old Indian was standing by the door.

"Compadre," Obregón hailed the man. "Can you tell us where we are?"

The man shook his head.

"But what place is this? What town are we near?"

Again the man did not know.

"Were you born here?" Obregón asked.

"Yes."

"And your wife also?"

"Yes."

"So you were born here, your wife was born here. You've both lived out your lives on this spot and yet you don't know where you are?"

"No," the Indian replied indifferently.

"José," said Obregón turning to Vasconcelos who was listening, "make a note of this man so that you can send him a complete edition of the classics you've just edited."[16]

Yet the classics were in keeping with the belief of Vasconcelos that a school did not live by the utilitarian but by the dream. He had scant regard for what he called the Robinson Crusoe attitude of the Anglo-Saxon mind. Mexicans, dreamers by nature, demanded another symbol, which Vasconcelos found in Ulysses. Mexicans needed a general conception of the universe, which the teacher had to help them find by transmitting the knowledge, the norms, and even the spirit to which Mexicans were to adapt themselves. Education might have a place for statistics, work techniques, and science, but it could not stop with these; it must be crowned by ethics and aesthetics.[17]

For Vasconcelos, education was first and foremost a defense of culture, rather than a matter of economics, which the Positivists had stressed under Díaz. He envisaged a school seeking to further Mexico's own brand of culture, which he visualized along Hispanic lines, essentially Spanish and Latin-European. His scale of values excluded the Indian contribution. Mexico was Hispanic; when not, its civilization must be made so. To encourage the development of culture he went out of his way to sponsor Diego Rivera, José Clemente

---

[16]Millán, pp. 44-45.

[17]William R. Crawford, *A Century of Latin-American Thought* (Cambridge, Mass., 1944), p. 263.

Orozco, and David Alfaro Siqueiros, for whom he found funds and walls for their murals. Art was not only for the professionals, but it was an integral part of the school curriculum as well. Local art, too, received encouragement from Vasconcelos, who struggled to revive talents long ignored by others. Out of this art was born a native form of expression genuinely Mexican, far different from and more meaningful than the Hispanic forms visualized by the patron himself.

There was, however, another side, with roots in the work of the early colonial missionaries. Vasco de Quiroga and his cohorts had placed great emphasis on the practical activities of the school, teaching the Indian not only to read and write but to use his hands. From these holy men of the sixteenth century Vasconcelos adopted what practical ideas he had on rural education, ideas which he put to work with the help of others who developed them into specific programs. This was the origin of his famous cultural missions, peripatetic educational groups patterned after the missionary system of the Conquest.

Vasconcelos was the patron of the rural-school idea. Two remarkable pedagogues, Moisés Sáenz and Rafael Ramírez, both of whom became famous under Puig Casauranc, gave form and substance to his dream. Mexican rural education of the twenties, therefore, owes its origins and its early progress, which was substantial in some directions, to a trilogy of leaders. Vasconcelos had the vision; Sáenz and Ramírez, city teachers whom Vasconcelos imbued with the idea, turned the high-blown moral crusade into a down-to-earth attempt to do something about the everyday problems of rural Mexicans.

One other man left his mark on the rural school: Manuel Gamio, a social scientist and chief of Obregón's Bureau of Anthropology. Though not an educator and only briefly in 1925 a member of the Ministry of Education, he helped shape the development of the rural school with his ideas on "integral education." Gamio's theories, however, were never widely upheld until the 1930's.

Moisés Sáenz, undersecretary of education from 1925 to 1930, was a northerner, the son of a moderately wealthy family of Nuevo León. Like Obregón and Calles, whom he served loyally, he represented the cattleman and ranchero of the border states. He was a graduate of the normal school in Jalapa, Veracruz, the best at that time, and later was a student at the Sorbonne, Washington and Jefferson University, and Columbia University. His doctoral dissertation at Columbia Teachers College was a comparative study of secondary education in the United States and Europe.[18] Sáenz rose rap-

[18]Raúl Mejía Zúñiga, *Moisés Sáenz: Educador de México* (Mexico, 1956), pp. 5-6.

idly in the teaching profession, serving as director of education in Guanajuato, as head of the *Preparatoria* in Mexico City, and later as *Oficial Mayor* in the Ministry of Education.

Among the pedagogues of his time, Sáenz was unique. He was a Protestant, an ordained minister. He wanted to convert and save for Protestantism, often as much as he wished to save the peasants from ignorance and disease; hence his program of rural education was characterized by evangelical missionary zeal. Having studied at universities in the United States, he valued American ways, frequently using them in Mexico. Critics and friends alike called him a *pocho*, an Americanized Mexican. Pedagogue and Protestant, Sáenz was an intellectual, too. His books and essays covered a wide range of subjects; a majority dealt with rural questions, education in particular, and the Indian.

With a background similar to that of his patrons, Sáenz was a moderate; his views, nevertheless, reflected a realistic appraisal of the general picture and of reform. As a Protestant, he held to a theology that did not ignore economic questions. While he shunned radical ideas, refusing to support the leftists in the thirties, he recognized that Mexico's plight was the poverty of the countryside. In his opinion, education could not ignore economic problems; it must contribute to their solution. He endeavored to adapt his school to reality by meeting the needs of the village, but as a Protestant clergyman he was also a moral man, equally concerned with the salvation of Mexico's soul, which colored his blueprint for reform.

Sáenz developed a keen understanding of rural people and a genuine appreciation of Indians, whom he learned to prize as individuals and as a group. Like Vasconcelos, he wanted the Indian to take an active part in society; but, in contrast to Vasconcelos, who would have stripped the Indian of his culture, Sáenz sought to conserve the strong features in indigenous life and to combine them with the concepts and customs of the modern world. The Indian was not a ward to shelter or a beast of burden to exploit; he was a human being with a citizen's rights to participate fully in Mexican life and to contribute to the national culture. Translated into pedagogy, this meant the "incorporation of the Indian into civilization," but a civilization formed by merging the European contribution with the Indian background.

Not surprisingly, Sáenz the pedagogue rejected much of Vasconcelos' approach and put the school in the hands of professional educators. With much effort he sought to bring about better organization and more discipline in education, with the result that problems were taken from the bottom, or technical side, and then followed up to the top, or the broad aspect. Vasconcelos had seen the broad view and neglected the technical side. Now the technical phases were improved, but often to the detriment of the whole. Sáenz' struggle to standardize methods gave a certain formality to education but tended to emphasize technical aspects at the expense of the spirit of education. By 1931 more attention was being given to how to teach than what to teach.

Last of the trio was Rafael Ramírez. Lacking the glamour of Vasconcelos and the mystic qualities of Sáenz, Ramírez labored unrecognized behind the scenes. He left a monumental contribution; his admirers call him the father of the Mexican rural school. Proud and haughty, stubborn and difficult, demanding much of those around him, he gave his life to rural education. A man of deep moral convictions, a disadvantage in his relations with others of less integrity, he "swept from the temple that he built the faithless who dared profane it with their shameless presence."[19]

Like Sáenz, Ramírez was a graduate of the normal school in Jalapa, capital of his native state. His teaching career dated back to 1906; he had served as school inspector before the triumph of Obregón. He came to rural education through the cultural missions, which he helped to organize. There he made a name for himself. In 1927 he became chief of Cultural Missions and later head of the Department of Rural Schools, a position he held under Sáenz and his successors until 1935. A student of Dewey and other leading pedagogues, he was a scholar as well, writing numerous articles and books on education, and especially rural education. Some are masterpieces in their subject. A moderate reformer in the twenties, he became a militant exponent of change, the supporter of leftist leaders in the thirties. With abundant opportunity to enrich himself, he died a poor man.

There was the faith of the reformer in Ramírez. If Vasconcelos represented the Catholic preoccupation with the downtrodden and Sáenz the zeal of the Protestant missionary in a Catholic land, Ramírez, a Catholic liberal, was moved to help the poor and oppressed for no other reason than that they needed his help. His dream was a rural school by which to free the peasant of his shackles; "to educate is to redeem," he said. The three R's were not enough for him; he wanted a school concerned with the social and economic betterment of the masses. At first he saw this in terms of the individual, essentially what the moderates had in mind. Later he became an enthusi-

[19]Luis Alvarez Barret, *La obra educativa de don Rafael Ramírez* (Mexico, 1959), p. 1.

astic advocate of an education for the group or community, frequently overlooking the school's obligations to the individual.[20]

John Dewey found a receptive audience in Mexico through Sáenz and Ramírez. Accepting only what it wanted of Dewey, the ruling clique approved his belief in government leadership and his criticism of organized religion, which supported the clique's stand on political and clerical issues. Dewey's book *School and Society*, particularly, had a wide reading public among teachers who came to believe that the solution to Mexico's problems lay in his theory that a child learned best by actual participation rather than by relying upon books and teachers. By 1931, according to Sáenz, Dewey was gospel among Mexican teachers.[21]

The views of Sáenz and Ramírez met with a hearty endorsement from some and a hostile reception from others. Conservatives believed that excessive emphasis had been given to experimentation and science and saw danger ahead for the economic system and the Catholic faith. So there came about a kind of pedagogical war in Mexico between the "progressives" and the traditionalists. Partly because of the new education and the avowed anticlerical stand of Calles, which was aggravated by the adamant position of the church, a religious war erupted in 1927.

III

Mexico's contemporary rural school dates back to 1920. Vasconcelos, appointed rector of the National University by interim-president Adolfo de la Huerta, had accepted the post with the understanding that he had full authority to organize a system of public education. As he said: "No matter how much I should and do recognize the wisdom and knowledge of many professors, I . . . believe that any state . . . that permits extreme neglect to live side by side with great knowledge or wealth is . . . cruel, unjust, and totally barbarous."[22]

Before a federal program of education could be launched, however, a national law had to be written. Article 3 of the Constitution said nothing about a ministry of education, and Carranza had scrapped what federal organization there was in 1917. Vasconcelos began from scratch, revising Article 73 to permit federal officials to establish primary schools throughout the Republic, resurrecting and

[20]Ibid., p. 7.

[21]Sáenz and Priestley, *Some Mexican Problems*, p. 78.

[22]Universidad Nacional, *El movimiento educativo*, p. 6.

perfecting Justo Sierra's old ministry, and convincing Congress that his ideas had merit. Success called for the qualities of legislator, politician, and propagandist; Vasconcelos possessed them all.

Vasconcelos' delight was his blueprint for a federal Ministry of Public Education. He took full credit for it. The idea, he recalled later, had come to him while reading "what Lunacharsky was doing in Russia. But," said Vasconcelos, "I believe that my plan was more compact and organic, more simple in its structure, yet vast and complicated in so far as there was not a single theme which it excluded. I drew it up in a few hours," he went on, "and corrected it several times, but the complete outline came to me in a flash, like lightning that illuminates a complete edifice." So simple and coherent was the plan, confessed Vasconcelos, "that I have been told that when friends of D'Annunzio showed it to him in Italy, he said that it was a *bella ópera de acción social*. And the opinion of poets has always meant very much to me."[23]

Lunacharsky may have been Vasconcelos' inspiration, but there was precedent to build on, too. On the day that Porfirio Díaz was saying good-bye to Mexico from the prow of the *Ypiranga*, interim-president Francisco León de la Barra had affixed his signature to a federal school bill. This was the controversial Law of Rudimentary Education of June 1, 1911, authorizing the establishment of pre-primary two-year rural schools to teach the Indian-speaking population, without distinction as to age and sex, to speak, read, and write Spanish and to handle the fundamentals of arithmetic.[24] Accepted tacitly was the idea of federal responsibility for rural education; it was not the intention of the legislation, however, to supplant local schools with national ones, but simply to establish schools where there were none.[25] For the legislation Congress provided 300,000 pesos, a figure later cut in half. This plan raised a heated public debate, particularly between Gregorio Torres Quintero, distinguished pedagogue and chief of the Office of Rudimentary Instruction under Madero and supporter of the legislation, and Alberto Pani, Madero's undersecretary of education, who spoke for the critics.

The idea was a step forward, declared Torres Quintero. Without adequate funds, this was the only measure possible under the circumstances. Although the beginnings were modest and confined to one group, the program could be enlarged later to include all of the

[23]Vasconcelos, *El desastre* (Mexico, 1938), p. 26.

[24]Alberto J. Pani, *La higiene en México* (Mexico, 1916), p. 157.

[25]Gregorio Torres Quintero, *La instrucción rudimentaria en la república* (Mexico, 1913), pp. 3-4.

rural population. By establishing 1,000 schools annually—the hoped-for number—the needs of the rural population could be satisfied in thirteen years.[26]

Pani and his followers denied this. The plan was nothing more than a belated effort by the old guard to stem the tide of reform by catering to the spectacular problem of the Indian. Not only was the program late in coming, inadequate, and poorly conceived, but its philosophy was inspired by a blind faith in the power of the alphabet.[27] How would reading and writing solve the problems of the Indian, they asked. Even granting the need to read and write, how were two-year schools to teach illiterate Indian-speaking peasants from the hills what city schools had often failed to do in six years? Providing schools only for the Indian-speaking groups brought no benefits to the majority of peasants, equally illiterate.[28] Since school attendance was put on a voluntary basis, how were you going to get the children to come to school? The budget, Pani pointed out, was far too small for what was envisaged, providing one school for every 7,500 kilometers and every 38,000 illiterates.[29] A major error was the abstract character of the education proposed, which would have no practical impact on the community. Unaccompanied by any outside effort to raise living standards, the proposal would merely upset the equilibrium of the countryside. Unless hope for improvement was given the student, it would be a mistake to educate, for this would prepare the ground for demagogues willing to exploit the discontent of the half-educated.[30]

Why not begin with a limited program, asked Pani. Rather than teach the entire Indian population, confine the program to children of school age. Since the Indian had a language barrier, postpone building his schools until a program was organized for Spanish-speaking groups, where less effort and experience were called for. Instead of teaching abstract principles, offer a program with practical application in the rural community. Teach basket weaving and pottery, and give instruction in agriculture and manual labor; make the program of the school reflect the activities and possibilities of the local region.[31] Above all, warned Pani, every effort should be made to

[26]Ibid., p. 27.

[27]Pani, *Mi contribución al nuevo régimen (1910-1933)* (Mexico, 1936), pp. 53, 96.

[28]Pani, *Una encuesta sobre educación popular* (Mexico, 1918), p. 269.

[29]Ibid., p. 18.

[30]Pani, *Mi contribución*, pp. 79-80.

[31]Pani, *La higiene*, pp. 167-168.

bring about "the economic redemption of the proletariat," else education would merely "make men dissatisfied with a life of poverty."[32]

Whatever the merits of the rudimentary-school idea, little came of it. Although Madero and Victoriano Huerta accepted it, few schools were built. Much of the failure was due to the opposition of the states, and particularly of Coahuila, where Governor Venustiano Carranza, later president of Mexico, rejected the proposed schools on the basis that the law infringed the sovereignty of the states, even though less than a third of Coahuila's population could read and write.[33] What benefits there were came out of the controversy stirred by the bill. By debating the rural-school issue in public and writing books and pamphlets about it, Pani, Torres Quintero, and others advertised the problems of rural education and focused on questions later faced by Vasconcelos and his successors.

Something of the rudimentary-school experiment and of Sierra's bureau were incorporated into the proposal for the Ministry of Education that Vasconcelos submitted to Congress. There were to be three major divisions: one included the departments of Urban and Rural Education, with auxiliary offices of Indian Education and Literacy; the other two were Fine Arts and Libraries.[34] Once Congress had approved his suggestions, Vasconcelos proposed to erect his edifice in the old colonial convent of *Nuestra Señora de la Encarnación* on Calle Argentina, which he hoped to remodel as a symbol of what could be done with the past.

"Never in the history of Mexico," asserted *El Demócrata* (September 27, 1920), "had a proposal of such transcendental importance been laid before the public." This was the opening salvo of the long-awaited moral war against ignorance, which every progressive Mexican wanted to eradicate. Others echoed this view, but there was criticism, too. Some wanted a different organization, with greater emphasis on rural education; others felt that city schools would suffer. A minority believed that the Indian had been ignored.[35] But the chief criticism and opposition came from the states, whose spokesmen argued that the bill stepped on their local autonomy.

Friends of the bill rallied to its defense, pointing out that federal schools were preferable to no schools. If the states were worried about their rights, they asked, why had they permitted the govern-

---

[32]*On the Road to Democracy*, trans. J. Palomo Rincón (Mexico, 1918), pp. 123-124.

[33]Torres Quintero, pp. 4-5.

[34]Vasconcelos, *El desastre*, pp. 25-26.

[35]Ibid., p. 71.

ment to sponsor secondary and professional schools within their boundaries, a practice dating back to the nineteenth century? Was the training of engineers and lawyers by the federal government acceptable, but schools for the masses not? Since the states had neglected public education, often for lack of funds, who was to provide schools for the people?[36]

These arguments carried the day in Congress. The proposed Ministry of Public Education received congressional blessing, and federal officials won their battle to establish schools throughout the Republic. Local authorities, however, retained their right to have a separate system of public instruction. Relying on this right, they were later to act independently of the federal program, failing to support the national effort with funds needed to establish local rural schools. The result was often either local neglect of rural education or duplication and waste, a wide range of standards and methods, and litigation. Obregón, who had just assumed the presidency, appointed Vasconcelos chief of the new Ministry of Public Education.

IV

Adopting the blueprint was one thing; getting rural education under way another. Aside from the short-lived experiment with the rudimentary schools, which never got off the ground, there was nothing to build on. The colonial experiments of Vasconcelos' revered monks were far in the past, and Díaz had simply ignored the problem. How to begin? This was the question. Vasconcelos, who never evaded any problem, tackled this one with energy and imagination, seemingly oblivious of the magnitude of the barriers ahead. Without sufficient funds or materials, always in need of qualified and dedicated men, with only his faith in the missionary schools of the colonial era to sustain him, he put together the foundations of a rural school system that by its freshness and originality attracted the attention of the Western world. Determined to provide schools for the children of his native land, he declared—so legend has it—that if the devil had offered to establish schools, he would have welcomed him.

Before Vasconcelos could do anything, he had to recruit teachers, for there would be no schools without them. Where to find them? There was only a handful of pedagogues willing and able to carry

---

[36]"La discusión del proyecto de ley en la cámara," in Universidad Nacional, *El movimiento educativo*, pp. 290-291.

the new gospel to the thousands of tiny hamlets. By exploring every opportunity, by appealing to the spirit of patriotism and selfless effort, and by calling attention to the need for schools, Vasconcelos eventually gathered together a small cadre of volunteers willing to organize the program in the countryside. He called them his "missionaries." Somehow he also found teachers for the rural communities. The brunt of the work was shouldered by the missionaries, who became the helmsmen and supervisors. From village to village they went, by horseback, by mule, or on foot, spreading the idea and awakening the people to the need for education. They organized hundreds of schools in the villages, humble and elementary, but schools nonetheless, training teachers for them from among the local population. Poorly rewarded, left to their own resources, these early pioneers managed to lay the foundations for others to build on. It was a gigantic and novel undertaking, one that Vasconcelos watched closely. From this humble catch-as-catch-can beginning came what Dewey was later to call "Mexico's educational renaissance."

La Casa del Pueblo, the House of the People, Vasconcelos called his school. The *Casa* was for everyone, children and adults alike, on the theory that education must minister to all lest the neglect of the adults hinder the learning of the child. The children came during the day, the adults at night, after the fields were plowed and the animals fed. Both the practical and the traditional sides of education, which Vasconcelos stressed, had to conform to the reality of the countryside. Rural poverty, and that of the government, limited schooling to four years, and usually less. Life was a struggle for survival: the parents could not afford to send their children to school, and they were needed at home to help with the work. Limited by time and funds, the curriculum had no place for frills; every hour counted. Learning to read and write the Spanish language, simple arithmetic, a few fundamentals of geography and national history: this was the academic curriculum. The vocational side was equally elementary. To give as much as possible to students who would seldom go beyond the fourth year of school was the objective. These were elementary schools in every sense of the word, reflecting what was possible under the circumstances. Between 1921 and 1924, Vasconcelos' last year in office, hundreds of these simple schools were built. When Vasconcelos left the house he made famous on Calle Argentina, the beginning had been made. It was up to others to expand it.

This Sáenz and Ramírez did. Under their tutelage this sketchy, improvised beginning developed into a formal school. With Dewey as the new authority, the *Casa del Pueblo* became the School of Ac-

tion, the all-important title until Calles fell and Marx and his followers won the battle of education in the thirties. Vasconcelos had spoken
of cultural and traditional values; the School of Action reflected instead the social and utilitarian emphases of Sáenz and Ramírez, who
believed strongly in nonacademic activity and particularly in health
programs. Visits from doctors and nurses were encouraged; wells
to provide pure drinking water were dug; children were urged to
bathe and to bathe others. Seeking to build sound bodies, the school
gave athletics a prominent role to play. Hundreds of schools sponsored campaigns portraying the evils of alcoholism, the curse of rural
life. Out of the fight against pulque came the open-air theater. A so-
cially minded teacher conceived the idea of using dramatics to demonstrate the evils of pulque, so he wrote a one-act play and with his
pupils built a simple theater in the open air for the production. The
idea was a success, and the movement spread. Two years later there
were nearly 4,000 theaters in as many schools.[37]

Like Vasconcelos before them, Sáenz and Ramírez gave high priority to cultural growth. Their schools revived folklore and tradition,
sponsored community festivals, held song fests, and promoted the
native arts. Homage to what was Mexican—this was the temper of the
times. But where Vasconcelos had had a European model, Sáenz glorified the local or Indian contribution.

Local support of education, wooed by Vasconcelos, was assidu-
ously cultivated by his successors. Without it there could be no
school, for the school was of the community. The government, with
only a skeleton budget for education, provided the teacher and a bare
minimum of books and paper; from the community came the building—a humble hut but the best the village had to offer—the chairs and
tables, and often classroom supplies, too. The cost to the government
was low, reported Gruening, "one thousand pesos annually, of which
the teacher receives an average of 720—two pesos a day, the balance
going for school supplies."[38]

Some communities responded nobly; others ignored the call.
Among those that listened, Comaltepec, a village in Oaxaca, set a high
standard, but not a unique one. In less than two years it built and
furnished the school, planted an orchard on its ground, harvested and
sold a crop of corn for the school's benefit, purchased wire for the
animal pens, gave chickens to the students, donated a hand loom, and

---

[37]Katherine M. Cook, *The House of the People: An Account of Mexico's New
Schools of Action* (Washington, D. C., 1932), pp. 67-68.

[38]*Mexico and Its Heritage*, p. 522.

provided a lamp for the adult night class.[39] Each gift or contribution involved self-sacrifice on the part of the community. It was cooperation of this type that led John Dewey to declare that he was "willing . . . to say that there is no educational movement in the world which exhibits more of the spirit of intimate union of school activities with those of the community than is found in this Mexican movement."[40]

The extent of local support given education and the lack of public funds, paradoxically, led the government in 1929 to an experiment that threatened to undermine what progress had been made in rural education. Lacking funds with which to establish more schools, Sáenz conceived the idea of circuit schools, schools supported entirely by the community. The idea was to get local communities to hire and pay their own teachers and to provide almost everything else needed for a school. A visiting teacher from a nearby federal school (the local schools formed a circuit around a parent institution), who came to check on the local situation occasionally, was the extent of support offered by the government.

The circuit-school idea, which was in keeping with Sáenz' belief that any school was better than none, had a number of weaknesses. So poorly paid were the teachers in them that only those unable to find jobs elsewhere asked for the positions. Also, the full burden of education fell upon the already poverty-stricken community. Since final responsibility rested with the community, school policy was left in the hands of ignorant and inexperienced leaders, who frequently gave the landlord or priest control of public education. These shortcomings, and others that developed, led to the abandonment of the circuit-school idea; eventually the government had to abolish the worst of these schools and bring the best ones into the federal system.

V

By 1932, despite countless disappointments, the Northern Dynasty had accomplished much in education; considering the challenge, the effort was praiseworthy. The apparatus of a modern educational system had been dropped into place. "At the end of ten years," wrote Eyler Simpson (p. 281), "the battle had been joined on many a front;

---

[39]Secretaría de Educación Pública, *El esfuerzo educativo en México: La obra del gobierno federal en el ramo de educación pública . . . (1924-1928)* (Mexico, 1928), I, 88-89.

[40]*Impressions of Soviet Russia and the Revolutionary World: Mexico—China—Turkey* (New York, 1929), p. 158.

the territory of the enemy had been invaded and here and there the first ramparts had fallen."

On the credit side of the ledger there were impressive gains. Statistically, the northern patrons were kind to education, as a comparison with the past brings out clearly. Under Díaz there had been almost no federal rural schools and no funds for them. The states were equally negligent; only occasionally did a governor provide funds for schools, as in Puebla, Sonora, and Veracruz. With the coming of the conflict of 1910, matters worsened. Madero's budget for education was 8 million pesos; Victoriano Huerta's was half of that, only a fraction of which reached its destination; Carranza abolished federal education. A new era appeared with Obregón. There was little improvement in 1921; military considerations curtailed expenditures. But in 1922 the government set aside two and one-half times what Madero had allotted for education and in 1923, 45 million pesos, four times that given by any other administration. Although corruption and rebellion reduced this by a third before the year was over, the money earmarked for schools was greater than ever before.[41] Between 1921 and 1931 national expenditures on education rose from 4 per cent to nearly 13 per cent of the budget, of which almost a third was spent on rural schools. There was only a handful of rural schools in 1921; ten years afterward there were 6,796 federal rural schools with 593,183 students, children and adults, and 8,442 teachers.[42] The federal effort had come a long way.

But there was a negative side, too. Instead of limiting itself to a narrow but thorough program, which would have been in harmony with its capabilities, the government attempted to carry out an extensive effort, sacrificing quality for quantity, in keeping with public demand. Yet quantitatively the achievement was short of the need. Even adding local rural schools and those under Article 123 to the federal total, there was still an appalling shortage. By government figures alone, 81 per cent of the 72,164 communities of less than 4,000 population had no schools.[43]

Nor were the schools always satisfactory. Classrooms were insufficient and poorly constructed. Buildings varied according to the resources of the community; but most communities were poor, so most schools were small adobe huts. More than 82 per cent had just one room. All were lacking in equipment; less than half were passably equipped with benches, desks, blackboards, and textbooks. Over 28

[41]Gruening, "Emerging Mexico," p. 683.
[42]Simpson, pp. 281-282.
[43]Ibid., p. 283.

per cent of the schools had no farm land, despite the supposed emphasis given agricultural instruction; 54 per cent had no libraries; 32 per cent lacked playgrounds; and 81 per cent were without shops of any kind.[44]

Equally alarming were figures on registration and attendance. Less than a third of the children of school age in rural communities enrolled in school. Registering students was one problem, getting them to come to school regularly another. From Monday through Friday the teacher rang the bell about eight. "But no one came to school until the stock was watered, the alfalfa cut, the goats sent off to pasture, the corn ground, the tortillas made, and the babies tended."[45] More than likely, school began at nine, and stragglers drifted in after that. Of fifty or more children registered, perhaps thirty-five came on any given day. On a national average, approximately one third of the students never attended. From 1920 to 1930 all but 2 per cent of the students left school before completing their course of studies, usually during the first two years.[46]

On the instruction side, teachers were overworked and inadequately trained. Classes were large: seventy students per teacher on the average, and 81 per cent of the schools with only one teacher. All students usually studied together, without regard to age or ability. Nearly 90 per cent of the rural teachers had no teaching certificate or diploma of any kind. More than half of them were women, in a role that demanded experience in agriculture and crafts, traditionally the prerogatives of the male in a society that relegated women to the kitchen. All teachers were poorly paid.

The unwillingness of many communities to accept "mixed" (coeducational) schools multiplied the school and teaching problems. So that the sexes could study separately, forlorn villages, reached only by riding horseback over a rugged and lonely trail, supported two schools, each duplicating the work of the other. Villa Alta, one of many villages in southern Tlaxcala, was typical of them. "Behind a low fence of organ cactus," wrote Gruening, "two adobe huts form the village schools with forty-three boys in one, forty-two girls in the other—the entire school population. The children range from six to eleven years, are divided into two grades, though but a single room and teacher serve each school. While one grade is instructed, the other studies—or waits." In Santa Justina Ecatepec, on the side of a

[44]Ibid., p. 284.

[45]Helen M. Bailey, *Santa Cruz of the Etla Hills* (Gainesville, Fla., 1958), p. 146.

[46]Ignacio García Téllez, *Socialización de la cultura: Seis meses de acción educativa* (Mexico, 1935), p. 23.

"brown and barren hillock," a "boys' school with forty-four pupils, and the girls' with thirty-eight," had two grades, "though ages range from five to fifteen. Both schools lacked books, pencils, even benches."[47]

Poorly equipped, understaffed, their activities isolated from one another, the Schools of Action lacked realistic emphasis. Their work relied almost exclusively on the enthusiasm and goodwill of community, students, and teachers, which did not take the place of training or substitute for a coherent, comprehensive program of rural reform. "The intent is excellent," wrote Gruening. "But in practice as I observed it, there was little else than the old routine teaching—of the Three R's, geography, national history, with one child reciting while fifty were non-participant."[48] The immediate needs of the community were ignored. Less than half of the schools cultivated vegetable gardens or raised chickens, only 12 per cent kept bees, less than 14 per cent raised rabbits, nearly 55 per cent had no classes in arts and crafts, and, despite the emphasis on thrift, more than 70 per cent had no savings banks.[49]

Divorced from the day-to-day life of the community, the schools tilted at windmills, a fact that Gruening's description of San Andrés Cuamilpa illustrates perfectly. Water for the village, situated on top of one of the thousands of hills that dot the Tlaxcalan landscape, came from the canyon below. Every drop was carried up "three hundred feet after laborious lifting from the depth of a sixty-foot *pozo* (well) by means of earthen *ollas* (water jars) attached to ropes." Almost impossible to imagine, he continued, was the "dominating—the literally desiccating—effect of this obstacle on the life of the village." Cleanliness became nearly impossible "and health well-nigh unattainable." Unable to drink water, the inhabitants used pulque, obtained from the maguey plants.

Without a solution for the water question, there was no remedy for San Andrés and no place for the school. "Better abandon the rural school for four years," counseled Gruening, "and invest the four thousand pesos thus saved in motor, pump, and piping! Running water," he concluded, "would prove more 'educative' than the best teacher's unassisted struggle against the odds erected by Nature and man's ignorance of how to extricate himself."[50] Water was the problem of San Andrés; other communities needed a few miles of road to

[47]*Mexico and Its Heritage*, pp. 523-524.
[48]Ibid., p. 529.
[49]Simpson, p. 286.
[50]*Mexico and Its Heritage*, p. 530.

link the local market with the highway, a dam, perhaps, or malaria control along the tropical coast. Meeting these diverse needs, all of which were often found in one pueblo, required the coordinated effort of every ministry of the federal government, not just that of the Ministry of Education working alone and unaided.

A beginning had been made in this direction in 1925 under Calles, who had appointed as undersecretary of education Manuel Gamio, a Columbia University–trained archaeologist and anthropologist. Gamio had spent eight years working among the population of San Juan de Teotihuacán, site of a famous pre-Columbian city. "For the first time," wrote Gruening upon learning of Gamio's appointment, "a tried, scientifically worked out educational program will be applied to the redemption of the Indian."[51]

Through his work with the people of the pyramids of Teotihuacán, Gamio had come to the conclusion that only an "integral education" covering every activity of an entire community had value in rural Mexico. For a people at varying stages of cultural development, whose civilization lacked the homogeneity of Western life, the three R's were incongruous. There was no logic in teaching verb usage to students whose poverty-stricken parents planted their corn with a hoe by the light of the moon, shared their homes with burros and pigs, and died in the arms of a witch doctor without ever having known a physician or a nurse. Ways and means to ease the burdens of life were called for; what the Republic urgently needed was an education by which to integrate the village with its neighbors and bring all into the national current.

Scientific planning was the key to Gamio's concept of "integral education." Where a school was contemplated, a careful survey of the region was carried out, for "the requirements of groups living under widely diverse climatic and physiographic conditions, with differing antecedents and contacts, and in distinct stages of development" varied radically.[52] By examining the region from every angle, the architect of reform became familiar with the people and their problems; by learning something of the peculiar characteristics of their psychology, he could adapt his methods to the character of the region and its inhabitants and bring about their spiritual and physical well-being through intelligently applied self-help.

Gamio put his theory to work at San Juan de Teotihuacán, with funds provided from fees charged tourists who came to view the

[51]"The New Era in Mexico," *Century Magazine*, CIX (March 1925), 656.

[52]Gruening, *Mexico and Its Heritage*, p. 520.

pre-Columbian temples and pyramids. His numerous reforms were community-sponsored. He established a school, a clinic for prenatal and infant care, and a simple community theater. With them came guidance in land use, crop control, and fertilization. In order to improve the livestock, which was generally poor, he purchased a blooded bull and boar and kept them at stud, selling their services for a small fee. Unable to afford cow's milk, local mothers had fed their babies pulque; Gamio imported goats, inexpensive to buy and simple to care for, in order to provide a substitute. For years the Teotihuacanos had manufactured an inferior pottery, brown or black and porous and brittle; Gamio introduced new colors and techniques without destroying the native designs. Housing in the villages, as in all Mexican hamlets, was short of every convenience necessary for health; Gamio built a model home with separate rooms, a chimney for the fireplace, and windows along the walls. The average hut had none of these.[53]

Unfortunately for reform, Gamio's stay in the Ministry of Education was short-lived. After five months in office, he was dismissed by Calles for political reasons and replaced by Sáenz. The new undersecretary did a magnificent job, one that deserves accolades, but Gamio's loss was a serious blow, for Mexico could ill afford to lose a trained and dedicated reformer. After Gamio's departure, his theories were, frequently for lack of imagination, more honored in the breach than in the observance.

Yet had boldness and imagination been found to put Gamio's ideas into practice, the funds with which to carry them out on a national scale were not there. Despite the neglect of professional and university education, justified on the grounds that rural needs had priority, there were never sufficient funds to go around. In 1932, an above-average year in terms of federal expenditures, approximately 9 million pesos were spent on rural education.[54] This was a per capita expenditure of about 54 centavos, only a fraction of that spent by Mississippi, the poorest state in the Union. With this amount Mexico was supporting an existing plant and trying desperately to enlarge it. A figure twenty times the sum spent would not have been excessive. The lesson was obvious. Until Mexico had prosperity, as Gruening says, only a fractional effort was possible, and a majority of children would be left "without schooling or schooling so slight as to be negligible."[55]

[53]Ibid., pp. 520-521.
[54]Simpson, p. 663.
[55]*Mexico and Its Heritage*, p. 529.

Chapter III

THE SOCIALIST SCHOOL

I

OFFSPRING OF MODERATE THINKERS AND LANDED PATRIARCHS, the rural school of the twenties came to life in an era of optimism and hope; that of the thirties was born of the Great Depression, the collapse of old values, and the despair that followed in their wake. Rising out of an age of criticism and experimentation, the educational philosophy of the thirties relied heavily on the collectivist ideologies sweeping the restless world.

The Great Depression descended upon Mexico with catastrophic effects, bankrupting an economy tottering on the edge of disaster since the Gonzalo Escobar uprising of 1929. On the business front, the major industries collapsed, petroleum output fell off, and mines shut down. Equally gloomy was the agrarian scene, where milksop legislation left the *status quo* undisturbed but frightened the *hacendados*, who retaliated by curtailing production or replacing foodstuffs with export crops, for which a tariff-ridden world paid poorly.[1] Droughts in 1929 and 1930 complicated the picture. By 1931 Mexico was importing large quantities of lard, eggs, corn, and wheat yet had no funds with which to sustain the heavy purchases. Seeking to close the breach in the economic crisis, Plutarco Elías Calles took the country off the gold standard, a move that paralyzed commercial operations, inflated the price of consumer goods, and shattered public confidence.[2]

Growing political and social unrest followed on the heels of the worsening economic situation, which spotlighted the poverty of the countryside and the failure of reform. By 1932 the Revolution was history, but the peasants had nothing to show for their sacrifices. The Revolution had been waged for land, yet less than 2,000 families held one third of the national domain.[3] Peonage, which the Revolution had struggled to eradicate, survived nearly everywhere, frequently

[1]Simpson, p. 507.

[2]Carleton Beals, "The Calles Plan," *New Republic*, LXVIII (Sept. 2, 1931), 64-65.

[3]Beteta, "Some Economic Aspects of Mexico's Six-Year Plan," in Herring and Weinstock, eds. *Renascent Mexico*, p. 94.

on the haciendas of former revolutionaries. In the face of the darkening picture, Calles procrastinated. Unwilling to accept drastic change, distrustful of even moderate reform, he sought to distract public attention from the economic question by resurrecting the religious issue, which a bitter and backward clergy eagerly grasped.

Demagoguery failed to stifle the unrest. So Calles, always the master politician, fell back upon a policy of concessions. Having placed the conservative Pascual Ortiz Rubio in the executive chair, he removed him in 1932 for Abelardo Rodríguez, a northerner less identified with the reaction. In a celebrated interview with Ezequiel Padilla, former secretary of education and now senator, Calles followed this up with some ideas for a comprehensive blueprint of government action. Despite these concessions, Calles had merely postponed the inevitable. The spirit of reform was on the march; awkward and hesitant at first, it gathered speed slowly and then broke loose.

Half-hearted steps rather than fundamental change characterized policy under the cautious Rodríguez. The interim chief of state, grown rich as an obedient servant of the Sonora clique, was watched closely by Calles, who pulled the strings from his home in Cuernavaca. Rodríguez accepted the need for new agrarian legislation but granted land to a limited number of villages. His successor dumped Calles and the Northern Dynasty and removed all restrictions on land reform.

Out of the collapse of the Calles machine and the frustration that followed in the path of the Great Depression rose a program of rural education reflecting the agrarian philosophy of the new rulers, men who believed that the capitalistic order of middle-class society had failed in Mexico and elsewhere. Where Vasconcelos and even Sáenz had steered the school in the direction of the individual, the new architects of education put their emphasis on the group and the community, in keeping with the collectivist doctrines popular in Europe and particularly the Soviet Union. By 1934 the "socialist school" had replaced the School of Action and the House of the People of the twenties. The death of individualism in Europe had been felt in the New World, where a people different in background and temperament, but with a communal heritage of their own, fought to blend the collectivism of the Indian with modern doctrines.

II

The new education began with the Six-Year Plan of the *Partido Nacional Revolucionario* (National Revolutionary Party), a vague, confused program for national action in the era from 1934 to 1940, to which Calles had given his blessing. Striving after the Soviet and New Deal experiments, the plan reflected the state-planning trend of the thirties.

Amidst high-sounding phrases about "collective development" and the "class struggle," the Six-Year Plan, product of hard times and agrarian discontent and an aging Calles fighting to hold on to the reins of power, set off to "socialize Mexico." A bundle of contradictions from start to finish, the plan approved "socialist education," cooperative farming, and other measures which if carried out fully would have transformed the entire social system; on the other hand, the plan gave protection to private property, only mildly opposed foreign capital, and accepted capitalism as an economic system. These ambiguities, however, did not conceal the awakening of a new social consciousness that went beyond demagogy.[4]

The Six-Year Plan had four principal aims: the full utilization of the national wealth, higher incomes for peasants and workers, industrialization, and a self-sustaining autonomous economy. As in the past, the agrarian problem received the lion's share of attention. Favoring economic solutions over political answers—so ran the tenor of the argument—the plan heralded the question of land ownership and use and the welfare of those who tilled it as the most pressing issues of the day.[5] Not until the public demand for land was satisfied would the government rest, the plan declared. On the surface, only small property received guarantees against expropriation.

Despite the boldness of its language, the Six-Year Plan had not departed from the route marked out by the Northern Dynasty. What it proposed was to carry out Calles' limited concessions as outlined in his talk with Padilla. In the face of victories won by the agrarian opposition—an autonomous agrarian department and an agrarian code—the plan was conservative on the major issues; the emphasis was on the independent farmer and on the private ownership of property.[6] Following the pattern set in former years, the peon on the hacienda was denied the legal right to petition for the land he lived on, which left the majority of haciendas, with much of the arable land, safe from expropriation.

Orthodox in the landholding sense, the plan had a progressive side. Proposing a scientific reorganization of the agrarian picture, its au-

[4]Millán, p. 72.

[5]Partido Nacional Revolucionario, *Plan sexenal de gobierno ... 1934-1939* (Mexico, 1934), p. 3.

[6]Simpson, pp. 454, 463.

thors laid special emphasis on collective action and particularly on agrarian cooperatives. Giving the peasants land would not alone solve the agrarian muddle, they announced. What was called for was the total reconstruction of the rural economy through the cooperative, making possible community purchases of machinery, fertilizers, and seeds, as well as the introduction of modern farming methods.[7]

Two developments sabotaged the moderate stand taken by the architects of the plan: the worsening economic conditions, which made radical action almost mandatory, and the election of Rodríguez' successor, Lázaro Cárdenas. Until 1934 the rulers of Mexico—with the exception of Ortiz Rubio—had come from the northern states; Cárdenas' home was the central zone. Unlike the northerners, Cárdenas placed his faith in the Indian and his communal system.

All of the plan's fathers agreed on the primary position of the rural school, which was given preference over other forms of education and particularly over professional and university work.[8] For the success or failure of the blueprint of 1934 depended almost as much upon the rural school as on reform in general.[9] The rural school was especially important to the conservatives, whose platform centered around a program shorn of any economic change. Yet, paradoxically, the *ejido* goals of the radicals, who appropriated the plan and made economic change their goal, put even greater demands on rural education. Their collectivist designs, complex in theory and more so in practice, called for wholehearted public cooperation and enlightened and selfless leadership, which only a literate and homogeneous population could provide.

An ambitious building program of federal rural schools was plotted: 1,000 new schools in 1934; 8,000 in the years from 1935 to 1938; and 3,000 in 1939. The total: 12,000 new rural schools by 1939.[10] Since there were approximately 7,000 federal rural schools in 1933, the program represented a gigantic undertaking, calling for a 5 per cent increase in the budget set aside for education by 1939.

But the Six-Year Plan went beyond a mere demand for more rural schools. Having adopted the stand of the conservatives on the land question, the architects of the educational provisions, spokesmen for the anticlerical extremists from Tabasco and Veracruz, paradoxically called for a radical revision of Article 3 modeled on the "socialism of

[7]Partido Nacional Rev., *Plan sexenal ... 1934-1939,* p. 5.

[8]Ibid., p. 15.

[9]Chester Lloyd Jones, "The Six-Year Plan: A Criticism," in Herring and Weinstock, eds. *Renascent Mexico,* p. 118.

[10]Partido Nacional Rev., *Plan sexenal ... 1934-1939,* p. 14.

the Revolution."[11] Nothing was done to define what was meant, perhaps because there was no unanimity of opinion, a fact demonstrated later by the debates in Congress, where every member had his particular version. Some thought socialism signified social justice in the framework of capitalism; others believed it synonymous with economic nationalism; a minority defined socialism as the classless society of Marx.[12]

Some general agreements were apparent, nonetheless. Accepted implicitly was the materialistic interpretation that man's lot depended upon his ability to support himself; therefore economics was the problem. Since the working class was the pivot of national policy, the ultimate objective of the educational system was the emancipation of the proletariat. The capitalistic worship of competition and private profit had to go, its place to be taken by a cooperative psychology that would open the way to a more equitable and just regime. From the point of view of practical politics, the revision of Article 3 was a political weapon with which to combat the clergy and foreign capital and woo labor.[13]

According to the revision, the rural school was a social institution; as the genuine representative of society, the government had the sole authority to define its mission. Without the approval of the government, no individual had a right to establish and direct educational plants, as "would occur with a false and exaggerated concept of personal liberty." Utilitarian in character and stressing technical education, the socialist school excluded all religious teachings, substituting true, scientific, and rational knowledge and providing an "exact and positive concept of the world and society."[14] No one took the trouble to say what constituted an "exact" concept of the universe, a philosophical question as old as man.

A Pandora's box of hothouse panaceas was opened by the amendment. Characteristic of them was a diluted dialectical materialism announcing the death of traditional liberalism. The dialectical bent of the era opened wide the door to those "isms" of salvation so typical of countries wracked by misery and psychological despair.[15]

With the amendment also came a storm of protest. The Catholic

[11]Ibid., p. 2.

[12]Nathaniel and Sylvia Weyl, *The Reconquest of Mexico: The Years of Lázaro Cárdenas* (London, 1939), p. 315.

[13]Victor F. Calverton, "Red Rule in Mexico's Schools," *Current History*, XLIII (Dec. 1935), 263-266.

[14]Partido Nacional Rev., *Plan sexenal . . . 1934-1939*, p. 14.

[15]George F. Kneller, *The Education of the Mexican Nation* (New York, 1951), p. 63.

Church jumped into the fray from the start, joined by conservatives and even moderates. Thousands of parents withdrew their children from the public schools and denounced the revision as the work of the devil. Intellectuals, too, protested. The reform, wrote one of them, had come from Calles, who had seen fit to "establish an ideological dictatorship sanctioned by law in keeping with the political orientation of the State." No one in education had been consulted, he declared, and the revisionists had known nothing of educational matters.[16] Others labeled the revision a smoke screen raised by the Calles machine to obscure failures elsewhere.

III

As befitted these years of experimentation, education fell into the hands of men dedicated to the idea of state planning. Narciso Bassols, the first of the socialist-oriented planners and the darling of Mexican radical intellectuals, became minister in October 1931. For more than two years he labored to reorient the educational system. When he left office in May 1934, he had laid the basis of the school of the thirties. For his efforts, Bassols was opposed on all sides. Teachers revolted when he began to weed out incompetents from their ranks. His belief in science, his support of coeducation, and his acceptance of the wisdom of birth control angered Catholics. Parents in Mexico City kept their children out of school. In the United States newspapers printed stories of the atrocities supposedly committed in the schools under his regime. Confronted with a growing opposition, virulent and well organized, Bassols eventually gave up the struggle, resigning in 1934. He was the last of the great ministers to rule the house that Vasconcelos built.

This controversial figure was the caricature of the intellectual in the public image. He was young, short, nervous, and nearsighted, a condition he overcame by wearing heavy, dark, horn-rimmed glasses; a fringe of brown hair circled his balding head. "He had all of the appearance of a friar, a modern friar, to be sure, marked by devotion to his cause but thoroughly disciplined by years of legal training," wrote Verna Carleton Millán (p. 50). An impetuous man of tremendous energy who spent fourteen hours a day in his office, he was the outstanding figure of the Rodríguez cabinet. Like Moisés Sáenz before him, Bassols was keenly interested in rural education; as minister he frequently left the capital for the countryside, where he

[16]Samuel Ramos, *Veinte años de educación en México* (Mexico, 1941), pp. 65-66.

found satisfaction in helping the peasants. Thoroughly honest, he was as poor when he left office as when he entered, a significant achievement in the graft-ridden days of Calles. Never afraid of controversy, the author of numerous unorthodox studies, he had little, if any, public support among the well-to-do.

Bassols was an economic determinist. He believed that man's life was essentially an economic struggle. Shunning classicists and Deweyites alike, he placed his emphasis on "practical knowledge," substituting the economic for the social in pedagogical theory. Satisfying the material necessities of the rural class, not the incorporation of the Indian into society, was the objective of rural education. "The issue," to him, "was a concrete one; a hungry Indian cannot be turned into a good scholar, and, furthermore, his studies only have value in so far as they aid him completely to transform his economic life."[17] With three fourths of the population engaged in agriculture, Mexico needed schools to prepare farmers to use the soil wisely for the benefit of self and country. Here, in this agrarian thesis, was the essence of Bassols' pedagogy.

Long a believer in state planning, Bassols belonged to a minority of public figures who knew what socialism implied; later, for the benefit of others, he translated John Strachey's *Theory and Practice of Socialism*. He believed in a school favoring the transformation of "the systems of production and distribution of wealth along frankly collectivist lines."[18] Instead of an education for the individual, based on competition and personal success, he prescribed a formula for the "economic education of the whole nucleus of the peasant population considered as units."[19] Yet, paradoxically, he did not support the "socialist" revision of 1934. In private he expressed surprise over the proposal and later, seeing the difficulties and pitfalls that lay ahead, tried to halt it before it became law.

Among Mexican public figures, Bassols was far ahead of his time, advocating even population control to alleviate social and economic problems. While scholars had long recognized the correlation between reform and population growth, Bassols alone of the men in office had the courage to face the issue. His effort, ill-conceived and doomed to failure from the start, and confined almost entirely to Mexico City (and about which factual information is almost un-

[17]Millán, p. 51.

[18]Secretía. de Educ. Públ., *Memoria relativa al estado que guarda el ramo de educación pública el 31 de agosto de 1933* (Mexico, 1933), I, 52.

[19]Millán, p. 52.

available), raised a storm of protest from the church and Catholics. Mexico was not ready for a planned-population approach, despite the growing need for it.

Bassols surrounded himself with able men. Jesús Silva Herzog, one of Mexico's gifted economists, became his assistant. He left Rafael Ramírez in charge of the Department of Rural Schools, his post since 1925. Ramírez served him loyally, accepting his dicta as gospel, testimonial to Bassols' ability as leader and thinker. Unfortunately, Ramírez' dictatorial methods and his penchant for meddling in the affairs of his teachers eventually involved Bassols in a conflict with their trade unions. On Ramírez' recommendation, Bassols cracked down on irresponsible leaders, stirring protest and rebellion, including the resignation of Sáenz from a special project. Angered by Bassols' policies, Sáenz accused him of subverting rural education and of being hostile to the rank-and-file teachers. Neither charge was justified, for Bassols raised rural salaries, using funds earmarked for public buildings and urban teachers' salaries.[20] Sáenz' defection, however, was a tragic loss, for Mexico could ill afford to lose a man of his stature and experience.

The architect of the rural school of the thirties was Bassols. Lázaro Cárdenas, whose election marked a resurgence of reform, was the builder. Despite his known sympaties for education, his zealous support of rural schools surprised nearly everyone. Hardly a soul had pictured this mild-mannered military officer as a dynamic leader, least of all Calles, who picked him and who had publicly declared that his disciple was no extremist.

In 1934 there was almost no reason to dispute the verdict of Calles. The new president, a quiet, unassuming man, was a native of Jiquilpan, a small town in Michoacán. Without fanfare or notoriety, he had won prominence as an aide of Alvaro Obregón and Calles. Later, as a favorite of Calles, he became governor of his native state, chief of the PNR (National Revolutionary Party), and minister of war in the cabinet of Rodríguez. Throughout nearly all of his career he was a loyal and orthodox supporter of the Northern Dynasty. He was known, however, as something of a reformer, a reputation he had won by encouraging land distribution and rural education as governor. No one questioned his honesty. With the nomination of Cárdenas in 1934, Calles felt that he had outwitted his opposition again. Here was a man easily manipulated yet acceptable to a majority of the discontented group. Calles was mistaken. By 1935 the

[20]Unpublished letter from Narciso Bassols to Moisés Sáenz, Mexico City, Feb. 4, 1933. Private collection.

man elected as another puppet president had won the backing of peasant and worker, ousted his mentor, established himself as master of Mexico and apostle of reform, and emerged a Gandhi-like figure.[21]

Cárdenas talked revolution and, unlike his predecessors, practiced it. He took the Six-Year Plan, and particularly its socialistic jargon, literally, much to the amazement and anger of Calles and his supporters, who had expected nothing more than propaganda from them. For him, wrote Luis Cabrera, "the Revolution was indivisible and continuous."[22] Like Zapata, whom he fought in Morelos only to recant later, Cárdenas saw Mexico's wealth in her rural population and especially in the Indian, the beast of burden of parasitical urban classes. He had a simple goal in mind: to give the peasants and workers a decent standard of living. For the peasants this meant land.

By accepting the *ejido* as the ultimate goal and not as a transitional stage, Cárdenas departed again from the ideas of the Northern Dynasty. The *ejido* provided a golden opportunity to blend collectivist ideas with existing pre-Columbian land systems. Two types of *ejidos* were organized. Where tradition, contemporary practice, and the character of the terrain favored the Indian communal system, the independent village *ejido* was established, particularly in central and southern Mexico, where mountains and valleys divided the region into small and isolated farming communities. Their small size, four hectares on the average, required intelligent, resourceful farmers, able to squeeze every benefit from the soil, if the hacienda were not to be replaced with subsistence agriculture.

Alongside of the traditional unit, a new type of *ejido* was organized. Where the land and crop systems favored the use of machinery and planting in common, as in the Laguna in Coahuila and Durango, collective farms were laid out. The individual villages farmed collectively, laboring in units to produce a cash crop: cotton in the Laguna; henequen in Yucatán; rice, wheat, and corn in the Lombardia of Michoacán. Each peasant received a share of the profits from the harvest; the amount received was determined by his labor contribution. Management was in the hands of the *Banco Ejidal*, which financed the crops. Through the collective *ejido*, Cárdenas endeavored to fulfill the land promises of the Revolution and, at the same time, to avoid the pitfalls common to small landholdings.

With the distribution of over 50 million acres of land in six years, three times the total given out before 1934, came the downfall of the

---

[21]William Cameron Townsend, *Lázaro Cárdenas, Mexican Democrat* (Ann Arbor, Mich., 1952), p. vi.

[22]*Veinte años después,* 3rd ed. (Mexico, 1938), p. 215.

hacienda.[23] Its death was sealed by the departure from earlier legislation that barred the peon on the hacienda from petitioning for its land. When the peon was made eligible, the sacred hacienda became a thing of the past. With its demise, peonage as a formal institution, the curse of Mexico for centuries, collapsed. Millions experienced freedom for the first time.

Land was one step. To provide the *ejidatario* with credit, for the purchase of seeds, fertilizers, and equipment, an *ejidal* bank was opened, almost as a charity institution, willing to lend money with little expectation of repayment. Eager to help the *ejidal* farmer, Cárdenas had discarded traditional banking practices, believing that the hazards of lending without assurance of repayment were compensated for by the greater national welfare. To overcome the chronic shortage of water, small and large dams were constructed, and the Department of Irrigation was given additional importance. Seeking to organize the peasants for their own protection, Cárdenas sponsored the first Republic-wide rural union: the National Confederation of Peasants (CNC), whose members were encouraged to form militias for the defense of *ejido* and school. In the hands of Graciano Sánchez, an eloquent spokesman for the agrarian sector, the CNC became a powerful force in national life. Successful management of the *ejido*, and state planning and control, called for literate peasants and officials trained for a system of cooperatives and collectives, which put new emphasis on rural education and particularly on its socialist goals.

There was one major difference between the programs of Bassols and Cárdenas. Both focused their attention on economic matters, but Cárdenas, long disturbed by the plight of the Indian population and more sensitive to cultural values, revived the Indianist program, forgotten since the departure of Sáenz. From 1935 until 1940 the Indian became the pivot of a large-scale and much-publicized reform effort. Many prominent Indianists played leading roles in this campaign; among them was the historian Luis Chávez Orozco, undersecretary of education and later chief of the Department of Indian Affairs.

Cárdenas watched closely over his rural schools, taking time to visit them frequently. His cabinet heads, Ignacio García Téllez, who served six months, and Gonzalo Vásquez Vela, whose activity raised angry outcries from conservatives, rarely made major decisions. Orders came from the top, from a politician who believed that the

[23]Betty Kirk, *Covering the Mexican Front: The Battle of Europe versus America* (Norman, Okla., 1942), p. 119.

noblest figure in Mexico was the rural schoolteacher. Swayed by his sympathies for the rank and file, and a firm believer in union organization, Cárdenas accepted the advice of critics of the aging Ramírez and dismissed him as chief of rural schools. Nearly everyone accepted this decision as wise and inevitable; if rural education was to have new ideas and be more than a one-man show, now was the time for younger leadership. Unhappily for Cárdenas and Mexico, Ramírez' successors were not his equal.

IV

Reformers in the thirties believed that the rural school had waged a useless and uphill battle, a belief even Sáenz shared by 1933. Appointed director of the Carapan experimental project in rural education by Bassols in the summer of 1932, a shocked Sáenz acknowledged that something had gone wrong with his revered school. "I am," he wrote in his *Carapan: Bosquejo de una experiencia*, "convinced of the futility of the countless sporadic and puerile activities of our so-called School of Action." Critics, he confessed, had referred to the ill-equipped and poorly led rural schools as schools of reading, writing, and arithmetic; those in Carapan, symptomatic of the majority, did not merit even this contemptuous epithet.[24]

Despite the inadequate and limited character of their academic plan, however, this was all the schools offered in most cases. Few of them had experimental gardens, and the much-heralded shops were conspicuously absent. Instead of emphasizing the practical, the schools had taken refuge in methodology, Sáenz lamented. Led by teachers with scant preparation or interest in their work, they had lost contact with community, parents, and local leaders. As community centers the schools had failed. Almost nothing had been done to transform the cherished ideal of adult education into a reality, and without it there could be no effective schooling for the young in the village.[25] Calling upon the people to give up their vices, furthermore, was no simple moral crusade. The addiction to pulque, for example, often had its roots in the waterless character of Mexico. When the teacher attempted to combat it, he ran into obstacles beyond his control, as one school inspector learned. During one of the periodic anti-alcoholic campaigns of the twenties, he had stopped in a village notorious for its pulque-drinking inhabitants. There he had called

[24] (Lima, Peru, 1936), pp. 245, 95.

[25] Ibid., pp. 95, 130.

the people together and lectured them on the pitfalls involved in their use of pulque. He urged them to drink water. His audience listened attentively, saying nothing. After he had finished, the villagers asked him to eat with them. At the table he noticed that his glass contained rancid and muddy water. Surprised and angered by this, the inspector demanded an explanation. "Maestro," they answered, "this is what you have asked us to drink." For miles around, there was nothing to drink but water from stagnant pools. The people drank pulque instead.

Determined to correct these shortcomings, the men of the thirties fell back on Manuel Gamio's cherished integral education. Seeking to formulate a concrete and practical blueprint, reflecting the mundane necessities of the community, the planners called for coordinated, large-scale reforms, giving every federal office a part to play. Unless the different ministries worked together, knowledge alone would solve little. Without roads and water, the electrification of rural villages that the darkness of night separated from the world of books, and rural credit, for example, the school waged an isolated struggle. Nor could it remain a mere center of learning, divorced from the day-to-day activity of rural life. For these leaders who worshiped the common good and who lived by the code of state planning, the school spoke for the underdogs, pleading their case before the tribunals of social justice that allocated the lands and waters and protected political rights. "We want," to quote Ramírez, "to make our school a proletarian school, reflecting the interests, aspirations, and ideals of the workers and tillers of the field," where individual development is not the end, but the "means toward social perfection."[26]

With these revised objectives there followed a further de-emphasis of traditional pedagogical methods, a trend that already characterized the school of the twenties. Learning, productive work, and social action were linked even more closely together, and additional stress was given to subjects of first importance to the community, especially agriculture and the cottage industries. Community needs received preference over individual demands. Entire regions were mapped out for the combined efforts of the various federal branches, particularly the Yaqui of Sonora and the Mezquital of Hidalgo, home of the destitute Otomíes, whose poverty threatened to become a national scandal. The initial step was to provide the inhabitants with land; Cárdenas visited both regions, personally supervising the Agrarian Department's activity in the Yaqui. After the land question was settled,

[26]"The Six-Year Plan in Education," in Herring and Weinstock, eds. *Renascent Mexico*, pp. 138-139.

other federal departments stepped in. Communications built roads and bridges; Irrigation dammed streams and dug canals and ditches; Agriculture supplied seeds and fertilizer, technical assistance, implements and draft animals, and frequently milk cows, chickens, and pigs for breeding purposes; Education and Health provided schools and teachers, medical facilities, doctors, and nurses. The Department of Indian Affairs supervised this activity in the Indian zones.

In the Mezquital, among the Chamulas of Chiapas, the Laguneros of Coahuila and Durango, and wherever the federal banners were planted, the cooperative was introduced. It was initially conceived as a means of using collective action to obtain what the school needed; then the cooperative's scope was enlarged to include the solution of community problems in general. By 1940 over 800 societies had been organized.[27] The cooperative movement led to a bitter clash between the schoolmaster and the *acaparador*, the local middleman who purchased neighborhood products at next to nothing and later sold them at fantastic profits. According to many observers, this was the heart of every conflict between the rural school and its many foes. When the schoolmaster attempted to upset the monopoly of the *acaparador*, frequently an unscrupulous local political boss with influential connections who was willing to exploit even the religious issue to protect his business, he incurred the wrath of the most powerful figure in rural Mexico, whose prerogatives dated back to the Indian caciques of colonial days. There could be no compromise in this struggle, for the *acaparador* had everything to lose. Without prominent friends upon whom to rely and isolated from the authorities in Mexico City, the teacher usually tasted defeat.

Indoctrination in the ideals of the Revolution, long characteristic of the rural school, became the pivotal point of education in the thirties. A barrage of propaganda, oral and written, explaining and justifying the logic of the government's case, descended upon students and parents. There were books on socialism, pamphlets on the classless society that came with state planning, and leaflets on every conceivable subject deemed worthy of the student's attention; all were profusely illustrated with vivid scenes from the utopian future that was promised if only the reader would cooperate. What was left undone by the written word, the teacher was supposed to fill in. The school had become a political pawn.

Under Cárdenas, who stressed what he called "the equality of labor and intellectual activity," the curriculum of the rural school,

[27]Secretaría de Gobernación, *Seis años de gobierno al servicio de México, 1934-1940* (Mexico, 1940), p. 223.

confined to a limited number of academic subjects until then, was put on a par with that of the urban school. All differences between them were eliminated; the needs of community and national citizenship came before regionalism and provincial effort.[28] For the academic program of the first two or three years, this gave the rural school equal standing with that of the city, on paper at least. The old Department of Rural Schools was abolished and its place taken by a General Office of Primary Rural and Urban Education. The ideal was more honored in the breach than in practice.

Militant spokesmen for peasants and workers, the socialist-minded planners demanded that high-income groups carry their share of the school burden. From this view came the enforcement of Article 123, the labor code of the Constitution, which required *hacendados* and businessmen to establish and support primary schools for the children of their workers, if there was no school within the radius of three kilometers and there were more than twenty school children on their property. Mute testimony to the failure to destroy the haciendas, these institutions were called "schools Article 123," being controlled by the states and supervised by the federal Department of Labor. Neither had enforced the legislation. A study compiled in 1932 indicated that fewer than half of the 4,000 communities covered by the legislation had the schools. More than 1,500 employers had ignored the statute. In the hands of poorly rewarded and ill-trained teachers, a majority of the hacienda schools fell below federal standards. Seeking to remedy this situation, the Ministry of Education asked Congress to transfer the schools to its jurisdiction. This was done in 1934. The Ministry appointed teachers, dictated programs, set salaries, and compelled employers to build schools and support them.[29] Federal supervision multiplied their number until the tempo of land reform made many of them unnecessary.

Convinced that supervision and direction from Mexico City held the answer to Mexico's ills and that planning on the national level entailed federal control, the leaders of the thirties undertook to unify federal and local systems of rural education. Since Vasconcelos, three systems had existed side by side. There were federal, state, and municipal schools. About a third of them were under local jurisdiction. While the federal system was beset with politics and budgetary inadequacies, the local schools, especially those municipally supported, were taxed by chronic political wrongdoings, lack of funds, and a

[28]Kneller, p. 54.

[29]Secretía. de Educ. Públ., *Memoria . . . de educación . . . 1933*, I, 30.

host of other sins. The quality of education rose and fell with the character of the governors, and most of them could not "be depended on for disinterested public service," recalled Ernest Gruening.[30] Uniformity was lacking in education, teaching standards, and objectives. Teachers outside of the federal system were at the mercy of local caciques and their friends at the state capitals. Their salaries were poor and tenure virtually unknown. A few governors set aside half of their budget for education; others, as little as 1 per cent. With the founding of federal schools, some governors closed theirs. In one state, Calles reported, where the federal government had opened 150 schools, the local authorities closed an equal number.[31] Were the educational program left to the states, concluded Gruening, "no certain progress" lay ahead.[32] Aside from this, the duplication achieved by the states led to waste and inefficiency.

Before unification could be achieved, there were numerous obstacles to overcome. Jealous of their prerogatives and unwilling to share their income with federal authorities, the provincial bosses opposed any merger. Local teachers presented another problem. Many of them lacked the qualifications for a federal appointment. Having only minimal schooling, they feared that unification would cost them their jobs. The qualified ones, on the other hand, formed the vanguard of the merger movement, which they saw as the means to security and better salaries. By supporting unification, they exposed themselves to persecution from local authorities, and some even lost their lives, as Nathaniel and Sylvia Weyl testified (p. 322).

Serious attempts to unify the systems were begun in 1930. A few states reached tentative agreements with officials in Mexico City but did not ratify them. Not until Bassols were permanent steps taken. Two patterns were adopted. Some states kept ownership of their schools, supporting them with local funds, but entrusted their supervision to the federal government. These were called "coordinated schools." Five states accepted this pattern. Four others released their schools to the central government, agreeing to contribute half the cost of their upkeep. These were "federalized schools." Only nine states accepted these formulas. Nothing was done in the others, and many adamantly refused to participate in any joint program and stopped building schools when federal authorities began to establish

[30]*Mexico and Its Heritage*, p. 528.

[31]Robert Hammond Murray, trans. and ed. *Mexico before the World: Public Documents and Addresses of Plutarco Elías Calles* (New York, 1927), p. 91.

[32]*Mexico and Its Heritage*, p. 528.

them within their borders. If figures for all primary schools were tabulated together, therefore, there were fewer schools in 1940 than ten years before, despite the stepped-up activity emanating from Mexico City.[33] Local authorities had simply abdicated their educational responsibilities, preferring to have outsiders establish schools for them. Since a majority of the schools involved in this controversy were rural, the peasants were the ones to suffer. Nothing had been done by 1962 to correct this situation.

V

With the expropriation of the foreign-owned oil companies, the era of reform came to an end. The petroleum question compelled the president to forsake rural affairs and to give his attention to oil. Unfortunately, the government had not prepared plans for the operation of the oil industry, and sales declined. Federal income dropped sharply, and rural education felt the pinch.

At almost the same time the liberal renaissance of the thirties lost its vigor. The ideological battles raging in Europe and mirrored in the United States found an audience in Mexico. General Franco's victories in Spain, especially, heartened conservatives, who became increasingly vocal in their denunciations of public policy. In the countryside the *sinarquistas* raised the specter of religious strife again, frequently aided and abetted by the clergy. Teachers and parents lost their lives, and schools closed. As Betty Kirk has written (p. 264), "the battle of Europe versus America" began in Mexico.

Blame for this turn of events lay partly with the administration. With the socialist reform of Article 3, self-styled Marxists opened a vituperative attack on almost every tradition cherished by conservatives, frightening them and inviting retaliation. Scores of them invaded the house that Vasconcelos built on Calle Argentina, "boring from within, landing themselves fat jobs for which they gave no service but only agitated," to quote Kirk (p. 264). To the conservatives the Ministry of Education had become the headquarters of the Comintern in Mexico, whence an insidious propaganda filtered out into the provinces. Although few of the "Marxists" had any connection with either Moscow or Communism—Ambassador Josephus Daniels called them protestants-against-the-*status-quo*[34]—their class

[33]Humberto Lombardo Toledano, "Proyecto de reorganización de la Secretaría de Educación Pública," *Revista mexicana de educación*, I (Dec. 1940), 421.

[34]Introduction to Kirk, p. xiv.

propaganda jeopardized the activity of the Ministry and angered moderates whose support was essential to its success.

Aware of the growing problem, Cárdenas cracked down on demagoguery, bidding his subordinates to think before making statements. Teachers were told to teach and to leave politics and the church issue alone. Radical textbooks were withdrawn from the schools "after both Catholics and Communists had protested against them, although for different reasons."[35] After 1938 democracy found new friends, and socialism lost many a former admirer. The policy of moderation had a strong impact on education. By 1940, to quote Millán (p. 234), the socialist school had a program "about as radical as that undertaken by progressive schools throughout the United States, which place a great deal of emphasis on a scientific concept of life."

Cárdenas' retreat from radicalism was reflected on the political scene. To forestall a split in the national party, which he had organized as the *Partido de la Revolución Mexicana* (PRM), a kind of popular front, he endorsed the candidacy of the conservative Manuel Avila Camacho. Having stopped the religious strife that he inherited, he made peace with the clerical hierarchy.

No peace reigned in education, however. Until the day that Cárdenas left office, political and ideological differences split the Ministry into warring factions. Liberals, "Marxists," and reformers in general supported the government; moderates vacillated and often deflected; conservatives were unanimous in their condemnation of the efforts of the past years. The dissension at the top reverberated among the rank and file of teachers, whose factional strife and political bickering plagued their efforts at union organization. With the backing of officials in Mexico City, local teachers carried their battle for recognition to the provinces, and their quarrels followed them. All disputes eventually came before federal tribunals. Although Cárdenas offered dynamic leadership as the behind-the-scenes chief of education, of a kind never seen before, his subordinates frequently failed him.[36] With the exception of Luis Chávez Orozco and one or two others, his principal assistants did not rise to the demands of the time. Cárdenas' weakness, his admirers readily admitted, was his inability to surround himself with men of talent.

When economic difficulties appeared with the oil expropriation, the architects of school policy, who shared the spotlight with the agrarian planners, became the whipping boys of the critics, particu-

[35]Millán, pp. 236-237.

[36]Jesús Silva Herzog, *La revolución mexicana en crisis* (Mexico, 1944), p. 19.

larly of the conservatives who cast about for a scapegoat for Mexico's ills. Angered by the favoritism shown leftist schemes, they lashed out at the failings and mistakes of the last years, singling out the rural school for special censure. By destroying the hacienda and making the *ejido* and small farm the heart of the reform, around which a school program was built, the utopian planners, they alleged, had spent money fruitlessly, neglected the intellectual training of the individual, wrecked the economy, and jeopardized the national food supply—criticisms partly supported by the rising cost of living, food shortages, and the neglect of urban secondary and professional schools.

Much of the criticism was unjustified. From the beginning Cárdenas had recognized that large-scale agriculture and technical training were indispensable to the modern nation. If professional and white-collar education suffered, Cárdenas, a strong nationalist, compensated by trying to make Mexico self-sufficient, which he assumed could be accomplished with village and collective *ejidos* and through industry. The National Polytechnic Institute, the first of its kind in Mexico, was established by him for the training of technicians for farm and factory. To Cárdenas the collective *ejido* symbolized large-scale agriculture; industrialization denoted the gradual development of light industries producing vitally needed consumer goods, rather than the overnight expansion of a heavy or luxury industry in the hands of private enterprise, paid for by the rural population. By a policy typical of the president, he encouraged private investment in industry but clamped tight controls on the activity of businessmen; there was no profit, he believed, in replacing foreign exploitation with a home-grown variety.

That mistakes had been committed even Cárdenas acknowledged. Despite the grandiose designs of the Six-Year Plan, the much-talked-about program of the state, the total effort developed in a disjointed and haphazard fashion. Without a broad, coherent plan intelligently applied, Mexico was simply unprepared for socialism or for any other social "ism" that called for coordinated leadership and public participation. There was confusion at the administrative level and disorder in the village, and both suffered from a shortage of trained and selfless leaders with which to offset poverty, ignorance, and indifference. The government had preached a form of agrarian socialism and had taken steps to carry it out; but by its own admission the task was just begun.[37] Millions still wanted land, but there was not enough land to go around; and, unless the labor of the past years was contin-

[37]Secretía. de Gob., *Seis años de gobierno . . . 1934-1940*, p. 233.

ued on a similar or greater scale, which would bring with it more dams, irrigation canals, schools, the reforestation of eroding lands, agricultural credit liberally granted, and a hundred other needs, the rural scene would continue victim of the Mexican heritage.

What was descriptive of the general picture was equally characteristic of education. Mexico was not ready for a socialistic school, whatever its meaning. As Millán put it (p. 234): "Mexican education, to begin with, never was, never will be and never can be socialistic, unless the entire social system is changed radically." This was not done. Even on the *ejidos*, the focus of the collective program, where a socialistic school was plausible, the effort bogged down for want of foresight and funds. Of the *ejidos* in 1940 nearly two thirds did not have schools. Although the fact that a third did have schools represented a marked improvement over former years, the number fell short of what was required even to speak of socialized education. As Eyler Simpson points out (p. 299), "land without schools in Mexico is almost as useless as land without water or agricultural credit," and, conversely, the school without the other resources served as a prime example of conspicuous waste.

Confronted with little more than a scholastic socialism, unsupported by material change and meaningless to him, the peasant often reacted apathetically. In the Laguna region, for instance, scene of Mexico's greatest experiment with collectivized agriculture, out of a school-age population of 28,621 only 15,335 on the average attended classes, much of the loss being due to lack of parental interest.[38] A similar situation prevailed in the Mezquital, where a major effort to build a coordinated program on many fronts eventually failed for want of funds and because of official suspicion and rivalries, poor planning, and the failures and weaknesses of the local population.

For analogous reasons, a similar fate befell the cooperative movement. In the face of some gains, it faltered, due as much to the lack of a well-planned and directed program as to the hostility of the *acaparador*. Nor did the peasants give their full cooperation, often accepting their ancient role of dupe rather than espousing a cause that threatened what security they possessed. In spite of their communal background, they frequently preferred to farm independently and lacked both the predilection and training necessary to handle their interests in common. Aside from these factors, the broken nature of the land, which made large-scale mechanized farming all

[38]Clarence O. Senior, *Democracy Comes to a Cotton Kingdom: The Story of Mexico's La Laguna* (Mexico, 1940), p. 30.

but impossible, the isolation of the village, and poverty destroyed much of the effort.[39]

There were setbacks at other points. In spite of a budget for rural education almost twice that of 1932, inflation and population growth outran it. According to the census of 1940 there were 2 million more illiterates than ten years before. Again, population increases, which better health and schooling facilities encouraged, outstripped the school effort, despite the undeniable fact that no other administration had ever devoted so much attention to education.

Viewed broadly, nonetheless, the thirties rejuvenated rural education, furnishing leadership willing to experiment with new ideas. Although the unrealistic goals of the Six-Year Plan were not reached, more rural schools were built between 1935 and 1940 than in any comparable era, and attendance was the highest on record. Nor did this tell the full story; other regimes would build more schools. The contribution of the Bassols-Cárdenas school lay elsewhere. By placing much of the responsibility for land reform with the teacher, who was told to encourage and guide the struggle for land, the men of the thirties offered the means to a goal long aspired to by the peasants but never reached: the ownership of their land. Now, with the land in the hands of those who tilled it, much was possible in the realm of education, for the foundations of a rural school intimately related to local needs were now laid.

[39] Townsend, pp. 157-158.

Chapter IV

BUSINESS IN THE SADDLE

I

WHATEVER MAY BE SAID about the years after 1941, they differed radically from the decade before. The collectivist reformers of the thirties stressed the welfare of the peasant, the communal holding of land, and the rights of labor; the period that followed belonged to business-minded leaders. Out of a quasi-socialist revolution emerged a dynamic free-enterprise society, combining the trappings of the state-directed planning and welfare ideology of the twentieth century with the practices of the American robber barons. By 1946, to quote Alexander H. Uhl, there was "far more Morgan in Mexico . . . than . . . Marx."[1]

Two decades had passed since the agrarian guard of the Revolution had overthrown Carranza. A new generation, which knew the Revolution only as students of history or politics, wielded power. Although professing loyalty to the principles of 1917, it had ambitions of its own. Once surface similarities were brushed aside, there was little about this group that resembled what an older generation had fought and died for. Under its tutelage Mexico gave less emphasis to the agrarian panaceas of the past and listened sympathetically to native and foreign businessmen.[2]

The men who wielded political power in the forties and fifties believed that industry offered the best way out of Mexico's difficulties. Only the factory could raise the standard of living of the Mexican people. There was little hope of social progress in the agricultural programs of yesteryear; natural handicaps were too formidable. What, they asked, could man do with climate and topography but submit? No such limitations were imposed on industry. What was good for industry was good for Mexico; this was the new gospel, wrote Sanford Mosk. Regardless of cost Mexico had to industrialize, a lesson World War II hammered home with powerful impact. There

---

[1]"The 19th Century Comes to Mexico," *New Republic*, CXVI (May 5, 1947), 16.
[2]Ibid.

was no alternative. Either Mexico would continue in the patterns of
the past, which had failed to provide a better way of life, or she would
find a new future through industrialization. To participate in the crusade for industry was the patriotic obligation of every Mexican. A
few were called upon to invest in the new enterprises; others would
furnish the skills; the majority—the consumers—were asked to carry
the burden, even if it meant the purchase of native goods of inferior
quality and higher prices.[3]

With the coming of World War II and the need to supply goods
formerly imported, there developed what Howard Cline called (p.
287) a "veritable industrial revolution." The boom gained momen-
tum after 1944 and developed swiftly from 1946 to 1952. Although
many members of the industrial group were hostile to outside competition, others welcomed foreign capital.[4] By 1952 there was more
American money invested in Mexico than at any other time in
history.

The industrial revolution described by Cline brought changes
on the ideological front. Free enterprise, Mexican style, received the
blessings of officials in Mexico City who continued to cloak themselves with the mantle of the collectivist Revolution, which often led
to confusion and even conflict among divergent groups in the economy. Cárdenas had spoken of rural needs, of an agrarian revolution
and the class struggle; the new men of power believed in a dynamic
industrial society, the rights of the individual, and Western political
principles. Harmony was the watchword, not a society ruled by
workers and peasants. Nowhere was the shift more apparent than on
the political scene. The National Revolutionary Party, a militant
leftist organization under Cárdenas, became the Institutional Party
of the Revolution (PRI), dedicated to developing existing institutions. The aggressive phase of the Revolution was over. Now the job
was to make the institutions work.[5] Reflected in these political
changes was the rise of a powerful urban middle class whose spokesmen ruled the PRI by 1946.[6]

Much of Mexico got a face-lifting under the tutelage of the new
rulers. A large-scale program of public works was inaugurated. Roads
and highways were built, giant concrete dams poured into place, and

[3]Sanford A. Mosk, *Industrial Revolution in Mexico* (Berkeley, Calif., 1950), pp.
33, 38.

[4]John J. Johnson, *Political Change in Latin America* (Stanford, Calif., 1958), pp.
146-147; Mosk, pp. 33-35.

[5]Cline, pp. 6, 309, 325-326.

[6]For the new middle groups see Johnson, p. 128.

cities renovated. Old buildings came down and new ones went up in Mexico City, Monterrey, and Guadalajara. "Not small buildings," either, wrote Uhl, "but eleven and twelve-story ones with huge signs telling you that Otis elevators . . . [were] being installed and that everything would be modern down to the last push button."[7] There were sport palaces, the world's largest bullring in Mexico City, stadiums, wide avenues lined with trees reminiscent of Maximilian's Paseo de la Reforma, and a University City costing millions of dollars. Hundreds of thousands joined the ranks of the wealthy and spent their newly acquired fortunes on palatial estates and vacations at luxury resorts. Neon lights flashed brilliantly in Acapulco and Mazatlán, illuminating a façade of progress and prosperity.

Beneath the shadows cast by the lights little had changed. The war and its aftermath had brought chronic inflation. According to two Mexican economists writing in *El trimestre económico*, the hardest hit were the rural masses, whose purchasing power fell 46 per cent between 1940 and 1950, a decline nearly twice that of the purchasing power of salaries in thirty-five basic industries and more than that suffered by any other group.[8] Nearly two thirds of all Mexican families, and almost every rural family, lived on less than 300 pesos a month[9]—or less than $24.00 at the exchange rates of 1955. Just one fifth of the national income went to agriculture, in which about half of the economically active population was engaged.[10] Driven by dreams of a better life and often by hunger (Mexico's fundamental problem, reported Jesús Silva Herzog[11]), millions flocked to the cities or swelled the ranks of the *braceros* laboring on farms in the United States. The poverty of yesteryear continued to live with the poverty of today. The tourist did not have to walk far in Mexico City to find dirt and abject squalor. Around the corner from the National Palace tiny youngsters slept huddled in doorways with only newspapers to protect them against the cold. Behind the magnificent houses of the rich, other Mexicans lived "in tiny wretched huts with dirt floors and pigs snorting through the garbage."[12]

Mexico's postwar boom was engulfed in a wave of opportunism.

[7]"The 19th Century," p. 16.

[8]Diego G. López Rosado and Juan Noyola Vásquez, "Los salarios reales en México, 1939-1950," *El trimestre económico*, XVIII (April-June 1951), 206.

[9]Emilio Mújica Montoya, "Los salarios en la economía nacional," *Investigación económica*, XVI, No. 4 (1956), 566.

[10]Salvador Calvillo Madrigal, "Política agraria," *El Nacional*, Dec. 17, 1952.

[11]*El agrarismo mexicano y la reforma agraria* (Mexico, 1959), p. 499.

[12]Uhl, "The 19th Century," p. 18.

This was the era of the new rich, of those who loved ostentatious displays of luxury, no matter who paid for them.[13] There was corruption at the top and at the bottom, particularly in the days of Miguel Alemán.[14] Huge fortunes were accumulated by businessmen. Governors, cabinet members, and others used their offices for pecuniary gain. Plagued by an inflation that reduced their meager salaries almost daily, hundreds of thousands of public employees emulated their patrons. Even teachers exacted bribes from parents waiting to enter their children in schools in Mexico City. If the parents did not pay what was asked, there was no place for their child in the classroom. Ill-gotten gains had always been part of revolutionary Mexico, but this was called corruption in the past. Now efforts were being made to justify bribes on the basis that tribute must be paid to those who had brought Mexico's recent and impressive developments. "We laid the foundation for Mexican capitalism," Carlos Fuentes had Federico Robles say in his novel *La región más transparente*. "What if we did get our percentage from every . . . contract? What if the collective farm directors do steal half the appropriations they are given? Would you," he asked, "prefer that in order to avoid these evils we had done nothing at all? I repeat," declared Robles, "because of what we went through, we are entitled to everything. Because we were born in dirt-floor shacks, we have the right now to live in mansions with high ceilings and stone walls, with a Rolls-Royce at the door." A man had to take advantage of his opportunities. "And if I hadn't," Robles continued, "someone else would have seized what I have seized, stand where I stand now, do what I do."

Unquestionably the great defection came in the agrarian picture; here the leaders of the forties and fifties veered away from Cárdenas' views. Postwar Mexico favored private ownership of land; less land was expropriated and less given to the peasants. Cárdenas granted 2,934,856 hectares of land annually; Avila Camacho 555,929; Alemán 669,378; and Ruiz Cortines 533,130.[15] There was less arable land to give, reported the policy makers. The solution was to develop marginal lands for farming and move the landless there. With this in mind irrigation projects were mapped out, boom towns built, and mountains and valleys pierced with roads linking village and city. Despite this, only a fraction of the landless population found new homes in the irrigated districts.

Cárdenas and his disciples left *ejidal* ownership to the state; their

[13]Cline, p. 285.
[14]Silva Herzog, *El agrarismo mexicano*, p. 544.
[15]Ibid., p. 535.

successors gave individual titles to the land. Alemán moved another step away from traditional agrarian reform. A few days after taking office he modified Article 27 by introducing legislation safeguarding certain kinds of property from expropriation. All privately owned land of less than 150 hectares—an increase of 50 hectares over previous legislation—was made safe from expropriation. Holdings of 300 hectares or less planted to bananas, sugar cane, coffee, henequen, rubber, cocoa, grapes, olives, vanilla, and fruit were included.[16]

A mixed reaction greeted these changes. The conservatives, a majority by 1946, praised them. The reformers, and particularly the agrarians, denounced them as a step backward. To them increasing the size of property safe from expropriation aggravated the land question. Millions of hectares were still in the hands of great landlords, and millions of people were landless. Land in the areas opened for farming, the reformers charged, had fallen into the hands of "nylon farmers," political cronies of the administrations. There was something strange, too, they added, in the fact that the lands excluded from expropriation, which were the most productive, were found frequently in the native states of Alemán and his favorites.[17] After these changes were enacted, according to the agrarian reformers, only a minority received land. For the rest there was nothing except to flock to the cities or to join the march across the Río Grande, further proof that the Revolution had failed.

Even if the agrarians had oversimplified the case, the fact was that the new policies marked the demise of a militant agrarianism that labored to nationalize the land and to build a quasi-*ejidal* economy. Now private property, large and small, was considered sacred. Advances in farming came from the use of science, irrigation, and mechanization, not from the *ejido* as an ideal, either the communal or collective type. This is not to deny the gains made in agriculture, especially after 1953.[18] These gains, however, did not spring from the small farms or the village *ejidos*, which remained largely unproductive; they came from the great estates that formed in the wake of the legislation of 1946 and the giant collective farms of the Cárdenas era, which were not disturbed unduly by the conservatives. The cash crops raised on this land were often sold abroad or, as in the case of cotton, were nonfood crops. The advances were not merely the result of postwar planning but were the rewards of years of labor.

Of the three presidents who ruled between 1940 and 1958 only one,

[16]Ibid., p. 493.

[17]Ibid., pp. 493, 522, 527.

[18]Ibid., pp. 501, 538.

Manuel Avila Camacho, had direct ties with the Revolution. Avila Camacho, a polo-playing general and Cárdenas' choice for the presidency in 1940, had seen almost no active duty but had spent nearly the entire Revolution as a minor clerical officer, rising through the ranks as a careful, plodding subordinate devoted to questions of organization. Never a very colorful figure, he won recognition as a protégé of Cárdenas. He represented the state of Puebla, where his family had lived for generations. "His father was a landowner, not very rich, not very poor," a leader in his community and a spokesman for the conservative, Spanish, and Catholic *bourgeoisie*, wrote John Gunther.[19] Pleasant and well-meaning, Avila Camacho was a transition president, standing between the political extremes of the past. Selected as a compromise, he slowed down the pace of reform, placated the church, and encouraged private enterprise.[20]

His successor, Miguel Alemán, personified the business-minded leadership of postwar Mexico. Where Avila Camacho had accepted the advice of the old guard, Alemán, a dynamic leader, was the "harbinger of the Economic Revolution."[21] Like Avila Camacho, whom he served as campaign manager in 1940 and later as minister of *Gobernación*, Alemán came from the southeast, having been born in Veracruz. "Alert, smooth and friendly," he was the "party fixer, the boss of the government machine."[22] A lawyer by training and a politician by dedication, he rode the Cárdenas bandwagon and then jumped to Avila Camacho's. Alemán was the first nonmilitary president of twentieth-century Mexico. While his father had given his life in the struggle, Alemán had no other connection with the holocaust. He spoke for the urban middle class and particularly the businessman. If Avila Camacho held mild agrarian views, Alemán was indifferent to the peasant. To him industry was the salvation of Mexico and private enterprise, foreign or native, the way to get it.[23] Convinced that the agrarian reformers had failed, he placed his faith in foreign capital and the businessman.

Last of the men from the southeast was Adolfo Ruiz Cortines, onetime governor of Veracruz, Alemán's campaign manager, and his minister of *Gobernación*. Old for a Mexican president—nicknamed *El Viejo*—he was a compromise between the choices of Alemán and Cárdenas, both of whom preferred someone else. A bureaucrat and

[19]*Inside Latin America* (New York, 1941), pp. 34-35.
[20]Kirk, pp. 183-184.
[21]Cline, p. 312.
[22]Gunther, p. 91.
[23]Robert E. Scott, *Mexican Government in Transition* (Urbana, Ill., 1959), p. 206.

administrator rather than a glamorous political personality, he rode to power on the coattails of the younger and dynamic Alemán.[24] Like Alemán before him, he spoke for the groups that captured power during the forties. Yet he broke with Alemán, whose business-minded administration had taken credit for an industrial boom but had ignored corruption and the continuing plight of the peasant. Avila Camacho was selected to consolidate the radical push of the thirties; Ruiz Cortines led a mild "liberal" reaction against Alemán, whose policies had frightened moderates by 1952. Scrupulously honest, he fought graft, brought to a close the era of frenzied industrialization, and gave greater emphasis to agriculture.[25] If little was done to aid the peasant farmer, as some believe, still agricultural production soared to new heights under his benevolent tutelage.

Whatever the personal differences between these three leaders, their goals were stamped with a common die. Differences in policy were matters of degree rather than principle. All three spoke for the urban classes and favored the ideal of industrialization. While they devoted time and thought to agrarian questions, the issues of the past were of secondary importance to them. The war forced Avila Camacho to neglect land problems after 1942; Alemán had to orient and direct a business boom. Not until Ruiz Cortines did the government again focus on agrarian matters, but interest in the *ejido* was not revived. None of these rulers was known as a great patron of public education, least of all the rural school, although all supported it. Like Obregón and Calles, they left school problems to others.

Perhaps, as many maintain, by 1946 the Revolution had become history. No matter how wise its policies, things were different now. "The administration of President Alemán," wrote Silva Herzog, "whatever anyone might say to the contrary, is no longer a continuation of former governments. For better or for worse . . . it is the beginning of a new era in the history of Mexico."[26] In the field of education, too, the rural school faced new challenges.

I I

At the blueprint level the men of the forties and fifties favored a middle-of-the-road solution to the educational issues of their time. Striving to divorce themselves from the "radical" planners of the

[24]Ibid., pp. 217-218.
[25]Calvillo Madrigal, "Política agraria."
[26]"La revolución mexicana ya es un hecho histórico," *Cuadernos americanos*, XLVII (Sept.-Oct. 1949), 14.

thirties, they fell back upon statistical proofs of numerical gains that satisfied urban public opinion and avoided controversy. In practice the ideological conflict of the period, which dated back to Cárdenas' time, hampered a neutral policy. Spurred on by the East-West struggle on the world scene, critics who saw the specter of Communism behind the ideas of yesteryear won the ear of the executives. By 1958 salient reforms had been purged from the record books or filed among forgotten legislation.

Where other administrations, including the conservative Northern Dynasty, had placed their stress on the country schools, the business-minded leaders favored urban schools and particularly higher and technical education.[27] Everything was done to make learning part of the industrial effort, a decision made simple by public indifference to rural problems. The leaders' dedication to the ideal of peace in the countryside brought the curtain down on the era of the teacher-leader, whose usefulness had declined after the oil expropriation of 1938. Legal and public sanction was extended to old enemies of public education. The National Confederation of Parents of Families, long hostile to the policies of the past, acquired official sanction.[28] What funds were available were channeled into special schools or into the construction of a university for the benefit of a half-dozen cities, whose graduates seldom bothered themselves with the peasant. Gross expenditures for education rose, but the percentage of the total national budget reserved for rural schools declined as funds were funneled off into roads and public works. Ruiz Cortines made a belated effort to remedy this picture, but his financial reforms fell short of what was called for.

Nothing better illustrates the shift away from rural education and left-wing solutions than the character and thinking of the men who charted the routes of the school in this period. Between 1940 and 1958 there were five men in the house that Vasconcelos built on Calle Argentina, three of them during the administration of Avila Camacho, when major battles were fought and lost by reformers. Of the five, two were moderates, one was a conservative businessman, and one spoke for the church. Only one represented the views of Bassols. With two exceptions, they had almost no experience with education.

Luis Sánchez Pontón, Avila Camacho's initial appointee, "quiet, well-educated [and] nonassertive," harked back to the thirties.[29] Be-

[27]Beteta, *Pensamiento y dinámica de la revolución*, p. 168.
[28]Kirk, pp. 149-150.
[29]Gunther, p. 95.

fore coming to the Ministry of Education in 1940, his first important federal post, he was governor of his native state of Puebla. Sánchez Pontón and his leftist undersecretary, Enrique Arrequín, served a brief ten months, during which they were censured sharply by critics. Their successor was Octavio Véjar Vásquez, a "pistol-toting" crony of the Avila Camacho family. He was a general with a law background, former judge of the Military Supreme Court, and later attorney general for the army. His friends, reported Betty Kirk (p. 150), were the conservatives. He was convinced that there were scores of expendable radicals in the Ministry, that the teachers' syndicate was too powerful, and that Christianity was being forsaken. By 1943 he had purged his house of "radicals," destroyed their organization, and won the hearts of conservatives.[30] Avila Camacho's last chief was a poet and diplomat. Suave and sophisticated, the antithesis of his predecessor, Jaime Torres Bodet adopted the middle road of compromise. He had served an apprenticeship under Vasconcelos as his personal secretary and later as head of the Department of Libraries, after which he was occupied with writing and diplomacy. The most competent chief after Bassols, he had to pick up the pieces of what was left of the Ministry after Véjar Vásquez had nearly destroyed it.

Manuel Gual Vidal, Alemán's choice and the successor to Torres Bodet, was a prosperous lawyer whose knowledge of educational matters was limited to teaching law and finance at the National University. He was chairman of the committee for the National Charity Agency, which distributed funds from the sale of pawned goods. Hostile to labor and indifferent to rural questions, he was selected with the hope of bringing business efficiency and support to the national educational program.[31] He was followed by José Angel Ceniceros, who, with Torres Bodet, was the only other minister of education with more than a cursory knowledge of school questions. Ceniceros had studied at the old National Normal School in Mexico City, from which he graduated in 1921, and for nineteen years had taught at the National Teacher's College. His failure, therefore, is the more disheartening. Ceniceros was also a lawyer, professor of law at the university, the author of books on criminal law and juvenile delinquency, and former editor of the government newspaper *El Nacional*. Well-intentioned and mildly liberal, he incurred the wrath of the Republic's teachers by his actions in the labor disputes of 1958. His departure was welcomed by a majority of teachers.

None of these figures, no matter what other qualities they may

[30]Townsend, p. 346.
[31]Kneller, p. 57.

have possessed, was a specialist in rural education or especially concerned with it. Sánchez Pontón had some experience with rural affairs but was no expert. Of his successors only Véjar Vásquez knew rural life; the others were urbanites, closely identified with their times. Outside of Torres Bodet, a writer in the spirit of Rubén Darío, all reflected the parochial views of Mexico City.

The retreat from the policies of Bassols and Cárdenas began with the presidential campaign of 1940. General Juan Andreu Almazán, the conservative candidate, centered much of his speechmaking around the school issue.[32] The schools, he declared, were godless and communistic. His bitter attacks aggravated an issue already critical, and his defeat at the polls did not calm the conflict. No sooner was Sánchez Pontón sworn into office than he became the target for attacks from those who saw him as a cabinet spokesman for Cárdenas. Some of the criticism he invited by speaking of the class struggle after a conservative tide had swamped the government. Much of it, however, rose out of his efforts to hold the school program together; he was willing to modify the program but not to abandon it. He was crucified for this. After ten months in office, during which he was unable to overcome persistent criticism from the outside and to heal the rifts in the Ministry, Sánchez Pontón resigned over a dispute involving his leftist subordinate Arrequín.

His departure from the hallowed halls on Calle Argentina hailed a conservative victory and closed the chapter opened by Bassols but did not end the strife. With Sánchez Pontón's demise the last of the "golden age" of the rural school vanished from the scene. Prophetically, perhaps, that same year Moisés Sáenz died in Perú, and Vasconcelos, morose and disillusioned, publicly joined forces with the enemies of a school he had helped to found two decades earlier, becoming an adviser to Véjar Vásquez.

With the appointment of Véjar Vásquez the schools of the past were put on trial before a hostile judge and found wanting. At last, after what seemed like ages of persecution, the day had come when believers would direct the fortunes of education, conservatives declared.[33] Véjar Vásquez, to paraphrase a statement in *Excelsior*, was above partisan strife, committed to no one, free to work out impartially the problem before him.[34] The conservatives had reason for their jubilation, for there was nothing of the reformer in Véjar Vás-

[32]Kirk, p. 144.

[33]Ibid., p. 151.

[34]"La renuncia de Sánchez Pontón," *Excelsior*, Sept. 13, 1941.

quez. His policies had flowered before the Revolution. Clerically minded teachers won key posts, two priests found places on the Committee on Art and Culture—in defiance of laws that said that no priest could hold public office—Jesuits got back school property, and Falangists were approved as directors of public schools.[35]

Unwilling to have anything to do with the school of the thirties, Véjar Vásquez offered a substitute: the school of love. Love would eliminate all conflict between classes; love would triumph over all obstacles. His "school would teach Mexicans to love one another despite differences in creed, party, or class."[36] As a substitute for the shops and tools that characterized education when economics dictated policy, Véjar Vásquez offered spiritual and moral values. To him the schoolmasters were a sort of clergy, and the school was a mission.[37] The problem of education, rural and urban, was a moral one.

Past policy stressed the group; Véjar Vásquez emphasized the individual. Group education, he felt, was communistic; to educate was to recognize the individual personality and enable him to fill his "hierarchic position in creation," as, according to him, there existed a well-defined and proper place for every human being, a kind of predestination. The school must develop abilities inherent in man, as modified by environment and history, in the hope of reaching a higher degree of natural perfection. Only when free reign was given to what was original did growth take place. Since all originality began with the Conquest of Mexico, there was nothing of value in the pre-Conquest heritage.[38] Stated another way, the Indian village must learn from the Spanish city, with the urban school serving as the model.

If love dictated pedagogical principles, there was none left over for the halls on Calle Argentina. Avila Camacho had forsaken Sánchez Pontón in behalf of national unity, but his military colleague precipitated a struggle that threatened to sabotage the system. Rather than close the gap between reformers and conservatives, Véjar Vásquez widened it. To Vasconcelos and his friends the school of love had replaced that of hate;[39] Bassols called Véjar Vásquez the dupe of the Franco-Fascist columns in Mexico.[40] In Congress Véjar Vásquez' policies stirred a nest of hornets. He was accused of discriminating

[35]Kirk, p. 150.
[36]Kneller, p. 68.
[37]*Excelsior*, May 16, 1943.
[38]Kneller, pp. 68-69.
[39]*Excelsior*, Jan. 12, 1943.
[40]*Excelsior*, May 19, 1942.

against rural education, of seeking to deliver the rural school into private hands, of being Vasconcelos' stooge, and of trying to bring religion into the classroom. He denied these charges but acknowledged that "the rural schoolmaster had not lived up to his obligations. He lacked the kindness, the virtue, the ideals that inspired the priest: the will to serve others."[41] Avila Camacho, unable to quiet the furor raised by his controversial subordinate, dismissed Véjar Vásquez in December 1943 and called in Torres Bodet.

The new chief of education faced a multitude of problems. To his credit, by 1946 he had silenced the critics and healed the wounds. He did this by offering something to everyone. For the conservatives and the rising industrialists there was the middle-of-the-road policy and a new emphasis on technical training. The church was pleased, because he looked the other way when clerics opened schools. To placate the liberals he supported publicly the revolutionary principles embodied in Article 3. When asked whether he favored urban over rural education, he replied that they were equally necessary to Mexico. His schools, it was often said, represented the accumulated wisdom of the past and the ideas of tomorrow. "Peace, democracy, and justice"—these were the cornerstones of the schools established by Torres Bodet.[42] Democracy and justice remained goals, but peace did come to the educational scene.

Virtually undisturbed were the blueprints left behind by Véjar Vásquez. The Ministry had an enlightened chief on Calle Argentina and a more realistic view of the political situation, but there was nothing left of center about policy, particularly after the factory-building boom began to demand technical training. Nor was Torres Bodet particularly interested in rural education. Only indirectly did he give his personal attention to the needs of the village school: through his efforts to improve teacher training, which involved working with the rural *Normales*, and the literacy campaign, a nationwide program.

Gual Vidal and Ceniceros, the successors to Torres Bodet, followed in his footsteps. Gual Vidal was institutionally oriented. Mexico was a mature nation with stable institutions, he asserted. With peace and order, which would permit the ideals of the Revolution to bear fruit, the future was assured. National standards had been achieved; now the need was for the codification of the laws. There was no social life, either national or international, without legal order.[43] "The liberty and dignity of man, the integrity of the family . . .

[41]*Excelsior*, Dec. 12, 29, 31, 1942.
[42]*Excelsior*, Dec. 25, 1943, Dec. 1, 1945.
[43]Kneller, p. 73.

and the sovereignty of the state"—this was the creed of Ceniceros. In his mind there was no room for radical measures such as the socialist reform of Article 3 that spawned a "historic materialism whose companion was Communism." He condemned pedagogical ideas that led to rifts between classes, particularly between city and country folk. Evolution, not revolution, was the way out. Six-year plans based on false panaceas were worthless; long-range plans that offered "decent and veracious" solutions were needed.[44] The school was to prepare the student for life in a democracy, the family, and a new world order, always in the minds of Mexico's postwar leaders. Ruiz Cortines ruled for all Mexicans, and his school was for everyone. There were no "lefts and rights" in the Ministry of Education, only professional service.[45] Like their predecessors, Ceniceros and Gual Vidal left rural education to their subordinates.

I I I

That there would be changes in past programs during this era was inevitable. That they would bring conflict was obvious. The battles revolved around three contemplated changes: the elimination of coeducation, the revision of the socialist amendment of 1934, and the unification of rural and urban educational programs.

Political warfare over the socialist school of 1934, which at times led to bloodshed, erupted in the election of 1940. Betty Kirk reported (p. 140) that the key campaign issue was the controversial law. Almazán, a wealthy general from Nuevo León, long shorn of his revolutionary fervor, was an old foe of the socialist doctrine. He had opposed its introduction in the public schools of Nuevo León, and he brought the issue into the election struggle.[46] Backed by Cárdenas and the reformers, Avila Camacho, never a supporter of the measure, paradoxically ran on a platform endorsing it. On the surface his victory carried the day for the defenders of the 1934 reform; but they had won a skirmish, not the war. Once in office, Avila Camacho made clear that his sympathies did not lie with what he considered an extreme piece of legislation. Nor were Almazán's supporters defeated, for they quickly returned to the fray after the failure of their candidate.

The battle revolved around what critics of the socialist amendment called *la libertad de enseñanza*, the freedom to teach, an ideal that

[44]José Angel Ceniceros, *Educación y mexicanidad* (Mexico, 1958), pp. 38, 33, 120.
[45]*El Nacional*, Dec. 17, 1952.
[46]Millán, p. 271.

many of them had rejected when the church controlled education. They wanted to purge the schools of ideas hostile to religion, Catholicism in this case. They believed, with some justification, that the reforms of 1934 represented an attack on the faith. Had they stopped here, all but the radical diehards might have joined their cause, but this was only the beginning of their demands. Above everything else, what they wanted was to revise Article 3 in order to permit the church to sponsor schools once again; in other words, they advocated a return to the constitutional principles of 1857. This, therefore, was not merely an attack on the socialist school but on the revolutionary thesis that only the state has the right to sponsor public schools, a view reflecting a clerical conflict centuries old. Not only was the socialist school at stake, but, more significantly, so were some of the basic tenets of Mexican education.

This was indicated clearly by the attack on coeducation, for the faultfinding came from the same quarter. Schools for students of both sexes had arisen under Vasconcelos, and their number grew after Sáenz had taken command under Calles. During the twenties coeducation was limited to the primary schools; Bassols extended it to the secondary schools. This raised a storm of protest from the clergy and their supporters. The reformers held fast to their principle, for coeducation represented more than just school policy to them. Classrooms for both sexes, in their opinion, symbolized the progress Mexico had achieved since the days of Porfirio Díaz, when colonial traditions dominated thinking. There were also sound economic reasons for coeducational schools: they were cheaper to support. In the rural village, furthermore, they struck at dual standards that made the wife a slave to her husband, a relationship the reformers hoped to destroy.[47]

The school for both sexes became a target of conservative attack almost immediately after Véjar Vásquez replaced his predecessor. Sympathetic to the demands of the conservatives, he encouraged them publicly, leading an American observer to wonder if the school of love would really surmount all class conflict. For, paradoxically enough, Véjar Vásquez' catholicity did not include both sexes. The natural requirements of men and women were so different, Véjar Vásquez believed, that he preferred to limit educational opportunity rather than follow the "socialist" policy of teaching males and females together.[48] Avila Camacho concurred.

Three months after Véjar Vásquez had taken office, Article 3

[47]Alberto Méndez Bravo, *La escuela rural mejicana* (Santiago, Chile, 1929), p. 103.
[48]Kneller, p. 68.

was shorn of its coeducational features. Coeducation was abolished over the protests of thousands of teachers and parents who pointed out that this step came at a time when the world was moving in the opposite direction. From a monetary angle the decision was also highly unrealistic, for now the budget would have to support two school systems.[49] Hardest hit by the legislation were the women of Mexico, who found themselves once again classified as second-class citizens. They were saved from the full impact of the blow by the inability of the administration to change over completely to the dual system for lack of funds with which to duplicate facilities.

Having won the battle over coeducation, the conservatives opened a nationwide campaign against the reforms of 1934. There was no letup after Véjar Vásquez left office. With the support of affluent businessmen and the church, conservative politicians demanded the repeal of the controversial amendment. Middle-class opinion rallied behind them.

Cognizant of the growing dissatisfaction with the school bill of 1934, the National Syndicate of Teachers (SNTE) convoked a conference in 1945 to discuss the question of revision. There was general agreement that concessions were called for; the public must be pacified. Among the teachers themselves there were serious objections to the law. It was inflammatory in character, and it left a host of questions unanswered. For example, how was socialism to be established in the school of a capitalist country? Willing to make some concessions, the majority at the conference recommended modifications of the objectionable features but no retreat from the premise of public control of education. A moving endorsement by Vicente Lombardo Toledano, leftist labor leader and teacher and intimate friend of the president, carried the day for the friends of revision. Among the foes of concession were Rafael Ramírez and Alberto Bremauntz, the framer of the 1934 version.

Since Avila Camacho and the conference were of the same view, congressional action followed quickly. Where just a few years before deputies and senators had pledged allegiance to socialism, the sole opposition to the change came from ten votes cast by the spokesmen for the Mexican Confederation of Workers, whose former boss endorsed the revision. The reform of 1934 had established a socialist school excluding all religious doctrine and demanding an exact and rational concept of the universe; there was nothing of this in the version of 1945. Education would "seek to develop harmoni-

[49]George I. Sánchez, "Education in Mexico," in Arthur H. Moehlman and Joseph S. Roucek, eds. *Comparative Education* (New York, 1951), p. 105.

ously the faculties of the human spirit, and at the same time inculcate a love of country and a feeling for international solidarity of independence and of justice." Education would continue to remain aloof from religious doctrine.[50] Nothing was said of socialism or the class struggle.

Less controversial, although equally meaningful as a commentary on the thinking of the times, was the question of a curriculum for the primary schools. Were country and city schools to have one program? Cárdenas and his advisers had advocated one program for both. Their opinion was that the country school should be the equal of the city school. This was not the view of former policy makers, who believed that the rural school was to prepare the country child for country living, not urban life.[51] By the late 1930's, however, hundreds of thousands of peasants had flocked to the cities. Even after they had attended school in the village, they were unprepared to cope with their urban environment. This was due to the elementary and limited nature of the rural-school curriculum, said the new pedagogues. The country school had not prepared its students for all eventualities; now, furthermore, the needs of the Republic were different. Technicians for factories and large farms were needed instead of peasants for subsistence agriculture.

What the pedagogues of the forties advocated for the rural school was the adoption of the more advanced urban curriculum. Their aim was to unite the village with the city and particularly with the industrialization program. Cárdenas and his supporters, who stressed agrarian reforms, paradoxically counseled a similar merger, but for different reasons. They sought to raise the level of education in the village by removing from the national scene a rural school recognized nationally as inferior to that of the city. There was, in addition, universal recognition that rural needs required independent attention, which the urban curriculum furnished only with extensive modifications. As matters worked out, little was done under Cárdenas. By 1946, on the other hand, Torres Bodet was able to announce that the rural school no longer formed peasants, but citizens of Mexico.[52] No matter where he went to class, every youngster now enjoyed the same fundamental instruction. With equal ease he could live anywhere.

The adoption of the one-school-for-everyone reversed the think-

[50]Kneller, p. 78.

[51]Ibid., p. 105.

[52]Ibid., p. 106.

ing of men like Sáenz, who had stressed that the routine of rural life differed radically from that of the city. In the face of the progress achieved since 1920, supporters of this view argued, rural Mexico still remained primitive and isolated. The city was another world. To make the schools in the villages a replica of those in Mexico City would cut them off from the countryside. When the rural school attempted to offer a full course of academic subjects, it had no time for the practical side of its program, which had distinguished it in the past. Nor did the average child in the rural community require an academic preparation for secondary schools. What was called for was a terminal education offering the knowledge and skills required by the village. These criticisms were ignored, although once again the inability of officials in Mexico City to implement their policy left much of the old rural-school program undisturbed. In practice, therefore, there was less change than the new theory called for.

IV

The educational architects of the forties and fifties focused their attention on two problems, which they felt were fundamental. One was the appalling illiteracy that two decades of activity had failed to eradicate. The other was the shortage of schools.

That illiteracy lay at the bottom of Mexico's educational problem was not an idea novel to the times. Mexican leaders had long been convinced that if they could teach everyone his ABC's all would be well at home. Thinkers on both sides of the political fence were fascinated by this idea of literacy as a cure-all. Vasconcelos had sponsored a national literacy campaign, and the Cardenistas had a mild flirtation with one. It remained for the spokesmen of the postwar era, however, to enshrine the panacea.

To Torres Bodet, as to Vasconcelos, the tragedy of Mexico was that millions were unable even to read a newspaper or to write a simple phrase. There were rural communities where no one could write his name. In 1940 more than half of the population lived and died oblivious to the written word. How to eradicate this evil when there was a shortage of schools and teachers? Here was the problem. Vasconcelos' solution, which the Cárdenas administration adopted, was the forerunner of the each-one-teach-one idea of Torres Bodet. Since there were only so many schools and teachers, said Vasconcelos, the way out of the dilemma was to employ all literate Mexicans as teachers. They would teach their neighbors to read and write. Vasconcelos put his idea into practice almost immediately after taking office in 1921. His short-lived program, calling on all Mexicans to fulfill what he called their moral duty, was a holy crusade against the great evil.

This pioneer program and that of the Cárdenas administration were emergency measures. Vasconcelos' was over by 1922; Cárdenas' program began in 1936 and was abandoned two years later. Torres Bodet's program, organized as a war measure, became a permanent feature under Alemán's administration, which established a General Office of Literacy and Out-of-School Education. The program began with the Federal Literacy Law of 1944, which exhorted every literate Mexican between eighteen and sixty years of age to teach one or more Mexicans to read and write.[53] The legislation was not a substitute for the school but a supplementary measure. Literacy centers were planned for all communities lacking primary schools or with schools that could not take all first-grade students. Still the emphasis was on teaching adults. According to Luis Chávez Orozco, the law was politically inspired, designed to quiet some of the discontent with the administration and to unite Mexicans in the war effort. This was a crusade around which Mexicans could rally; after all, who was not in favor of literacy?

These literacy drives were opened with much fanfare. There were speeches by presidents, governors, and mayors. Newspapers and magazines carried full-page pictures calling on the public to do its duty. Federal and local officials were warned to support the work. Public employees were forced to participate, and some states rewarded them for their work; others punished laggards. Durango, in the days of Avila Camacho, levied fines against employees who did not support the effort. Michoacán reduced the sentences of prisoners who learned to read and write, and Oaxaca offered to build a school in the village with the best record.

Many noteworthy examples of devotion were brought forth by these literacy programs. Ernest Gruening recalled seeing in a tenement in Mexico City "a girl of thirteen who had gathered some twenty-five children about her, marking letters and figures on the pink-tinted plaster wall, while the mothers paused in their washing around the central stone fountain to gaze with admiration and awe." The daughter of an illiterate plasterer "taught her father and 150 children to read and write."[54] One man carried books in a wheelbarrow for his neighbors to read and two years later had established a school

[53]Secretía. de Educ. Públ., *Ley de emergencia que establece la campaña nacional contra el analfabetismo* (Mexico, 1944), pp. 16-17.

[54]*Mexico and Its Heritage*, p. 518.

for 900 children.[55] There were similar examples in the thirties and forties. In San Pedro Arriba, a village in the state of Mexico, the local schoolmaster held his first class between four and five in the morning for 65 men. The children, the school's regular students, came from nine in the morning to one in the afternoon and again from three to five. From one to three the schoolmaster taught a class of women.[56]

From the outset, notwithstanding these individual performances, the programs were beset by difficulties. Public enthusiasm, strong in the beginning, lagged after the novelty wore off. The two early efforts were abandoned partly for this reason, after only a limited success had been achieved. Vasconcelos reported that 52,000 persons had learned their ABC's by 1922, the year of the program's demise; the Cárdenas administration claimed another 224,992 persons. At this pace there would be no victory in the battle against illiteracy, even if the figures did not err on the optimistic side. The leaders of the forties determined to do better. When a lag developed in 1945, soon after the program was organized, officials began to offer financial remuneration to persons teaching in the literacy centers. Torres Bodet, who had conceived the effort as a patriotic endeavor, was dismayed to find persons being paid to do what he considered an obligation; but as the program faltered he, too, accepted the need to pay for service rendered. By 1946 salaries of 60 pesos a month were common.

Waning public enthusiasm was one of several drawbacks. From the beginning the programs focused on urban and semiurban centers. Almost nothing was done in the villages. One reason for this, stated the SNTE, was that only one out of five persons was qualified to teach others to read and write; this fraction of the population usually lived in cities and towns.[57] The problem in rural regions was further complicated by the fact that many people there spoke only an Indian tongue. Numerical gains in the number of literate persons, therefore, were small and confined to the cities. The literacy program became less efficient in another way because of inflation. While the number of people learning their ABC's decreased between 1945 and 1959, the cost of teaching them multiplied rapidly. It required nearly twice as much money in 1954 to support 10,900 literacy cen-

[55]Frank Tannenbaum, "The Miracle School," *Century Magazine*, CVI (Aug. 1923), 505.

[56]Sindicato Nacional de Trabajadores de la Educación, *Conferencia pedagógica* (Mexico, 1945), pp. 215-216.

[57]Ibid., p. 211.

ters as it did to keep 37,722 in 1945.[58] Still more centers were called for; there were 40,000 localities in 1955 having from 20 to 300 school-age children without schools. What this came down to, Ruiz Cortines confessed, was that despite the drum-beating of the literacy exponents one out of every two Mexicans[59]—17 million in 1958—did not read or write, a number larger than that of any other era in the history of Mexico.

There were other negative factors. Between 1945 and 1958, the Ministry of Education reported, 4,570,578 persons learned to read and write in the program. On an annual average 326,541 persons completed their work successfully. But the yearly population growth was nearly three times that number, and the schools were not making up the difference. Even accepting the figures reported by the Ministry at face value, there was another question involved. Of the 4,570,578 who had learned their ABC's, what percentage retained them over the years? The problem was not just to learn them but to put them to use. Among a population beyond reach of books and newspapers there was reason to believe that many who had learned their alphabet seldom if ever put it to use and consequently forgot it after a year or two. By the Ministry's own admission one third of those previously certified as literate had for lack of practice forgotten by 1959 what they had learned.

By 1959 many had come to doubt the efficacy of the literacy panacea. Was teaching the ABC's the solution to Mexico's problems? More and more replied in the negative. The barrier was poverty, which literacy could never eliminate. Literacy was wasted where the activity of life centered on survival. Unless measures were taken simultaneously to correct the conditions that produced illiteracy, being able to read and write was of little value. Illiteracy was not a pedagogical ill but a reflection of deep-seated economic and social conditions. If the alphabet was to mean something, it had to offer specific advantages in terms of practical results, which could not be accomplished with poorly paid amateur teachers whose sole qualification was that they were able to read and write.[60]

Building schools was the other activity of the forties and fifties. Alemán announced during his presidential speechmaking that 24,000

[58]Secretía. de Educ. Públ., "Dimensiones y contorno del analfabetismo en México," *Escuela nueva*, I, No. 5 (Oct. 10, 1955), 154.

[59]Cited in Ignacio Mendoza Rivera, "Honda crisis de la educación en México," *Problemas de México*, I (Oct. 1, 1958), 243.

[60]Sindicato Nacional de Trabajadores de la Educación, "El problema de la educación extraescolar," *Problemas educativos de México*, I (April 1958), 16-17; Manuel Román Díaz de León, "Miseria y analfabetismo," *El Nacional*, Oct. 17, 1953.

new primary schools were needed;[61] his minister of education called for 70,000 classrooms.[62] Avila Camacho before him and later Ruiz Cortines made similar appeals. These schools were needed immediately; gone were the days, said the new policy makers, when the best school was the shade of a tree, as Sáenz believed. Modern education required well-built and fully equipped schools, which few rural communities had.

Granted that schools were called for, how was the administration to build them? Even critics conceded that the budget was stretched to the breaking point. There were no funds. Véjar Vásquez' answer was to revive the circuit-school plan of 1929, authorizing rural communities to establish schools and support their teachers. The Ministry of Education offered to defray part of the teachers' salaries as its share of the bargain.[63] In a capsule, the rural community was granted permission to establish independent schools. Behind this directive was the assumption that the way out of the school shortage lay in putting the burden of education on the local community. This idea had been of doubtful value in the past and remained so in 1942. Financially and otherwise, the village was not prepared to cope with the need. Schools had been built under the original circuit-school plan, but they had proved weak.[64] Most of their teachers were ill-trained and ill-paid, and standards were low. This was equally characteristic of those rural schools the states and municipalities supported in 1942.

Not only was the public unprepared for the challenge, but the climate of opinion was unfavorable. Hostile ideas long thought dead were enjoying a revival of popularity. Organizations antagonistic to reform, and to public schooling specifically, clamored for change. One American observer reported that there were 250,000 peasants among the *sinarquistas*, whose leaders condemned public education and expressed sympathy for Hitler and Franco.[65] To give them control of education would be to destroy it, reported the National Confederation of Peasants and spokesmen for the teachers.[66] This and similar indictments forced Véjar Vásquez to abandon his formula.

Torres Bodet's solution, which the Alemán administration developed more fully, was to call on private capital. With this hope in

[61]*El Popular*, July 5, 1945.
[62]*El Nacional*, March 20, 1948.
[63]*Tiempo*, July 24, 1942, p. 28.
[64]Unpublished letter from Narciso Bassols to Moisés Sáenz, Feb. 4, 1933.
[65]John Collier quoted in *Excelsior*, May 26, 1942.
[66]*Tiempo*, Aug. 14, 1942, p. 26.

mind Gual Vidal opened a national school-building drive urging businessmen in particular to contribute generously. The results of these attempts to solicit voluntary contributions from private sources fell short of the demand. From the time of Avila Camacho to that of Ruiz Cortines 4,156 primary and secondary schools were erected by these means.[67] Of the approximately 435 million pesos spent on these schools, 300 million pesos came from public funds.[68] Less than a third of the schools were erected in the provinces, most of them in cities and towns. Nearly twice that number of rural schools—7,939—were built under federal auspices; 4,764 of them were erected by the Avila Camacho administration, a transition government between a collectivist past and the age of free enterprise, before the formal school-building drive started. Between 1945 and 1952, on the other hand, with a campaign accompanied by the customary fanfare of every Alemán project, only 1,263 schools were established, less than 210 a year. An additional 1,912 were built under Ruiz Cortines.[69] Without fanfare the Cardenistas, with a smaller school population to worry about, had established 4,250 rural schools, a figure surpassed only by Avila Camacho.

Few persons would have denied the value of building new schools; but this was not exactly the problem in the villages. Schools were needed there; still the government had seldom built schools in rural communities. The communities had built them, while the authorities furnished teachers and leadership. More often than not, a community had with sacrifice erected a school and then waited months and even years for a teacher. Judging from the number of schools built in the Federal District, or along the highways where tourists could see them, there was some reason to believe that the government was not primarily interested in the plight of the village. Without denying the need of the cities and towns, the school crisis was more acute in rural areas. Of the approximately 5 million children in the primary-school age bracket, 4 million lived in rural Mexico. Of the 3 million children without schools in 1958, three out of four lived in villages.

V

Somewhere between 1941 and 1958 the ideal of Vasconcelos and Sáenz, which Bassols and Cárdenas cherished, lost its vigor. With this weakening of spirit came a crisis in education. Errors were com-

[67]*El Nacional*, Nov. 10, 1958.
[68]*Excelsior*, Sept. 2, 1958.
[69]*Excelsior*, Sept. 3, 1958.

mitted in the past, declared Jesús Silva Herzog, but the general orientation of school policy was sound. There was need to correct, to adjust, to perfect.[70] Now, wrote Ernesto Galarza, there was a climate of opinion unsympathetic to the fundamentals of the past.[71] What was left of the ideas of yesteryear, to quote George I. Sánchez, whose *Mexico: A Revolution by Education* worshiped the school of the twenties and thirties, was "reminiscent more of the days of Díaz than of those of Obregón and Cárdenas.[72]

Who was to blame, asked Silva Herzog. Clearly responsible were the architects of school policy since Avila Camacho.[73] Guilty, too, were the industrialists and businessmen whose goals only indirectly coincided with the needs of the rural people and whose mentality envisaged progress in terms of the sale and purchase of articles.[74] Equally at fault were the reformers who had lost faith in themselves and in the ideals of the Revolution. The ideological confusion and moral collapse of the age left policy planners bereft of a program and leadership to offer.[75] "We have no formulas or solutions for any problem or preconceived ideas on any question," confessed Ceniceros and his followers upon taking office in 1952. "What solutions we adopt will spring from the nature of the question before us."[76] After three decades of countless studies by experts, of experimentation and crisis, this confession augured ill for the future. This was not the attitude that began the program in Vasconcelos' time.

It was clear by 1958 that the last cycle of education, which found the gospel of industry king in a land where two out of three Mexicans lived in villages, had not overcome the educational difficulties of the past. There was, as a matter of fact, reason to believe that the rural school was worse off than before.

[70]*La revolución mexicana en crisis*, p. 35.

[71]"New Molds for Latin American Youth," in *Some Educational and Anthropological Aspects of Latin America*, University of Texas Latin-American Studies, No. 5 (Austin, Tex., 1948), p. 35.

[72]"Education in Mexico," in Moehlman and Roucek, eds. *Comparative Education*, p. 106.

[73]*La revolución mexicana en crisis*, p. 36.

[74]Miguel Salas Anzures, "Las nuevas formas socio-políticas y el programa de la escuela rural," *El Nacional*, March 29, 1948.

[75]Silva Herzog, *La revolución mexicana en crisis*, p. 36.

[76]Mendoza Rivera, "Honda crisis," p. 245.

Chapter V

TWENTIETH-CENTURY MISSIONARIES

I

WHEN CONGRESS ACCEPTED NATIONAL RESPONSIBILITY for public education in 1921, there were few schools in the countryside and only a handful of teachers. Officials in Mexico City began from scratch, constructing schools and finding teachers for them. Of these two tasks the latter proved more difficult. Without teachers there could be no schools of any kind.

Finding rural schoolmasters was a formidable undertaking. They were scarce, and the qualifications for the job were stringent and difficult. Rural schoolteachers—those called upon to redeem the deserts of Coahuila and Nuevo León; the pest-ridden territories of Guerrero, Oaxaca, Tabasco, Campeche, and Chiapas; the barren and empty wastelands of Durango, Lower California, and Quintana Roo—wrote Manuel Gamio, had to be men and women free of the "metropolitan environment, with all its suave and artificial routine." Holding classes in these lands, he added, demanded natives of the regions, "tempered to the burning suns of the lime plains or the sandy deserts," able to eat the *tortilla* and chili of the sierra and to sit on a horse and handle a plow. There was no place for the traditional teacher, unable to teach anything beyond the abstract knowledge he had mastered in the city, who could not tell his pupils how to cultivate their lands and raise their livestock.[1] Those chosen for this calling, stressed Frank Tannenbaum, had "to carry on lacking outside stimulus, where there is no one to talk with, where there are no books, no newspapers, where isolation is as complete as it would be on an island in mid-ocean."[2] A person from the city, Gamio concluded, "must inevitably prove a weak, anemic, exotic, and artificial transplantation."[3] Nor had the learned of the metropolis abandoned their luxuries for the discom-

[1]Vasconcelos and Gamio, *Aspects of Mexican Civilization*, pp. 146-147.

[2]*Peace by Revolution: An Interpretation of Mexico* (New York, 1933), p. 275.

[3]Vasconcelos and Gamio, *Aspects of Mexican Civilization*, p. 147.

forts of the village, confessed Rafael Ramírez, for the National University and the normal schools of the time seldom prepared individuals for this challenge.[4]

José Vasconcelos began his search for rural schoolmasters with seventy-seven messiahs—*misioneros*, he called them—a tiny cadre of volunteers from the *Preparatoria*, the city normal school, and the university. Unlike the majority of their companions, these young men were emotionally attached to the Revolution, which had offered them the opportunity for dedicated service in behalf of their fellows in a way that was novel to Mexico. Many had followed Villa, Zapata, and Obregón. Having "tasted hardship and bitterness in camp and battle-field," Tannenbaum wrote, they were ready to break with the customs and traditions of urban life in order to find men and women for the classrooms the Republic desperately needed. Leaving Mexico City behind them, this handful of dedicated pioneers struck out for the rural communities, spreading the gospel of the Revolution and calling for schools. These missionaries formed the vanguard of an army of teachers that invaded and settled rural Mexico.[5]

Once in the village, the *misionero* called the *campesinos* together. If they would provide a schoolhouse and a piece of land for it, he told them, officials in Mexico City would send a teacher. After the people accepted this offer, the next step was to make a census of the children in the community. Then a contract was signed with the local leaders, and the *misionero* wrote officials in Mexico City, telling them "that such and such a village, in such and such a place, of such race and language, had so many children and was willing to receive a teacher, willing to provide a school building," as Tannenbaum recalled (p. 276).

Having promised teachers, Vasconcelos and his staff had to provide them. Once again the leaders of Mexico fell back upon the Revolution. The conflagration of 1910 had attracted hundreds who, stirred by its ideals of social justice, were eager to accept the challenge of teaching in a rural school. They could read and write and knew something of the fundamentals of arithmetic. More important, their parents had tilled the soil for generations. Although they lacked training and formal schooling, they offered leadership, initiative, and character tempered by years of strife, reported Tannenbaum (p. 276). Their trademark was common sense. The *misionero* gathered these people into groups, teaching them what they would have to

[4]Secretía. de Educ. Públ., *Las misiones culturales en 1927* (Mexico, 1928), p. 25.

[5]*Peace by Revolution*, pp. 275-276.

know in order to teach others. Then he left them on their own in the village.

For the young teacher left behind, the job was enormous. He had to win the confidence of his neighbors, long distrustful of strangers with modern ways. Then he had to find a schoolhouse, perhaps the unused church annex, the town hall, or even the jail. Sometimes nothing was available, so he gathered his pupils under a tree until the community erected a schoolhouse. Equally simple were the supplies and equipment he used: a blackboard he made himself, a few pieces of chalk, and the two or three books he brought with him. Then school began. By 1922 there were hundreds of these miracle schools and teachers in rural Mexico.

Cognizant that willingness to serve was no guarantee of performance, that close supervision was called for, Vasconcelos and his successors converted the *misioneros* into a corps of federal school inspectors, whose activities gradually assumed an administrative character. Coordinating and directing the expanding system of schools demanded experience and imagination, which the *misioneros* provided admirably. By changing the duties of the *misioneros*, however, officials in Mexico City left no one to carry on their old functions, which were still necessary. Some system of teacher training was urgently needed if education was to take root and grow.

None of the established institutions offered a way out of the difficulty. Rural normal schools were on the drafting boards, and guidance and training from Mexico City or a provincial capital threatened to divorce the program from the needs of the countryside. Some agency for the rural areas had to be found immediately to train teachers and stimulate them, George I. Sánchez has written. Poorly trained, the average rural schoolmaster needed someone to show him how to build his school, how to put the garden plot to use, how to chart his daily activities, how to formulate a system of education for adults and community, and how to combat poor health and unsanitary conditions.[6] No one offered this kind of advice. To borrow from the past or to copy foreign methods left unanswered Mexico's peculiar requirements, which were those of an underdeveloped land bent on creating a national system of public schools, formerly the prerogative of the prosperous and powerful.

Vasconcelos found his answer in the activity of the Spanish friars of the sixteenth century, who had forsaken the Spanish towns to establish schools in the Indian villages. Unencumbered by family obli-

[6]*Mexico: A Revolution by Education* (New York, 1936), p. 70.

gations, the peripatetic friar served as a jack-of-all-trades: teacher of the three R's, agronomist, master craftsman, even social worker. Now, Vasconcelos reminded his followers, there were no friars, just heads of families with their own obligations. No family man could do the work of the individual friar, so Vasconcelos organized experts and teachers into groups, each called a *misión cultural*, a cultural mission.[7]

Like so much in the history of Mexican rural education, previous practices, peculiar local demands, and lack of experience, which called for experimentation and new ideas, gradually shaped an educational institution radically different from that of Vasconcelos' monks. Rafael Ramírez, who stamped the effort with his ideas, also deserves credit.

Behind the missions lay the experience of the early *misioneros*, whose weakness was their lack of organization and their small numbers. By building on their efforts, the Ministry prepared the groundwork for the cultural missions, whose activities resembled those formerly undertaken by the *misioneros*. The first cultural mission was organized in 1923 to offer guidance and training to the teachers of Hidalgo, where rural schools had been established by the *misioneros*. This group was a special unit formed for a specific project. Its success led to the organization of other groups; their success, to the formation of permanent units.[8]

Improvisation and the demands of the moment left their mark on the missionaries, the members of the unit. The original mission and those that followed drew specialists together. There were seven of them in Hidalgo. Besides serving as the director, Ramírez was the pedagogue. Assisting him was a soapmaker, a master tanner, an expert on farming, a teacher of folk songs, and a physician who vaccinated the teachers and directed the physical education program. The soapmaker, the tanner, and the agronomist were selected in response to the special needs of the people of Hidalgo. The second mission, also under Ramírez, which went to Morelos, dropped the physician, the tanner, and the soap man but had two agronomists, a master carpenter, and a home economics teacher. As other missions were organized, different professions and crafts were added, depending upon local needs and the personnel available.

In practice the missionaries were not always experts in the formal sense. Often they were individuals with some training and experience

[7]Vasconcelos, *El desastre*, p. 169.

[8]Secretía. de Educ. Públ., *Las misiones culturales*, p. 24.

whose outstanding qualification for the job was their complete devotion to the cause they represented. Few had been to the normal schools. They were frequently chosen as a compromise between those who could teach but had nothing practical to offer and the specialist who either could not or would not teach. There were often persons better qualified but lacking the will to serve others. Nor were officials in Mexico City always saddened by this fact. Many believed that men of no formal education from the villages made excellent missionaries. These men, they maintained, did better work than the graduates of the normal schools. One of these practical teachers, Lloyd H. Hughes was told, had come from a farm owned by an Italian farmer in Michoacán. Raised on the farm, he learned everything from his employer, who was an excellent farmer. The Mexican did all of the work on the farm himself, however. Impressed by the excellence of his work, a passing official from one of the missions asked him to join the system, and he did. Although he proved a poor teacher in the classroom—he could barely read and write—his demonstrations of what he could do with a farm stamped him as an outstanding agricultural missionary.[9]

At first the activity of the missions was conceived solely as the in-service training of teachers, but almost immediately it was expanded to embrace the community. From the beginning, public interest in what the mission was doing dictated a change of plans. When the mission gathered at Azcualtipan, Hidalgo, reported Ramírez, the inhabitants asked to participate in the courses offered by the missionaries. They were particularly impressed by the work of the farm expert, who had taken the teachers into the orchards to show them how to bud fruit trees.[10] The second mission had a home economics teacher whose activity proved immensely popular with the women of the community and began the mission's program in behalf of the rural household. From these chance developments a close relationship was formed between the mission and the community. Eventually the community became the focus of the mission's program, where the teachers of the surrounding villages under the guidance of missionaries found solutions for scores of village problems by solving the one they had before them, and where the people learned to help themselves by cooperating with their teachers.

Once the community and the local school had become the center of attention, holding the institutes (as the class activity of the mission

[9]*The Mexican Cultural Mission Programme* (Paris, 1950), p. 65.

[10]Secretía. de Educ. Públ., *Las misiones culturales*, p. 24.

was called) in the state capitals or provincial cities no longer sufficed. When Moisés Sáenz and Ramírez began to stress local affairs, it became necessary to hold the institutes in rural communities. This, in turn, gave the mission's activity an informal, experimental flavor, which Sáenz regarded as essential to its success. Keeping out the formalization of methodology demanded an approach reflecting the immediate needs of the local school and community, Sáenz maintained. By holding to this line of thinking, he wrote, there could be no talk of an ideal rural school, nor of abstract scientific principles. Facing the mission was a school, such as it was; the missionaries and their pupils had to learn how to make that school more effective. Equally important, the social program entrusted to the teacher was not studied in the abstract, but in the local neighborhood, thus transforming the community into a laboratory. In this way learning was acquired under normal conditions, that is, under the conditions that the student teacher faced every day.

The first institute lasted three weeks. This period proved too brief. To cover everything demanded of them, the missionaries pushed themselves and their pupils to exhaustion. Successive missions had similar experiences. Often the missionaries arrived in the community simultaneously with their pupils or even after them. They were thus forced to launch their program hurriedly, without sufficient time to study local conditions. Lacking time for planning, they committed mistakes. To overcome these mistakes the length of work was increased to four weeks, and later more time was added.[11] By 1932 their schedule had been lengthened to four months, and one experimental nontraveling group was established in Actopan, Hidalgo.

Experience dictated other changes. In the beginning two states were mapped out for every mission. This was too much territory to cover. Therefore, as the missions grew in number—there were fourteen in 1932—the provinces were divided into regions, approximately one hundred miles square, but varying according to population and topography, which gave the missions opportunity to concentrate their efforts somewhat. At first the program was opened to all teachers in a particular zone. Their large numbers made the institutes awkward and unwieldy, so their numbers were reduced. By 1928 the program was limited to fifty teachers selected from the neighborhood. The missionaries could then give individual attention to their pupils, as had not been possible before. When more formal supervision became necessary in 1926, a Department of Cultural Missions

[11]Ibid., pp. 14-15.

was established under Elena Torres, a social worker and teacher; Ramírez replaced her in 1927. The department also supervised the rural teacher-training centers then being built. Having close contact with rural schoolmasters, it was felt, the missionaries were uniquely qualified to direct the *Normales*.

The site for each mission's activity was selected carefully. The village chosen was typical of the area, small but large enough to furnish lodging for the visiting teachers. There was one local school and others in the neighboring communities. The schoolmaster, who was the host, kept his school in session, permitting the missionaries to use it for practice and demonstration during the institute. Once the site was chosen, the teachers were notified. They arrived with their clothing, their cups and plates, and a mat for a bed. Shelter was provided by the community: the schoolhouse, the home of a leading citizen, and even the huts of the common people. Getting the schoolmasters to mix with the villagers, Sánchez emphasized, was a triumph in itself, for it required surmounting local antipathies and distrust. More important, it permitted teachers and peasants to live together, to exchange ideas of benefit to both. This relationship enriched the entire program. By sharing the households of the village, the teachers were in a position to transmit some of their knowledge and training to the peasants—the use of mosquito netting in malarial regions, for example.[12] When the institute was over, the teachers returned to their respective schools until the following year, when they again met with the missionaries.

After the changes of 1926 and 1927 the missionaries arrived in the community before their pupils. They spent their first days on the scene getting acquainted with their schoolmaster host, the village, and local problems. Individually and as a group they met the villagers, visited their homes, and won their confidence. Every effort was made to interest the people in the forthcoming activity. With the advice of local leaders special projects were outlined: a house for the teacher, a community electric-light plant, a well for drinking water. Meanwhile the missionaries kept close tabs on local public opinion, hoping to avoid frontal clashes with the social and political forces that prevailed in the community.

When this was done and a blueprint drawn, the teachers arrived. Now the formal work began, from six in the morning until late in the evening. Classroom study and outside activities occupied all of the visiting teachers' time. The missionary, for his part, guided the

---

[12]Sánchez, *Mexico: A Revolution by Education*, p. 78.

discussions and led his pupils in the group activity of the institutes.[13] Resourceful as he was, he took advantage of every opening available, improvising and experimenting as he went along. There were classes in rural pedagogy, history, and geography. Groups of teachers ventured out into the fields with the agronomist, who discussed methods of soil care with them, introduced new crops and seeds, and taught them modern farming techniques. At the urging of the social worker, owners of livestock fenced the animals off from the homes and no longer permitted them to wander about; steps were taken to protect the water supply and to eliminate the breeding grounds of malaria-carrying mosquitoes. There were sewing and cooking classes for women. "If the peasants come to the school—so much the better," declared Sánchez (p. 82). "If they don't—the school will go to them, into their homes, into their kitchens, their barns, and their fields." At the same time, the music teacher was organizing choirs and folk-dance groups and practicing with the local musicians. Games for children and adults were introduced by the physical education instructor, who organized dances and tournaments among the neighborhood villages, breaking down old feuds and prejudices. By sponsoring basketball games between teams from different villages, holding dances, and even putting on horse races, the missionaries brought the local communities together and furnished them pleasure and relaxation. Classes in pottery, weaving, canning, tanning, and similar arts, depending upon the nature of local resources and skills, were opened to the community, whose participation was encouraged.

What "a revelation to watch the missioners at their work," an impressed Sánchez emphasized (p. 77), "to see how much they are able to accomplish in so short a time." He wrote that after a week or so "the missioners lose their status as strangers, they adapt their dress to local customs, they worm their way into the confidence of officials and citizens, they become accepted members of the community. I was dumbfounded," he confessed, "at the complete change that had occurred in *misioneros* whom I had known in Mexico City and who had fitted into the cosmopolitan sophistication." Once "in the rural village, it was difficult to distinguish them from the peasants of the community." In a matter of days, he continued, "they were so definitely entrenched in the good graces of the *campesinos* that they seemed to know all the gossip and all the problems small and large, that confronted the individual peasants and the community as a whole."

[13]Ibid., pp. 77, 81.

In the final analysis, everything had come from the community itself. The local host, the visiting teachers, and the people had learned to cooperate for mutual benefit. To carry out their program the missionaries had received a modicum of aid from Mexico City: their salaries, some utensils and tools, and one or two pieces of equipment. National poverty compelled them to teach the people to improvise with what was available. The tangible rewards were self-evident; the intangible gains, often of greater merit, were more difficult to evaluate. "They must be viewed first hand to be appreciated," concluded Sánchez (p. 81); "they can be measured only in subjective terms by those who can appreciate the difference between the old order and the new, between colonial Mexico and revolutionary Mexico."

Once examinations were out of the way, the mission prepared to move on. This was the signal for a celebration, which attracted people from the entire zone. A gay and festive mood reigned in Tula during the last day of the mission, remembered Katherine M. Cook. Brightly colored ribbons decorated the buildings of the village, and the streets were filled with people and animals on their way to the exhibits. "Food was cooking and on sale along the streets and in the market square." There were displays from "the school gardens, canned fruits and vegetables, all types of handicrafts, including furniture, baskets, pottery, weaving, and the like, which the . . . teachers would be promoting in their school communities." There were games, native dances, and a performance at the theater, tribute to the purpose and spirit of the institute in which the entire community had participated.[14] The celebration over, the mission moved on to another community.

This was not to deny that the missions on occasion faced distinctly different receptions and farewells. Not all communities received them with open arms; some placed insuperable obstacles before them. Communities here and there, Sánchez was told, "largely because of fanatical confidence in the political views and activities of the Church, will take every means to thwart the efforts of the missioners, sometimes going as far as armed opposition and physical violence." Some turned the missions away. The inhabitants of one hostile community drove the missionaries out with stones; but they came back, Sánchez learned, led by an old army sergeant who refused to accept defeat.[15] Local hostility was not always overcome with a change of chiefs, however. At times the missionaries and their pupils were com-

[14]Cook, pp. 27-28.

[15]*Mexico: A Revolution by Education*, p. 85.

pelled to wear sidearms and to sleep with rifles by their beds, particularly after the *cristeros* fanned the flames of revolt in the late twenties and early thirties.

I I

Notwithstanding what had been accomplished, the ingenuity of the effort, and the changes that Ramírez and Sáenz had enacted over the years, not all was well with the program. Its weaknesses, which Narciso Bassols and his staff analyzed in detail and attempted to overcome (perhaps failing to do so), were significant not only because of their implications for the missions, but because they illustrated perfectly the enormous complexities involved in developing institutions to bring about the transformation of the rural community. The careful analysis of these difficulties by Manuel Mesa Andraca, one of Bassols' principal lieutenants, therefore deserves thoughtful study.

Despite some excellent performances, his report began, the overall program had been "thinly spread and weakly enacted."[16] What the missionaries were asked to do was beyond their capabilities. From the pedagogical side they were told to provide professional guidance to thousands of teachers scattered the length and breadth of the Republic. Of the four months spent in the community, only six weeks were devoted to the institute for teachers. This was not enough. A pedagogue might teach his class reading techniques, offer some general observations on health and hygiene, and demonstrate games and dances, but who could furnish the teachers with the skills and experiences demanded by the local scene? This was what the teacher needed most to know. There were other limitations. Every missionary labored at a different pace; some got more done than others in the same amount of time. Some subjects were more complex than others; it was far simpler to teach weaving than farming. Since Mexico had wide regional variations, the missionaries had to know the local picture: the natural resources, the social and economic structure, and village politics. This was particularly true of the agronomists, who offered wise advice on the basis of intimate knowledge. While regions shared common problems, meeting them required time. Not all teachers were of the same age, background, and level of schooling; putting them in one class complicated the picture. The limited time at the disposal of the teacher-pupils compelled them to take courses and activities on many subjects, which taxed their ener-

[16]Secretía. de Educ. Públ., *Memoria . . . de educación . . . 1933*, II, 45.

gies and reduced their accomplishments, particularly since most of them had only a modicum of education.[17]

On the community side, even greater difficulties confronted the missions, the report went on. Given the precarious economic and social conditions of the rural community, it was impossible to produce permanent changes in the space of weeks or months. Nor could the hoped-for transformation be brought about by education alone; the participation of all branches of government, resources of every type, and technicians to study each aspect of the problem were required. The difficulties of rural communities, particularly those of the Indian-speaking groups, represented complex and deeply rooted ills, which educators were powerless to combat.

Taking the hypothetical case of an agronomist in the lower Mixteca of Oaxaca, the report outlined specifically what the problem was. Upon reaching the Mixteca, the agronomist found himself among Indian-speaking people where only the exceptional person spoke Spanish. Farming in this dry and mountainous region consisted primarily of planting corn in the minuscule valleys formed by the giant ravines or on the sides of the steep mountains, where there was no opportunity to use even a team of oxen or the Egyptian plow, where farmers employed the ax, the machete, and the wooden stake to dig holes for their seeds. No matter how enthusiastic the agronomist might be, he could not transform this scene in four months. Mexico, the report continued, had to rid itself of the belief that apostles of learning could do what only thorough planning and ample resources could accomplish over the years.[18] As Eyler Simpson wrote (p. 288), the idea of the missions was good, but enthusiasm had outrun capacity. The missions were facing "a stone wall of ignorance and poverty—a wall which they were charged to tear down with their bare hands." With what they had at their command, "this they simply could not do."

This did not imply, Mesa Andraca and his assistants hastened to add, that the effort had been totally wasted. On the contrary, much of value had been carried out. The missionaries had furnished the teachers with new ideas and clarified their responsibilities; they had stimulated the work by giving attention to the teachers' multiple needs; and they had put teachers in contact with each other. Through their travels hundreds of missionaries had reached every corner of Mexico; by their investigations of the rural scene they had come to

[17]Ibid., II, 45-46.
[18]Ibid., II, 48-49.

know the national maladies. They had compiled folklore and native traditions, preserving them for the future. Last but not least, by helping the community to build open-air theaters, public parks, septic tanks, and schoolhouses, the missionaries had left behind a modest but highly useful contribution.[19]

Measures to expand the missions' efforts, to increase their benefits, were now called for. Bassols' answer was the Regional Peasant School, uniting the cultural missions, the rural normal schools, and the agricultural schools, recently transferred to the jurisdiction of the Ministry of Education. More than any other organization of the thirties, these institutions represented the thesis of Bassols and his supporters that schooling alone faced insuperable barriers in the rural community, that education was helpless without concurrent economic and social changes. The Department of Cultural Missions was abolished and a Department of Agricultural and Normal Education formed, further evidence of Bassols' belief that educational progress depended upon improvements on the agrarian scene. By placing the missions permanently in the region of the parent plant, which prepared men and women to teach and farm at the same time, and by providing them with the time and equipment necessary to draw blueprints and enact them, Bassols hoped to eliminate past deficiencies. These changes, Bassols and his men acknowledged, meant sacrificing the extensive approach of the past for a small, more compact effort. The emphasis was placed on the training of teachers, rather than on the reconstruction of the community. The latter would come once the country had able leaders in the country schools and a different economic system.

As their name implied, the Regional Peasant Schools represented planning along regional lines. Bassols, Mesa Andraca, and men of similar opinion believed that fruitful results came through long familiarity with local problems, mapping out solutions, and charting programs around them. Planning, for these men, was an ideal. They prided themselves on their scientific approach to questions, refusing to undertake any activity before an investigation was made, stressing that intimate knowledge underlay the success of any enterprise. Underdeveloped nations, these men said, had few precedents to follow; unless they learned to recognize their needs, they ran the risk of imitating foreign systems of scant value to them.

Once community needs were defined and a program was designed for them, some organization had to carry it out. This was a job for the cultural mission, now called the Institute for Social Action. No matter how good the school was, declared the policy makers, it labored in a vacuum if its benefits did not extend beyond the walls of its classrooms.[20] Contacts with the outside were necessary, for only the bold and energetic teacher-leader who understood and sympathized with the problems of his people could help them to destroy the bonds that tied them to the past. To prepare the teacher for this role by working with him in the community and taking up local problems and solving them on the spot—this was the role of the mission.

Linking the classroom with the outside, the mission became a laboratory where abstract knowledge was applied in practice, an annex similar to those where fledgling teachers in the normal schools learned to teach. There were institutes for the training of teachers, but they were held in the classroom with adequate facilities or at some strategic village for the study of a particular question. The schoolmaster and the rural institution of higher learning were brought together in this way, thus developing a much desired bond. Through the mission the rural teacher was kept under the watchful eye of specialists who offered advice and guidance, a procedure that had not been followed systematically before. There was also a program for the community, modeled after that for the teachers, emphasizing agriculture and local crafts.

Group organizations, stressed the Department of Agricultural and Normal Education, opened the way for united action on a multitude of fronts. Compliance with this view led the missions to organize the population into groups of all kinds, to watch over them, and to put them in touch with the local school. Special importance was attached to cooperatives, "the only effective method to bring about the economic betterment of the community."[21] There were also mutual insurance groups, guilds, groups for social action, and organizations for the benefit of the home, the child, and art, as well as for the encouragement of some particular project such as sanitary measures. Whether organizing groups or building a schoolhouse, the missions solicited the support of the ministries of Agriculture and Communications, the Department of Public Health, and any other government branch whose aid was essential to the success of rural reform.

Bassols' changes added depth to the missions' program. As non-traveling groups the missions accomplished much that was not done

[20]Ibid., II, 94, 89.
[21]Ibid., II, 93.

before. The teachers and communities around the Regional Peasant Schools profited most. Bassols' revisions, however, left the vast majority of rural communities outside the scope of the program. His successors said that this was a mistake, that the missions offered more to the nationalizing process in their role of traveling teacher-training schools. "The choice," reported Sánchez, "was between quality and quantity, between regional values and national values." Having decided that the missions' principal role was to destroy provincialism and cultural barriers between classes and regions, Cárdenas' policy planners separated the missions from the Regional Peasant Schools and made them mobile again.[22] Hoping to keep some of the previous advantages, they divided the Republic into zones and distributed the missions among them. Efforts were made, meanwhile, to endow the Regional Peasant Schools and the rural normal schools with some of the activities formerly undertaken by the missions. Nothing was done to change the political character of the missions, a heritage of the days of Bassols. Engaged in vast agrarian reforms, Cárdenas demanded dynamic rural leadership in behalf of the *campesino*'s struggle for land, which the missions offered.

Need for radical leadership persisted until the dispute with the oil companies in 1938. Once petroleum questions had taken the spotlight away from agrarian matters, there was need for peace and national unity. Confronted with foreign enemies who threatened his position at home, Cárdenas called a halt to agitation in the countryside. Spokesmen for provincial interest groups menaced by the activity of the missions had also persuaded him that peace would not come until the power of the missions was curtailed. Convinced that the mission program engendered jealousies and rivalries that disrupted the peace he desired, Cárdenas disbanded them. To this date opinion is divided on the wisdom of his action. Those who believed in the missions have roundly condemned Cárdenas; their critics support the presidential decision. Whatever the truth of the matter, Cárdenas ended a program that dated back to Vasconcelos. The end came, as perhaps it should have, with the death of rural reform.

III

In 1942 supporters of the missions won the backing of officials in Mexico City, who revived the Department of Cultural Missions. Their benefactor was Guillermo Bonilla, an old hand at rural edu-

---

[22]*Mexico: A Revolution by Education*, p. 87.

cation. Moderate and prudent, he left politics alone, wisely acknowledging that past political entanglements had raised powerful enemies.
Compelled to placate Octavio Véjar Vásquez, a conservative with
no taste for radicals who tampered with the *status quo*, Bonilla left
land reform and similar questions to others. Faced with opposition
from the rural normal schools, whose directors objected to sharing
their program with others, he dropped the teacher-training functions of the missions. These changes confined the mission's program
to the community and cut it off from the rural school, the logical
institution to direct and coordinate local change. Now cooperation
between mission and school frequently depended upon the whims
of each.[23] After Bonilla's departure from office the missions were
merged with the General Office of Literacy and Out-of-School
Education, which cost them their independence and tied them to the
literacy program.

Two basic deficiencies continued to plague the missions. One was
poor salaries. Anxious to include more of the population in the program, Bonilla and his successors increased the number of missions,
from thirty-two in 1943 to seventy-eight in 1959. There was little
corresponding increase in the funds earmarked for them.[24] In 1959
the individual mission operated on a yearly budget of 60,000 pesos,
or less than $5,000 at current exchange rates, nearly all of which went
to salaries. The nine doctors attached to the missions, one for approximately nine groups, received a monthly stipend of 950 pesos, or
$76.00. Poor salaries hampered the hiring of personnel with the skills
and qualities of leadership urgently needed, while the unattractive-
ness of life in an isolated community further complicated the situation. Since the families of staff members were frequently left behind,
Nathan L. Whetten pointed out, only individuals imbued with the
spirit of the missionary accepted a position at the salary offered.
They were often poorly trained for their duties, for the gifted and
qualified found openings of every type in the cities.[25] Luis Alvarez
Barret charged that the poor salaries left the mark of the tradesman
on the missions. Those who joined their staffs were carpenters, construction workers, and teachers of trades, empirical teachers with
little or no formal preparation. Home economics teachers, nurses,
agronomists, and teachers with valid certificates were frequently
absent, as Hughes indicated (p. 65).

[23]Hughes, p. 67.

[24]Rubén Castillo Penado, "Las misiones culturales de México," *Escuela nueva*, I, No.
1 (June 1955), 9.

[25]*Rural Mexico* (Chicago, 1948), p. 440.

Another weakness was the lack of time. Since the days of Bonilla the missions had adopted a policy of spending from one to three years in a rural community. This was a compromise between Bassols' system and that of the twenties. Despite this, time was still lacking for the projects outlined. "The objectives," Whetten emphasized (p. 440), "are so broad and so far reaching that, in many cases, it would require an entire generation to accomplish them." The job was simply too big for the individuals, a fact that Bassols had recognized and Whetten supported now. Bonilla attempted to provide more time by having the missions move "just over the hill" from the preceding area of operations, permitting the missionaries to return periodically to direct the local inhabitants whom they had left in charge of their former activities. Like the policy planners of 1935 who had reversed Bassols' ideas, officials in Mexico City chose to spread their efforts thin rather than focus their attention at a given spot.

By 1960 the cultural missions represented thirty-three years of educational effort. They had offered a service performed by no other agency. As teacher-training institutions in the twenties and thirties they had kept thousands of rural schoolmasters in touch with Mexico City and with each other, furnishing unity and common direction to a dispersed effort and often the knowledge and techniques that spelled the difference between success and failure. Through the missions the rural community had come into contact with the men and ideas of a society beyond it. As a symbol of what the Revolution was waged for, no other organization had so faithfully demonstrated the change that was possible with initiative and leadership. In the face of problems and weaknesses in organization and administration, to cite Hughes (p. 76), once allowances were made for what was possible, the missions were "doing an excellent job with the funds and materials" that they were given.

Chapter VI

SCHOOLS FOR TEACHERS AND FARMERS

I

To ESTABLISH A NATIONAL SYSTEM of rural schools, thousands of teachers were necessary. This demand could be satisfied only by institutions especially equipped to prepare them—in other words, rural teacher-training or normal schools. The first of them, the *Escuela Normal Rural* of Tacámbaro, Michoacán, opened its doors in 1922; others followed, and by 1932 there were seventeen of them.

Unlike the traditional institutions in the cities, which prepared young men and women for the schools in the capital and the provincial towns, the *Normales* were called upon to produce teachers for the children of rural communities. Although Enrique C. Rébsamen, the noted Swiss educator, had introduced modern teacher-training methods to Mexico in the 1890's, nothing was done to build a program for rural areas. Beginning with his school in Veracruz, Rébsamen had confined his activities to the urban centers. Therefore, the architects of the rural normal school, many of whom had studied under disciples of Rébsamen, had no precedent to build on. By necessity, the *Normales* that they established rose in response to needs and the experience acquired during the early years of the rural-school program. Offspring of experimentation and improvisation, the *Normales* did not always match objectives with performance.

Their planners, including Moisés Sáenz, designed the *Normales* with three basic goals in mind. They wanted to prepare rural schoolmasters for the thousands of classrooms that would be built. Having appointed hundreds of schoolteachers who lacked the formal background demanded by their profession, they wished to provide them with such training. Hoping to spread the benefits of education beyond the confines of the classroom, they wanted their *Normales* to incorporate the surrounding tiny communities into their program.[1] To carry out these goals, rural *Normales* were organized. Their blueprints called for farm lands and the equipment necessary for a pro-

[1]Secretía. de Educ. Públ., *Memoria ... de educación ... 1933*, II, 41.

gram in agriculture, which would provide the students with the practical knowledge and experience required by the rural community.

The *Normales* were small institutions. There were facilities for approximately one hundred pupils with four years or more of rural schooling selected from the sons and daughters of *ejidatarios* and small farmers of the region. Faced with the need to train teachers as rapidly as possible, the planners limited the program of the *Normales* to two years. A faculty of about eight instructors offered courses in history, arithmetic, literature, music, art, and the social sciences. Special emphasis was placed on pedagogy for the rural schools: practice teaching in a neighboring school, the principles of rural education, small-school organization and administration. Besides the academic and pedagogical program, the policy makers hoped to offer vocational activities: courses in agricultural practices, the domestic sciences, and the trades and cottage industries. The blueprints called for the hiring of shop teachers and farm experts in addition to pedagogues.

Like the schools they were preparing teachers for, the *Normales* were simply built and run. Several of them were in abandoned or partly destroyed haciendas and convents. Many of their instructors and first pupils helped to build them, sometimes with the aid of the the local community. Equipment and supplies were limited and inexpensive, often acquired by the school itself. Some, as Katherine M. Cook noted (p. 43), were a "lesson in what enthusiasm and determination can accomplish without money."

Despite modest gains, these early institutions were not entirely successful. Mistakes were committed from the start. Forced to build the schools rapidly and lacking the resources with which to equip them properly in rural communities, the planners established some in urban or semiurban centers. This was particularly true of the *Normales* in Puebla, Chiapas, Nayarit, Sonora, and Nuevo León. A majority did not have the personnel and equipment required by their agricultural program. Some lacked lands or had postage-stamp-size plots. The school in Erongarícuaro, Michoacán, for example, had only two and a half hectares of tillable land; that of Tlatlauqui, Puebla, had three hectares; that of Tixtla, Guerrero, had seven. None of the others, with the exception of the school in Cerro Hueco, Chiapas, had more than seventy hectares.[2]

Equally if not more detrimental to the success of the program, the pupils were not always inhabitants of rural communities. The policy

[2]Ibid., II, 42.

planners had insisted that entering students must have four or prefer-ably six years of schooling. Only a handful of rural schools had these grades, so students from nonrural communities were chosen. In addi-tion, officials in Mexico City had asked for students in certain age brackets: the minimum age for boys was set at sixteen and that for girls at fourteen; these were the lowest ages permissible if the insti-tutions were to have graduates old enough to teach at the end of two years. Unhappily, these groups were seldom found in the rural school, where the pupils dropped out before reaching the prescribed age. This further impeded finding students in the rural schools.[3] By accepting applicants from towns and cities, however, the policy makers lost many graduates of the *Normales* to other pursuits, for the town- or city-bred individual rarely braved the isolation of the rural community.

Nor had the *Normales* implanted the type of education called for by their blueprints. In the face of the emphasis put on agriculture, a majority of the instructors knew almost nothing about farming. There were few agronomists on the staffs, and they were frequently unfamiliar with local characteristics. Much of the blame for this situ-ation could be attributed to the poor salaries offered the agronomists, who received 182 pesos a month, 37 pesos less than that paid by the Ministry of Agriculture. Without training in agriculture the gradu-ates of these institutions were unprepared to offer the skills and ex-perience required to orient and direct the communities they served. Lacking the means by which to make their influence felt in the pre-dominantly farming community, the graduates dissipated their ef-forts. This was disastrous, declared Narciso Bassols and those around him, who stressed that it was the teacher's duty to guide and mold the economic and social progress of the community. He could not do this in the absence of the proper background.[4]

Alongside of the teacher-training institutions there developed a system of agricultural schools, the *Escuelas Centrales Agrícolas*. For Mexico's problem was that of producing not just teachers but farm-ers, too. Although nearly two out of three Mexicans lived from the land, they were not farmers, as agricultural statistics testified. There were communities where the level of farming had not gone beyond that of primitive peoples. To make efficient use of Mexico's land demanded men and women who had mastered modern techniques. One way to get trained people was to set up agricultural schools. The first was established in 1925, and by 1932 there were six.

[3]Ibid., II, 42-43.
[4]Ibid., II, 43.

As conceived in the beginning, these *Centrales* were to satisfy the demands of the region around them. Each offered three years of practical training and experience in farming and related pursuits to approximately 200 students from rural communities. Their purpose was to instruct small farmers and *ejidatarios* in modern agricultural techniques. Upon receiving their diplomas, the students were to be given lands by the agrarian authorities and funds to purchase equipment and supplies from the *ejidal* agricultural banks established alongside of the *Centrales*.

Their architects, like those of the *Normales*, committed mistakes from the start. Political pressures and the need for haste compelled them to locate the institutions on the central plateau. The original plan called for schools in a wide variety of climatic regions. In 1932 only the *Central* of Tamatán, Tamaulipas, was in a semitropical zone. One *Central*, that of Champusco, Puebla, embraced two entirely different zones, one producing wheat and the other sugar cane. Students who came to the school did not always receive the type of training required by their communities.[5]

Errors were made in the selection of students. The policy makers stipulated that only the sons of *ejidatarios* and small farmers of the region were qualified to attend the *Centrales*. This policy was not followed. Of the 583 pupils registered in 1928, only 20 per cent were the children of *ejidatarios* and 39 per cent those of small farmers. The others represented *hacendados*, businessmen, merchants, and professional men. They had no intention of farming the lands of Mexico but hoped to move on to schools of higher learning upon graduation. Nor were the students always representative of the region. In the *Central* of Guanajuato in 1928, for example, students represented twenty-two states: 12 were from the Federal District, 15 from Michoacán, 8 from Oaxaca, 2 from Sonora, and some even from Veracruz. This situation had worsened by 1932 when the *Centrales* became the property of the Ministry of Education. At that time the *Central* of Guanajuato had only 60 pupils, less than a third of its capacity, fewer than half of whom came from the state. Of the 572 pupils registered in the *Centrales*, only 3.68 per cent came from *ejidos*.[6]

This picture was complicated by the wide range of schooling represented by the students. With the noble aim of making certain that the children of *ejidatarios* and small farmers gained admittance, of-

[5]Ibid., II, 56-57.

[6]Ibid., II, 58-59.

ficials in Mexico City had refrained from demanding a specific number of years of schooling for entrance to the *Centrales*. Just about anyone could apply, and students of every kind did. As a result the academic preparation of the students varied enormously. There were some with only a grasp of the fundamentals, along with others who had completed the *Preparatoria*. Much of this error had arisen from a ruling in 1929 stipulating that scholarships to the National Agricultural College at Chapingo would be granted to students from the *Centrales*. Thus the *Centrales* were turned into preprofessional schools, where everyone flocked who wanted a higher technical education.

From the beginning the *Centrales* were "palace-type" institutions. Led by a generous impulse to give the son of the *campesino* the best that Mexico had to offer, the administrators of the twenties built institutions foreign to his needs. Many were equipped with modern buildings, tools, shops, and some of the finest purebred stock in Mexico. "At one stroke," to quote George I. Sánchez, "they sought to raise Mexican agriculture from a medieval stage to the level of the twentieth century."[7] Nothing was spared in building them. "Of all the units in the postrevolutionary system of rural education," added Eyler N. Simpson (p. 288), "relatively more money was spent on and greater things hoped for from the Central Agricultural Schools than from almost any other type of school." Impressed by the agricultural colleges in Texas, their planners copied American ways. Students were outfitted with costly uniforms of gabardine, Texas-style hats, and leather boots. Their food, to cite the testimony of Narciso Bassols and his men, consisted of oatmeal and coffee with cream or chocolate for breakfast, and similar dishes for lunch and dinner.[8]

Such practices were alien to the local inhabitants; the planners had sought to modernize the schools with methods far ahead of the people's development in these primitive rural sections. "I have visited agricultural schools," Sánchez reported, "where the tractors and gang ploughs that were to replace the oxen and the Egyptian plough now lie abandoned in rust and neglect. I have heard," he continued, "how the pure-bred chickens, pigs, horses, and cows which were imported from foreign countries have fallen victims to the rigours of climate and the inroads of local insects and diseases."[9] Of course, conceded Bassols and his supporters, one of the goals of education was to introduce students to new ways of life, but this had to be done slowly,

[7] *Mexico: A Revolution by Education*, p. 145.
[8] Secretía. de Educ. Públ., *Memoria ... de educación ... 1933*, II, 60.
[9] *Mexico: A Revolution by Education*, pp. 145-146.

without alienating them from their environment. With what the *Centrales* offered, the students acquired customs and needs satisfied only in urban centers, so they fled the countryside after graduation.[10]

Politics and not just mistakes in planning partially accounted for this situation. As the *Centrales* were originally designed, the *ejidal* agricultural banks were to furnish their graduates with the funds and equipment necessary to farm in the manner that they had mastered in the classroom. Then, out of political considerations, the banks and the schools were separated. Once the banks went their way, the students were left to their own resources. Now the schools offered technical skills to their students but did not provide them with the resources to put these into practice. Since the students had not been prepared to cope with the local rural environment, they left for the city. The minority that returned home to farm lived as before. On the other hand, to complete this circle, when the banks offered funds to the *ejidatarios* and small farmers, few of whom had attended the *Centrales*, they could not take full advantage of the money because of lack of training.

The failure of the *Centrales* to spread their activity over the entire zone was another weakness. None of their budgets provided funds for this purpose. The result was that their extension service was either poor or nonexistent. Divorced from the needs of the countryside, the *Centrales* and the rural schools around them went their own ways, without taking advantage of what the other offered. Had they worked together, they could have compensated for their weaknesses. When the *Central* lacked the means to extend its benefits to the surrounding communities, the rural schoolmaster could have acted as its representative; if he did not have the training and equipment to offer courses in elementary agriculture, the *Central* could have helped with guidance and the simple tools necessary.

New institutions that they were, designed for a type of instruction that had never been offered before, the *Centrales* had need for special teachers. In the beginning their planners thought to provide them with professional agronomists and teachers from the *Normales*. Neither worked out well. Specialized in limited areas of agriculture and usually poor teachers, the agronomists lacked the breadth of knowledge required to teach every phase of farming. The pedagogues could teach but had nothing practical to offer. Troubles, meanwhile, had arisen between them. The agronomists scorned teaching, while the pedagogues looked down on the agronomists.[11]

[10]Secretía. de Educ. Públ., *Memoria . . . de educación . . . 1933*, II, 60.

[11]Ibid., II, 61-63.

II

Bassols and his collaborators were determined to eliminate these weaknesses. This, they concluded, could be accomplished only with the reorganization and consolidation of the entire structure of rural higher education. They based their decisions on a number of considerations, which underlined the philosophy of the thirties. The education of the peasant, they emphasized, had to stress economics, that is, to minister to the life needs of the rural classes. With this as the objective, it became imperative that those entrusted with it, the rural schoolmasters, have a special ideology and preparation. This type of teacher was produced by an institution where practical problems were studied and resolved, whose students represented the elite of rural youth.[12] Thus the *Escuela Regional Campesina* was established, uniting the *Normales*, the *Centrales*, and the cultural missions under the Department of Agricultural and Normal Education. Bassols entrusted supervision of the new institution to Manuel Mesa Andraca, an able agronomist and teacher.

Through the *Regional Campesina*, Bassols and Mesa Andraca launched a frontal attack on the old weaknesses. Hoping to bar the doors of the *Campesina* to all but the sons of *ejidatarios*, small farmers, and local craftsmen, they demanded proof of background, selection by a rural school, and approval by the *Campesina*. To overcome the age and academic limitations of former years, the age requirements for boys and girls were fixed at fourteen and twelve, two years less than before, and a special one-year program covering grades five and six was established for those who had not completed their rural school, a requirement for entrance. Wishing to anchor the schoolmasters to the local community, Bassols asked Congress to permit them to share the village lands with the *ejidatarios*. By furnishing them land, Bassols expected to identify their interests with those of the people they served, while providing them with an extra income. They would also encourage others to emulate them by farming their lands properly.[13] Upon graduation, therefore, the student majoring in education received a teaching appointment to a federal rural school and, Bassols hoped, land in the local community. Land and the equipment necessary to farm it were provided students who majored in agriculture. There was little that Bassols and Mesa Andraca could do about staff weakness, except to continue with the same personnel and wait for the *Campesinas* to produce well-rounded teachers for themselves.

[12]Ibid., II, 66.
[13]Ibid., II, 44.

The problem of distributing the schools was solved by drawing a regional map of the Republic and praying that political pressures would permit its adoption. Because Mexico had limited funds, and since some of the old institutions were still useful, Bassols began his building program slowly, utilizing what was ready and available, seeking to achieve through coordination and concentration at strategic spots what could not be done on a national scale without more money. The objective was to build new *Campesinas*, to transform the *Centrales Agrícolas* into *Campesinas* where location and the institution permitted, to incorporate some of the *Normales* into the program, and to furnish other *Normales* with agricultural curricula.

The *Regional Campesina* was a boarding school for both sexes, with facilities for one hundred to two hundred students. Its curriculum revolved around a two-year program in agriculture and the small industries. Those who finished it left as practical farmers. With Bassols and Mesa Andraca stressing what they called the obligation to train women, the *Campesina* offered girls courses in the domestic sciences, which prepared them for their duties in the home. This had not been done systematically before, yet no change was possible in the rural home until its mistress was willing to accept it. For those students who demonstrated unusual qualities of leadership and scholarship while taking the basic preparation in agriculture, there was a two-year teacher-training program. This was not intended to make the agricultural program a stepping-stone to the normal school, for both shared equal recognition. What was done was to mold a teacher-training program around the skills that the teacher would need in the rural community. Now he was a practical farmer—not just a master of the three R's—a community leader whose influence extended to the fields and homes. For the gifted student who did not want to teach yet desired additional training, the *Campesina* offered advanced study in agriculture, which prepared him for a position with the agricultural banks or the cultural missions.

As in other Mexican institutions, the students at the *Regionales Campesinas* participated actively in their management. Convinced that students learned best if they did things themselves, Mesa Andraca and his assistants entrusted all of the agricultural enterprises to them, forming cooperative societies for nearly every activity, "much as if they were all members of a communal enterprise," reported Sánchez. There were expeditions to the surrounding villages, where reforms were undertaken by the students, first under the guidance of a cultural mission and later under school initiative and direction. Substantial responsibility, Sánchez observed, rested with the students for the improvement of local rural conditions, a responsibility that provided abundant "opportunities to display qualities of leadership in real-life situations." Having witnessed the students' activities in the communities, from sweeping the streets to presenting musical fiestas, Sánchez testified that this training was of prime "value to them as citizens and as teachers or farmers." By combining the preparation of teachers with agricultural training and offering possibilities for social action on the spot, he concluded, the *Campesinas* offered the skills and enthusiasm necessary to strike at the conditions that blocked the development of rural Mexico.[14]

Throughout the thirties the *Regionales Campesinas* stood in high favor in the halls of government. After Bassols left office, his successors multiplied their number rapidly. There were 900 students in ten schools in 1934 and 4,116 in thirty-three schools in 1940.[15] Their location had improved; more of them were rural, and nearly all of Mexico's geographic regions were represented. Of all the rural institutions of higher learning, the *Regionales Campesinas* most closely approximated the ideals of Manuel Gamio's almost universally accepted integral education.

Still not all was well. The planning was there, but execution lagged. Here and there old evils survived. Determined to do everything possible for the peasants in the six years given them, the Cardenistas built many of the *Campesinas* hastily, without providing the necessary equipment and supplies. Little was accomplished to overcome the chronic shortage of qualified staff members; in 1940 the first graduates of the *Campesinas*, who were counted upon to fill this gap, had just left the classrooms. While some accepted positions with the *Campesinas*, they represented a tiny fraction of the personnel called for, and most of them lacked the preparation demanded by their activities. Although the classrooms had a higher percentage of pupils from rural areas than before, those with urban backgrounds were still there. Despite the precautions taken by Mesa Andraca and Bassols, the *Campesinas* failed to get their quota of applicants from the rural schools, for the great majority had less than three years of schooling. Only a fraction of the rural students ever went beyond three years, even where six grades were offered. The *Campesinas* prepared more rural teachers than ever before, but their pedagogical victories destroyed their agricultural program. By 1940 approximately three out of four students chose teaching as a profession; yet only a tiny mi-

[14]*Mexico: A Revolution by Education*, pp. 148-149.
[15]Secretía. de Gob., *Seis años de gobierno . . . 1934-1940*, p. 253.

nority decided to major in agriculture. Many of the teachers deserted their rural schools for the urban centers; others used the *Regionales Campesinas* to gain admittance to other schools.

These disappointing results had occurred in spite of efforts by able and experienced planners who had surveyed past weaknesses and mapped out blueprints to eliminate them. After having built a school that captured the applause of nearly every expert on rural questions, the architects won only a limited victory. Yet what had taken place, as Bassols had conceded earlier, would have occurred regardless of what was planned. Remedying the failure of the rural school to furnish qualified applicants, for example, was beyond the capabilities of the *Campesinas* or, for that matter, of officials in Mexico City. The inability of the *Campesinas* to produce farmers or to keep rural teachers on their jobs, regardless of how carefully they were kept in touch with the rural environment during their years of schooling, was traceable to factors beyond the scope of the program. These failures sprang from the hopelessness of the rural scene and particularly of the *ejido* and small farm. No man with any schooling wanted to farm; he could do better elsewhere. This applied also to the teacher who left the countryside for the city school. So long as the great contrast existed between the rural and the urban scene, as Bassols analyzed, those who acquired an education would always seek their fortunes in the city, for the village denied them a better way of life. The absence of persistence, finally, limited the success of the *Campesinas*, for no sooner were they established than the men of the forties abolished them, and seven years of labor were lost.

I I I

Confronted with these difficulties, and having turned away from the economic determinism behind the integral education of the thirties, the policy planners of the forties and fifties fell back upon the traditional system. The *Regionales Campesinas* were disbanded, and the old division between the *Normales* and the agricultural schools was revived. Once again teachers were trained separately from farmers and agricultural experts. Some changes were also made in the curriculums. Believing that teachers faced almost identical problems everywhere, officials in Mexico City gave the rural and urban *Normales* the same course of studies, making only minor concessions to environment. Their curriculum was extended to six years (in theory, that is), embracing grades seven to nine of secondary school and three more of specialized pedagogical study. The one-year preparatory course was continued temporarily. Similar revisions were made in the *Escuelas Prácticas de Agricultura*, the new name for the old *Centrales*. These were vocational schools of agriculture. In the first two years their students completed grades five and six, the next two years emphasized agricultural training, and the fifth was open to those who indicated aptitude for advanced study.[16] Aside from these changes, the new architects had revived the program of the twenties, which had major weaknesses.

The failure to come up with new ideas, or to continue the system of *Regionales Campesinas*, Luis Alvarez Barret believes, hurt rather than helped higher education in rural Mexico. By destroying the unity of the thirties, the policy makers lost the geographical distribution achieved by Bassols and the Cardenistas. Entire regions remained without either *Normales* or *Prácticas de Agricultura*. Campeche, Tabasco, Yucatán, Chiapas, and the territory of Quintana Roo shared two *Normales;* Lower California, Sonora, Chihuahua, and Tamaulipas had three schools, of which two were in Chihuahua. As George F. Kneller indicated (p. 152), "the regions unpopular with the rank-and-file teachers are just the ones that have few or no normal schools." A similar situation existed among the *Prácticas de Agricultura:* twenty-six zones were without them. Many of the *Normales* were in urban or semiurban areas. Established during the haste-ridden days of the twenties and thirties, these *Normales* saw the villages around them turn into towns, where the local population lived by selling food and supplies at exorbitant prices. Local politicians also profited. The municipal president of El Mexe, Hidalgo, for example, controlled sixty scholarships to the *Normal*. Although there was no longer a shortage of qualified candidates from rural schools, particularly for the *Normales*, where as many as ten applications were received for every scholarship,[17] a majority of students at both schools came from nonrural communities. When officials in Mexico City attempted to compel students at the *Prácticas de Agricultura* to major in agriculture, many protested, maintaining that they did not intend to farm.

Both the *Normales* and the *Prácticas de Agricultura* suffered from the emphasis given the academic side of their program. Some of the agricultural schools had turned their lands over to private citizens

[16]Departamento de Enseñanza Agrícola, *Escuelas prácticas de agricultura* (Mexico, 1946), p. 36.

[17]José Santos Valdéz, "El artículo tercero constitucional," *Magisterio: Revista de orientación pedagógica*, I (April 1959), 78.

to farm. All of the *Normales* rented their lands to others; the students observed but did not farm the land themselves. Where attempts were made to keep the practical side alive, other obstacles intervened. Few of the schools were equipped for the job. After a survey of the *Normales* in 1944—conditions remained virtually unchanged in 1960— Jaime Torres Bodet confessed that their situation was unsatisfactory. "Why speak of laboratories or shops," he asked, "when . . . we have not been able to supply them with farm animals or implements," when the libraries have no books.[18] There were exceptions, of course. Yet the average *Normal*, lacking shops and equipment, offered little beyond the three R's.

Staff and student problems complicated this picture. Qualified instructors were difficult to find for the *Normales* and, increasingly, could be obtained only for the better institutions. At the *Prácticas de Agricultura*, where the curriculum stressed land use, there was one pedagogue for every sixteen students but only one agronomist for every hundred students.[19] The directors of the *Normales* were burdened with duties that required their attention from Monday to Saturday, while their counterparts in the city had a thirty-six-hour week and the same salary, which they often supplemented with outside jobs. The fact that since 1941 the *Prácticas de Agricultura* had been under ten different department heads made a coherent and consistent program difficult. A majority of the institutions, particularly the *Normales*, suffered from irresponsible student activity. Unlike students in the United States, who seldom evinced any interest in school affairs or politics, Mexicans had always looked upon participation in these activities as their prerogative, frequently demanding and winning an equal voice in the running of their institutions. There were strikes and protests by leaders of the National Student Federation, political rivalries (often reflections of national ones), and personal quarrels that hindered study.

With the growth of the population, more schools and teachers were called for; yet there was no corresponding increase in the *Normales* or the *Prácticas de Agricultura*. For a rural population of approximately 4 million of primary-school age, there were 9,000 students in 32 *Normales* in 1959; only 2,000 of these students were majoring in education. Of those finishing grades seven to nine, only 18 out of every 1,000 completed the teacher-training program.[20] The

[18]*Excelsior*, April 24, 1944.

[19]Ateneo Nacional Agronómico, *Problemas agrícolas actuales* (Mexico, 1955), p. 134.

[20]Data furnished by Secretaría de Educación Pública.

others used the *Normales* as stepping-stones to higher education, frequently the National Normal School in Mexico City. Money earmarked for the training of rural teachers, in the meantime, was spent on secondary schooling. Between 1953 and 1958 less than one fourth of the teachers required by rural Mexico left the classrooms of the *Normales*. Nor was the number of *Prácticas de Agricultura* adequate. There were only 12 in 1958, in the face of a growing rural population and the poverty of agricultural techniques on the *ejidos* and small farms. (At the same time 2,000 urban secondary schools served less than 20 per cent of the eligible population.) Of the 1.5 million young men between sixteen and twenty years of age in rural Mexico, only 2,000 were in the agricultural schools. According to the Office of Agricultural Education in 1946, at least 50 *Prácticas de Agricultura* were needed; yet officials in Mexico City converted 6 of the 12 schools to *Normales* in 1959.

Since the rural *Normales* did not keep pace with the demand for schoolmasters, there were 27,189 teachers in 1959 without teaching certificates, for which six years of primary schooling, three of secondary, and three more in a *Normal* were required. There were 8,491 teachers with fewer than six years of education and an additional 14,774 who had not completed their secondary schooling.[21] The teachers with certificates, 16,307 of them, formed the minority. Granted that a teaching certificate was no guarantee of competence or performance, it represented twelve years of education, not an excessive number for the demands put upon the schoolmaster by the rural scene.

The *Normales*, on the other hand, were not always responsible for the shortage of qualified teachers. The demand for rural schoolmasters had constituted a national emergency in the beginning, necessitating improvisations. The national budget was never large enough to cover the cost of training all the teachers needed. Lack of funds for adequate salaries also reduced the number of persons willing to teach and decimated the ranks of those in the profession. Since 1936 more than one third of the Republic's teachers in the primary schools had left the profession entirely or moved on to secondary education, where salaries were better.[22]

The plight of the teaching profession had a strong impact on the country at large. Gains in education were held to a minimum by the lack of trained personnel. Agriculture in particular felt the loss. One

[21]Instituto Federal de Capacitación del Magisterio, *Capacitación de los maestros en servicio no titulados* (Mexico, 1959), p. 4.

[22]Ibid.

of the hopes of the reformers was that the rural school would help to improve agricultural techniques, but improvement had never materialized. The rural schoolmaster had not provided the leadership or the techniques. Even Sáenz, whose advocacy of the empirical teacher was well known, confessed that many failures on the rural scene could be traced to the unprepared teacher. Unless something was done to correct this situation, industrialization would suffer; for the factory, even more than the farm, demanded a population able to master new techniques. From a nontechnical point of view, the insufficiency of qualified leaders in the village school stunted cultural growth and the development of democracy.

Officials in Mexico City had long recognized that measures were needed to improve the quality of the rural teacher. The cultural missions represented the pioneer effort, and later the *Normales* offered a similar program. In 1938 the Cárdenas administration established a *Normal* for noncertified teachers in Mexico City. Torres Bodet expanded this organization into a Federal Institute for the Training of Teachers in 1946; the demand for qualified teachers was as urgent then as in the early days of education.[23] The institute offered classes for teachers within commuting distance of Mexico City and correspondence courses for those in the provinces. Later eighteen provincial branches were formed. In 1959 there were 10,905 teachers taking courses with the institute; 14,152 teachers, federal and state, had qualified for certificates since 1945.[24]

IV

For the graduate of the teacher-training school, life in the rural village had not opened the gates to paradise. Few occupations were as demanding; no one grew wealthy, and the hours were long. "Teaching the three R's would be child's play," wrote Sáenz, compared to what the rural schoolmaster must do.[25] The children came early and stayed late, and their parents counted on him from Monday through Sunday every week of the year. There were gardens to tend, chickens and pigs to feed, and playgrounds to supervise. If there were social activities in the evening, someone had to direct them. There were always scores of official forms to fill out. Even with help

[23]Secretía. de Educ. Públ., *La obra educativa en el sexenio, 1940-1946* (Mexico, 1946), p. 217.

[24]Inst. Fed. de Capacitación, *Capacitación*, p. 2.

[25]Sáenz and Priestley, *Some Mexican Problems*, p. 71.

from other federal agencies, the average teacher was social worker, nurse, and doctor to everyone in the community.

Teaching in the rural village was a lonely career. The isolated hamlet offered little in the way of material comforts: housing was primitive, sanitary facilities meager, and recreational opportunities nonexistent. Not only was the teacher isolated; culturally he was separated from the modern world he had come to know in the teacher-training center. Far from the cities, he had to fall back upon his own resources, which often failed him. Though the federal government employed him, the gods of Mexico City were far away and local politicians close by. If the minister of education had his welfare at heart, the local cacique was his enemy. Nor were officials in the capital steadfast in their loyalty. Some were friends of rural education; others put their faith in the urban school and forgot the village.

With every shift of administration there were different policy makers in Mexico City, fresh panaceas for the ills of rural education, and new demands upon the teacher. In the early twenties the doctrines of Vasconcelos reigned supreme; the schoolmaster was told that he was a reformer, but not a radical, that for every problem there was a native solution. With the demise of Vasconcelos and the coming of Sáenz the teacher learned that the way out lay in Dewey's school of action, anathema to Vasconcelos and a mystery to the average teacher. No sooner was Dewey ensconced in the halls of the Ministry of Education than Bassols arrived with blueprints for a collectivist school. On the heels of the class-minded thinkers came the "school of love," which put the teacher back into the classroom and warned him to stay there. Peace in the countryside—this was the goal of the new men of power. Whereas Bassols had demanded leadership, now the teacher was considered an agitator if he petitioned for land in behalf of the village—a confusing shift, for the problems of yesterday were still there. If the teacher did not speak for his people, who would bring the doctor, agronomist, and road-building crew to the village?

Left on his own, betrayed by many, the teacher took steps to defend himself. To safeguard his interests he built a nationwide syndicate and fought incessantly for better salaries.

Union organization was an objective from the start. The example was set by the CROM (*Confederación Regional Obrera Mexicana*) and other labor groups, which Calles had backed. Associations of teachers were formed early in the twenties, and by 1930 practically all of Mexico's schoolmasters belonged to one of them. These groups played important roles in determining the policy of the Ministry of

Education toward the individual teacher. With numbers and the pooling of resources came advantages. One was the Civil Service Act of 1938. Before the passage of this legislation each federal dependency decided labor policy on its own. Now there were guarantees against arbitrary officials, uniform tenure regulations, and old-age and disability benefits. Retirement was set at fifty-five, although it was not compulsory. Length of service determined pension rates, with a full salary awarded after thirty years of service. There were loans for the purchase of homes, free medical service, and sick leave. Unfortunately the Civil Service Act was based on a system of seniority that placed emphasis on age rather than on performance. By 1959 younger men were finding doors closed to them; the best jobs were in the hands of men no longer sufficiently vigorous for the task.

Union organization brought intrigue and factional squabbles. Public educational policy paid dearly for this; scores of competent men abandoned the Ministry of Education, and programs bogged down in the morass of politics. José Manuel Puig Casauranc placed much of the responsibility for the chaos of 1931 on the teachers themselves.[26] In his letter of resignation of 1934, Bassols censured the teachers who had attacked his efforts to establish a uniform system of tenure and promotions based on ability and training.[27] Bassols' mistake had been his attempt to eliminate union control over appointments and promotions. Additional fuel was poured on the fires of political agitation by the reform of Article 3 in 1934. Some groups of teachers sympathized with the reform; others opposed it. Those in sympathy with it advocated dismissing the opposition, while the foes of the reform persecuted its supporters as Communists.

Powerful before 1934, the teachers and their representatives won a major victory under President Cárdenas. He did much to aid them to win public respect and security. Critics declared that he turned the Ministry of Education over to organizations dominated by radicals and supporters of the Soviet Union. Whatever the merits of this view, there was no question that the turmoil of the past was intensified. Conflict over Article 3 continued, and fresh divisions arose when the teachers raised the banner of agrarian reform. Cárdenas overlooked much of the turmoil, and the problem was inherited by his successor.

By 1940 the STERM (Union of Workers in Education of the Mexican Republic), a militant organization closely identified with

[26]Secretía. de Educ. Públ., *Memoria que indica el estado que guarda el ramo de educación pública el 31 de agosto de 1931* (Mexico, 1931), p. v.

[27]Francisco J. Gaxiola, *El presidente Rodríguez (1932-1934)* (Mexico, 1938), p. 103.

left-wing international groups, had apparently won the right to speak for the Republic's teachers. On the surface there was unity in the STERM, but underneath factions ranging from moderate to Communist were struggling for power. Critics said that extremists had the upper hand. So powerful was the STERM that even cabinet members bowed to its wishes. In 1936 the undersecretary of education and the director of primary schools were forced out of office because of their alleged sympathies for elements out of favor with the STERM.

Alarmed by this situation and frightened by the specter of left-wing control of education, President Avila Camacho set out to subdue his teachers. He began by reforming the Civil Service Act. The new legislation of 1941 cut into the power of the unions by enlarging the categories of employees with no right to strike against the government,[28] a right that Cárdenas had granted them. Avila Camacho kept these groups loyal by raising their take-home pay and thus alienated them from their colleagues who kept their right to strike but earned less money. What Avila Camacho had done, ironically, was to intensify the grip of union bosses over their rank and file. By reducing the power to strike, the reform undermined the union's effectiveness but left undisturbed its control over appointments and dues. Nothing was done to eliminate the ceaseless struggle for power among factions, while the ability of the union to go to the aid of the teacher was severely impaired.

The Civil Service Act of 1941 did not go far enough for Octavio Véjar Vásquez. A conservative with no sympathy for union activity, he lost no time in attacking what he thought were the seeds of the trouble. His target was the STERM, which he destroyed by dismissing many of its members during his term in office. With them went the leadership of the STERM, which collapsed immediately. Véjar Vásquez won a Pyrrhic victory. Angered by the attack, the teachers closed ranks. The battle between them and the minister raged throughout 1942 and into the next year and culminated in the dismissal of Véjar Vásquez, whose proclerical activities had cost him the support of influential groups. From the victory of the teachers came the SNTE (National Syndicate of Teachers), a more moderate group than the STERM but plagued with all of its defects. Victory had fallen to the teachers, but there was no return to the days of Cárdenas. Avila Camacho offered only concessions, and his successor, Miguel Alemán, spoke for hostile business groups. Alemán's min-

---

[28]Wendel Karl Gordon Schaeffer, "El control del aparato jurídico y de los sindicatos de burócratas," *Problemas de México,* I (Oct. 1, 1958), 41.

ister of education, Manuel Gual Vidal, had no sympathy for the SNTE or for unions in general. His successor punished recalcitrant teachers as no one had done since the antilabor days of Porfirio Díaz.

By 1959 the union movement had lost what independence it once had. Chosen by the national political party, SNTE leaders spoke for the Ministry of Education and not the rank and file. There was corruption at the top and unrest at the bottom.[29] Branches of the SNTE became pawns of state political machines; much of the opposition to unification sprang from local groups that hoped to gain by cooperating with politicians in the state capitals. Federal schools were built in urban areas under pressure of SNTE groups that wanted the comforts of city life while teaching; yet the federal program lagged in the countryside for lack of teachers and schools. When reformers in Mexico City sought to win control of the SNTE, its leadership sanctioned a police attack on them.

Poor and corrupt leadership—perhaps a reflection of the national scene—had repercussions in the countryside. Having learned from the example set by their leaders that the road of the reformer led nowhere, hundreds of teachers joined the ranks of those who lived by exploiting the peasant. There were villages where the pulque monopoly was in the hands of the local schoolmaster; in others the teacher was the middleman. Countless teachers, to cite the testimony of officials in Mexico City, did not live in the villages but in the nearest urban center. They commuted, arriving on Tuesday and departing on Thursday, leaving the school abandoned for the better part of the week. Almost any event served as an excuse for a holiday.

Censurable as the teachers were, the fault was not all theirs. Far more guilty were officials and policy makers in Mexico, whose indifference to the needs of rural education grew after 1941. A conservative public, hostile or apathetic to the plight of the Republic's teachers, was equally guilty. Abandoned by nearly everyone, the teachers found security on their own. Some made living in the countryside a business; others left the village for the city. Thousands of conscientious teachers spent their time in union activity, demonstrating in this way their protest against those who lived in luxury but demanded sacrifice and abstinence from the teachers.[30]

Much of the trouble in rural education could be traced to the salary question. From the beginning the rural teacher was woefully underpaid. Salary troubles began with Obregón; after launching the

[29]Otón Salazar, SNTE leader, quoted in *Excelsior*, Dec. 7, 14, 1958.

[30]Pedro de Alba, "Prólogo," in Ramón García Ruiz, *Hombres y rutas de México* (Guadalajara, Mexico, 1953), p. xv.

educational program, he cut the school budget by 22 million pesos, and first to suffer were teachers' salaries. Sáenz fought valiantly for rural education but sacrificed his teachers. He built thousands of schools and paid his teachers 27 pesos a month. With the Great Depression the salary picture worsened. Bassols attempted to improve the situation by raising salaries of rural schoolteachers to 55 pesos per month; Cárdenas raised salaries again. Neither increase matched the rising cost of living.

With the coming of Avila Camacho there was no longer a friend in the national palace. Businessmen and industrialists won the ear of the executive. Under Alemán, money, supplies, and encouragement went to technical and urban schools, as they had in the days of Díaz. In 1934, 38 per cent of the federal budget was spent on salaries; Cárdenas increased that proportion to 44.6 per cent; under Alemán the figure fell to 10.3 per cent. Of the officeholders since Avila Camacho, only President Ruiz Cortines had substantially improved rural school salaries. Despite the increase, teachers were in effect earning half as much in 1959 as in 1936, for the cost of living had doubled.[31] The burden fell on the rural schoolmasters whose 630-peso monthly salary was approximately 400 pesos below that of the teacher in the city, despite almost identical costs of living. Both earned less than factory laborers, whose income rose rapidly in the 1950's.

Inadequate salaries hampered the development of a healthy school program at almost every turn. No matter what other solutions were advanced, it was clear by 1959 that until the rural schoolmaster's salary was placed on a level with that of his colleague in the city, and both were raised substantially, the program would fail. On the basis of salary alone the federal government had not advanced far in education.

[31]Ernesto Lobato, "La burocracia mexicana," *Problemas de México*, I (Oct. 1, 1958), 34, 31.

Chapter VII

NATIONALITY, THE INDIAN, AND THE EDUCATOR

I

DURING "THE LAST TEN YEARS [the 1910's] . . . not . . . fighting but thinking has been our occupation. Violent deeds are only the signs of our mental effort to fathom the truth of our reality and of our ideals," wrote Moisés Sáenz. An era of national introspection emerged with the Revolution, as Mexicans began to analyze themselves and their society. "What are we? What would we like to be?" asked Sáenz.[1] "What is the right of the white man, of the mestizo . . . of the Indian in the new scheme of life?"[2] Specifically, there were two questions: what was the Mexican nationality, and what was the place of the Indian in society. Both confronted the rural school.

For the artists the answers were simple. The masses, Indian by "race," brown by color, peasant by class, were the essence of revolutionary Mexico. So Rivera, Orozco, and Siqueiros turned for inspiration to the peasant, depicting on canvas and wall his struggle for justice and equality. What the artist painted, the writer put into words. The literature of Mariano Azuela and his friends spoke of villages and peasants, of battles waged by cotton-clad warriors against the forces of city and greed. The brown peasant exemplified strength and virtue; city, landlord, and foreigner were his enemies. The lawmakers of 1917, too, recognized the Indian by giving a place in the national Constitution to the *ejido*, a village land system dating back to the pre-Conquest.

The issue, however, was not as simple for the architects of the national program of education, for the answers given would determine the orientation of the program, a matter of public concern. Public opinion, furthermore, was divided on this question, for the character of their nationality was a sensitive issue among Mexicans, hybrids of

[1]"The Genius of Mexican Life," in Herring and Terrill, eds. *The Genius of Mexico*, p. 26.

[2]Sáenz, *Mexico: An Appraisal and a Forecast* (New York, 1929), p. 9.

Indian and Spanish stock. Some thought themselves Spaniards, or basically European; others boasted that they were "pure" Indian. And after all, what were Mexicans by race, ideals, and culture? Fundamentally, the question was whether the relationship established by the Conquest—equality of races in theory but with the Spaniard superior in practice—still existed, or whether in four centuries one group had risen at the expense of the other. Had the Indian by sheer weight of numbers and loyalty to tradition overcome the Spaniard, or had the European triumphed over the Indian? The answer to this question would determine the nationality of Mexico, which the reformers sought zealously to define. On this issue of nationality, subject to diverse interpretations, the reformers split into two general groups: the Europeanists (for want of a better term) and the Nationalists, or *indianistas*, as they were popularly called.

Equally important was the place of the Indian in society—second of the two questions. The 1921 census counted 4,179,449 Indians in Mexico.[3] There were more than eighty groups, some small and relatively unimportant, others—like the Aztecs—numerous and significant. They were distinct in language, folklore, and culture. A few remained in the nomadic stage; some were barbarous and war-loving; the great majority farmed for a living. With some exceptions, the Indians lived in poverty, the victims of disease, malnutrition, and superstition.

Urban society, the aristocracy, and the majority of reformers looked upon the Indian as a problem. Materially he lived on the margin of the national economy, a status detrimental to his welfare and to that of the Republic. Ways had to be found to raise his living standard and to encourage his aspirations. On this point reformers were in substantial agreement; but they split over how to carry out this rehabilitation.

II

The attitude of the Europeanists on the issue of nationality and the Indian was clear; the character of Mexico had been shaped by the Conquest. "The Indian's door to the future," wrote José Vasconcelos, "was that of modern culture; there was no other door open to him but that already trod by Latin civilization."[4] All originality began with the Conquest; only events after this "act of salvation," Octavio

[3]Departamento de la Estadística Nacional, *Resumen del censo general de habitantes de 30 de noviembre de 1921* (Mexico, 1928), p. 62.

[4]*La raza cósmica* (Mexico, 1948), p. 25.

Véjar Vásquez added, had something to contribute to the natural perfection of the Mexican.[5] If the ancient land of Mexico had given birth to indigenous civilizations, independent of the Old World, they had fallen before the stronger, more virile culture of the conquerors and were now merely of historical interest.

While this view had points in common with the ideology of the prerevolutionary regime, there were fundamental differences between them. As reformers the Europeanists were dedicated to the welfare of the masses; the old regime was not. Although rejecting the indigenous contribution, the Europeanists accepted the Indian as a human being. To quote Vasconcelos, "I do not believe that there is any difference between the ignorant Indian and the ignorant French or English peasant; as soon as one or the other is educated he becomes a useful addition to the civilized life of his country and in so doing contributes to the betterment of the world in general."[6] Or as Fernando González Roa put it: "We do not deny the...despondency of the indigenous race, but such can surely be removed since the race is capable of enjoying the benefits of civilization."[7] What reformers of this group believed was that with their help the Indian would become an asset to society. This was a rejection of all that "Indian" implied except the Indian himself.

There was a further difference between the Europeanists and the rulers of the past. Díaz and his followers had made a sharp distinction between the downtrodden Indian masses and the urban elite of whites and mestizos. Not only did a majority of Europeanists reject the Díaz myth of the Indian's racial inferiority, but some even denied his existence. All Mexicans were alike. There were no Indians, said a distinguished educator of the twenties: "I deny the existence of the Indian in Mexico. . . . We have only one group and one class of people—the Mexicans." Despite "ethnic groups that must still be considered as apart from us . . . for all purposes—political and cultural, in fact and in intention—we are only one people. We are all Mexicans." Why employ valuable time making ethnic studies of the population? "We gain nothing and by thinking in that way we may be damaging our sense of a coherent and homogeneous nationality."[8]

As a group the Europeanists favored Western civilization in gen-

[5]Quoted by Kneller, p. 69.

[6]Quoted by Millán, p. 45.

[7]*The Mexican People and Their Detractors* (New York, [1916]), p. 77.

[8]Quoted by Sáenz, "Indian Mexico," in Herring and Weinstock, eds. *Renascent Mexico,* p. 168.

eral; as individuals many had a more specific ideology. Spain, not merely Europe, was the essence of Mexico. The mother country had forged the cultural patterns and the social institutions of state and faith; these were the bulwarks of society. "We shall not be great," announced Vasconcelos, "until the Spaniard of America feels as Spanish as the sons of Spain."[9] The formula lay in rejecting the empirical philosophy and the utilitarian morality of the Western world, in reviving the Catholic tradition, and in resurrecting the colonial heritage.[10] For the Conquest had brought a "clash between the democracy of the time—one of the most genuine . . . of Europe—and despotism—one of the crudest . . . of history—the despotism of Montezuma."[11] What was fine in Mexican life rose from the Spain of the sixteenth century. Weakness had come with the disappearance of Spanish ways. "I recognized this," said Vasconcelos, "as I stood admiring one day . . . the fine old homes . . . in the ancient city of Oaxaca. As I looked around me I saw that something had happened to mar the traditional beauty of the scene." Over the years "the Whites had disappeared and the Indians from the mountains, silent and impassive in their blankets, had enveloped the streets and squares. Then I knew," he concluded, "that the tragedy of Mexico lay in this displacement and exhaustion of the conquering and civilizing blood of Spain."[12]

Despite their deprecation of the native background, the Europeanists had an ambivalent attitude. Their ideology was the product of two worlds, nurtured on the nationalism of the Revolution. Many of them accepted the superiority of the Western world with reservations; they were too Mexican for anything else. When American dignitaries asked Vasconcelos where he got his ideas on education, he replied: "Not in Boston, but in Xochimilco. Watch the Indian there . . . see how he cultivates his tiny plot of ground to grow the finest vegetables in the world. Would it not be foolish to send him to study agriculture in Maine[?]"[13] In his controversial *La raza cósmica* he asserted (p. 25) that the reign of the whites was destined to collapse. Their mission was to mechanize the world and to lay the foundations for the era of the mestizo.

Nature had bestowed its blessings on the mestizo—the cosmic race —offspring of "two aristocracies, both products of nature's severe

[9]*La raza cósmica*, p. 19.

[10]Vasconcelos quoted by Crawford, p. 262.

[11]Vasconcelos and Gamio, *Aspects of Mexican Civilization*, p. 47.

[12]*El desastre*, p. 395.

[13]Ibid., p. 81.

selective process."[14] Here was a race free of the defects of other races. Since individual differences stemmed more from the ability to do certain things to the exclusion of others than from the degree of total development, the mestizo surmounted these defects by complementing the weaknesses of a particular stock through interchange and assimilation. "The great periods of history," meditated Vasconcelos, were the products of hybrids, "of peoples and cultures, rather than the contribution of any privileged pure-blood nation."[15] The myth of racial purity was the propaganda of rulers. Miscegenation, not purity, was the ideal, for "hybridism in man, as well as in plants, tends to produce finer types and tends to rejuvenate those . . . that have become static." Bridging the gap between past and future, between Spain and the pre-Columbian world, was the mestizo. He was a Spaniard at heart even when fighting Spain, an Indian in spite of a skin turned white through fusion with the blood of the Iberian Peninsula. Resembling neither of his parents, he could not turn back; he was "always directed to the future."[16]

As to what should be done about the Indian, the Europeanists felt that since after four centuries of interbreeding the Indian was a dying segment of the population, he was a subject for redemption and nothing more. He had nothing to offer society except himself. It was sheer intellectual snobbery to talk of reviving such things as native languages, exclaimed Luis Cabrera. Or, to paraphrase the famous pedagogue Gregorio Torres Quintero, there was no reason why the Indian should be given preferential treatment. Of course the Indian needed schools but not at the expense of the mestizo. For Mexico was no longer a colony governed by laws making the Indian a ward of the crown.[17] The way out was through the "incorporation of the Indian into society," a society in the European mold. If the Indian could be made in the image of his mestizo neighbor, Western in thought, the problem would be solved. With this in mind Vasconcelos cast an educational plan of universal outlook. In the name of unity, schools were built to root out cultural deviations from the national scene. The school, to quote Cabrera, had "to make the race a homogeneous one, fusing its inferior elements—the Indians—and its superior ones—the whites—in the mestizo race."[18] Like the conquerors

[14]Vasconcelos quoted by Crawford, p. 266.

[15]Ibid., p. 97.

[16]Vasconcelos and Gamio, *Aspects of Mexican Civilization*, pp. 85, 83.

[17]Torres Quintero, pp. 43-44.

[18]"The Key to the Mexican Chaos," in Herring and Weinstock, eds. *Renascent Mexico*, pp. 24, 28.

the Europeanists accepted the equality of the Indian before God, but like Cortés and his monks they strove to make the Indian into their own image.

Supporters of these views represented a heterogeneous lot. There were intellectuals, particularly philosophers and historians—Vasconcelos was one of them—politicians, military men, and professional educators—Rafael Ramírez, for example; all served the school movement. In general, they were urban- rather than rural-minded, more linked with commerce and business—and later industry—than with agriculture. Loosely speaking, they were heirs of the doctrines of *La Reforma*. Still they had no sympathy for the Comte and Spencer of the old regime, and some of their leading spokesmen rejected empiricism in favor of Bergsonism and a *rapprochement* with the church.

Patterned after that of the Northern Dynasty, their program was conceived in terms of recovery rather than radical social change. Their reforms accepted the capitalism of the Díaz days, modified here, strengthened there; evolution was the key, not revolution. Not the destruction of the economic system, but the protection of private property, animated them. Their crusade stressed the rights of the individual and the virtues of Western democracy, which were alien to the Indian, who spoke for communal property concepts foreign to the individualistic character of Western society, as Robert Redfield pointed out in his study of Tepoztlán.[19] Economics, too, hovered behind some of the Europeanist denial of ethnic differences in the population. There was mirrored the traditional refusal of the conservative —and the Europeanists were conservatives—to admit to the existence of class distinctions in a society of his own making.

This view, paradoxically, received strong support from some radicals, who found the stress on economics convenient. The Marxists, in particular, condemned as "bourgeois . . . think[ing] of the . . . Indian problem in juridical, pedagogic, moral or racial terms."[20] The question was economic. How logical this union of conservative and radical thought was, the case of Rafael Ramírez illustrates superbly. A middle-of-the-road thinker in the beginning, he veered left under the tutelage of Narciso Bassols. Yet this ideological shift did not alter his views on the question of nationality and the Indian. Both as a supporter of the middle-class state and as the champion of collec-

[19] *Tepoztlán, a Mexican Village* (Chicago, 1930), p. 21.

[20] Partido Comunista, *Hacia una educación al servicio del pueblo* (Mexico, 1938), pp. 113-114.

tivism, he never wavered from what was essentially the position of the Europeanists.

Decrying violent change, the Europeanists dictated a conservative program of rural education. For the wrong type of learning would upset the equilibrium between the mental and economic levels of individuals and groups and lead to chronic discontent by awakening desires beyond reach. This discontent was fertile soil for the seeds of demagogues interested in such radical measures as agrarian socialism. The wrong school would fan the flames of Zapatismo and lead to the destruction of the sacred principles of private property, observed Alberto J. Pani.[21] If there was danger in mass education, however, greater peril lay in ignorance. Ignorance held the masses in check, conceded Jorge Vera Estañol, minister of education under Victoriano Huerta, but it also rendered them easy prey to agitators.[22] The road to unity and peace lay in a moderate program of education that erased concepts of class, party, and race and left undisturbed the foundations of society.

III

These views received little support from *indianistas*. To them the nationality was Indian. Since three out of four Mexicans still lived in rural villages, the traditional home of the Indian, the great Mexican majority was Indian, wrote Manuel Gamio.[23] Though the Spaniard had triumphed militarily and as an individual, his civilization was not transmitted to the Indian. The Spaniard was always a minority, and even the mestizo was more Indian than European. So why not accept reality—intellectually, artistically, and otherwise—and build around it?[24] If the nationality was Indian, the Indian had a vital role to play, declared the *indianistas*. As heir to the pre-Columbian past, he had much to give the present; for, as Sáenz eulogized in one of his sentimental moments, the Indian represented "a civilization so high and delicate that at times ... one wonders if ... the coming of the white man ... was not a pity rather than a blessing."[25] There was, moreover, no reason to deny the continuing existence of the Indian, as some did. "We gain nothing and lose much by trying to reason the Indian

[21]*La higiene*, p. 162.

[22]*Carranza and His Bolshevik Regime* (Los Angeles, 1920), pp. 34-35.

[23]"Las pretendidas razas inferiores," *El Universal*, March 4, 1921.

[24]Sáenz, *Mexico: An Appraisal*, p. 14.

[25]Sáenz and Priestley, *Some Mexican Problems*, p. 73.

out of our reality," announced Sáenz. "Indeed . . . this attitude is responsible for the neglect in which . . . [the] Indians . . . have been left."[26]

The *indianistas* were a mixed lot, bound together by a common interest in rural life, a Jeffersonian faith in agriculture, and a belief in the masses. Their ranks included rural educators, anthropologists, farm experts, here and there a renegade historian, and a strange collection of artists and writers, antiquarians, and romanticists. When the political climate favored *indianismo*, which happened rarely, politician, general, and businessman echoed its sentiments. But the businessman was hardly a friend, for he had cast his lot with commerce and later with industry, traditional rivals of agriculture. At the head of the *indianista* movement was the rural expert, usually the anthropologist or the specialist on rural education, who came to know and admire the qualities of the peasants. Intellectuals with an intimate sense of rural life, they were the links between the reality of the countryside and the *indianismo* of the printed page.

Ironically, what was lacking in the leadership was the Indian himself. With few exceptions, the Indianist movement, never an organized affair, was the child of intellectuals interested in rural problems, but intellectuals who were certainly not Indian. Even at the grass roots the Indian seldom joined the crusade. Once educated, however, and therefore no longer an Indian in the Mexican sense, he often returned as a teacher or rural expert, having learned and adopted the doctrines of *indianismo*. But this was acquired or imposed doctrine, not something indigenous. While the Indian of the village usually joined in the folk festivals sponsored by a cultural mission and supported the native language program, this was not always the case. The village was often indifferent, as Ralph L. Beals pointed out in *Cherán*.[27] Yet the symbol of *indianismo*, if it had one, was Zapata, the Indian agrarian chieftain, whose struggle for land and schools was an important phase of the Revolution.

Usually out of power and therefore free of any responsibility, the *indianistas* frequently allowed sentiment to get the better of reason. Still they were an influential and vocal minority. Their writings left a mark on social and economic theory, and their activities colored the agrarian era of the twenties and thirties.

Historically speaking, *indianismo* came into its own with the Revolution; but its roots were old. The beginnings were laid in the pre-

[26]"Indian Mexico," in Herring and Weinstock, eds. *Renascent Mexico*, p. 169.

[27]*Cherán:A Sierra Tarascan Village* (Washington, D. C., 1946), p. 111.

Columbian era; the seeds of *indianismo* are also found in the scores of Indian uprisings of the colonial period and in the activity of Las Casas and his priestly cohorts, whose defense of the Indian was a cult. Certainly, the Hidalgo and Morelos uprisings had characteristics later associated with *indianismo*. Throughout the nineteenth century—especially in the early 1830's, later during *La Reforma*, and even under the Díaz regime—there were vocal individuals of *indianista* leanings. Still the movement was a more recent phenomenon.

IV

There were many factors behind the *indianista* concept of nationality. Foremost was a rising group spirit, an impulse for nationalism emerging after centuries of neglect and exploitation. In a symbolic sense, the rediscovery of the Indian gave substance to the desire to stand alone, to be free of Europe and independent of the United States, as Redfield asserted.[28] The new nationalism was a revolt against Spain the colonizer and master, four centuries after the Conquest. It was an emotional repudiation of centuries of imitation, a reaction against Comte and Spencer, against the prejudices of Western society categorizing the Indian, and Mexicans generally, as inferior people. Viewed from this angle, *indianismo* was pride of race —racial chauvinism in some cases. For as Antonio Díaz Soto y Gama boasted to a group of visiting students from the United States: "We prefer the Indian blood that runs in our veins to the small amount of white blood from European extraction."[29]

With *indianismo* there came an awakened interest in folk language, folk customs, and folk personality. The new interest stressed things native, using the Indian as a symbol of individual honor and pride, ideals sought by that generation. "We must take advantage of what the country gives us: men of dark skin . . . to govern us, *tequila, charanda*, and *aguardiente* . . . the beverages of plants as noble as the grape," José Rubén Romero had his Pito Pérez say. "Were the clerics to use *aguardiente* in place of wine for mass, they would be humble and kind to their flocks."

Basically, *indianismo* was a belief in the simple agrarian economy of the peasant, long forgotten by an industrialized world. The In-

[28] "The Indian in Mexico," *Annals of the American Academy of Political and Social Science*, CCVIII (March 1940), 138.

[29] "The Agrarian Movement in Mexico," in Herring and Terrill, eds. *The Genius of Mexico*, p. 179.

dian's communal system offered a way out of the dilemma posed by a lingering quasi-medieval colonial system on one side and capitalism on the other. By fusing the communal village with collectivism, the peasant would get the benefits of Western technology and avoid the dangers of capitalism or the limitations of an antiquated colonial system. Perhaps, in the final analysis, behind the cotton *calzones*, the *huaraches*, and the *ejido* lay an attack—Marxian or otherwise—on capitalism or what passed for it in Mexico.[30] The *ejido*—and the rural school—represented *indianismo* in the countryside.

It was no surprise, therefore, to find Ramón Beteta, still the idealistic schoolteacher, suggesting in 1935 that Mexico revise her land system in order to substitute the small communal holding for private property. He saw no reason why land reform should be used to create an agrarian *bourgeoisie*, which, though new to Mexico, was antiquated elsewhere. To redistribute the land and not to go ahead with its socialization, he considered a dangerous step. Unless carried to its logical conclusions, declared Beteta, the Revolution had won a Pyrrhic victory.[31]

Conservative hostility to Indianism was born of this attempt to meddle with the economic *status quo*. The conservative reformer had no quarrel with a weak and numerically insignificant group that suggested a return to a nebulous and ill-defined "Indian culture" and raised no protest when the Ministry of Education subsidized mural art critical of the middle class. But here was an attack on private property in the guise of a cultural crusade, and conservatives rallied to protect the old order.

In the light of this picture, the school-church issue of the twenties and thirties, which divided reformers, takes on new meaning. In general the conservatives remained loyal Catholics or at least gave lukewarm support to the church. With some exceptions, they were ready to accept the church as vital to the future of Mexico, and some were willing to accept modification of Article 3 of the Constitution, which dealt with education. After all, the church gave tacit approval to the *status quo* and, since the days of Juárez, had posed no threat to the middle class. So long as the church refrained from political intrigue harmful to the social order, which it was willing to do if its own position was not threatened, the conservatives were ready to share education with the church.

On the other hand, the *indianistas* considered the church a vested

[30]Redfield, *Tepoztlán*, p. 21.

[31]"Some Economic Aspects of Mexico's Six-Year Plan," in Herring and Weinstock, eds. *Renascent Mexico*, pp. 101-102.

partner of the *status quo*, thus a logical target. If the school was to achieve its purpose—the transformation of society—the church, as constituted, had to go. As Sáenz wrote, "If religion is to function in a constructive way in the life of our people, the church-to-be must be willing to deal with the realities of the present life in accordance with the *social* and *political* ideals [italics mine] for which we are striving."[32] There could be no enduring harmony while there existed an ambivalence between present and future life, between material and spiritual values. Viewed from this perspective, *indianismo* was an extension, often with collectivist undertones, of the anticlericalism of the nineteenth century, which was rooted in the struggle for power between church and state.

Further, unlike traditional anticlericalism, which was neither anti-Catholic nor anti-Christian, *indianismo* denied both the faith and the church. The village—so ran the argument—while deeply religious, was neither Christian nor Catholic; its faith was a strange mixture of pagan rite and Catholic worship, both degenerate and misunderstood. Christianity, instead of replacing the ancient cults, had merged with them. Why not accept this fact and blend the two, asked Sáenz, for "out of pagan feeling and Christian conception and practice, a new manner of religion may come about where a complete synthesis of life will be realized."[33] Or, as Gamio asserted, the destruction of many aspects of pre-Conquest worship was regrettable, not especially because of their religious character, "but . . . because of the originality, the significance, and the rare beauty in the work of art which pre-Columbian mythology [had] created." Nothing since the Conquest had artistically equaled or surpassed "the decoration of the Maya temples, the bas-reliefs of Palenque, the plumed serpents of Teotihuacán, [and] a thousand other marvels." Since the mixture of Catholic dogma and pre-Hispanic pantheism had not produced anything equal to that art born of the union of aesthetics and mythology in the ancient world, why not replace "classic occidental mythology" with courses in school on the mythology of the New World?[34]

What these *indianistas* asked was that the church support their social order and accept the school's right to blend pagan worship with Catholicism. While the conservative reformer was familiar with the paganism of the village and with anticlericalism, this was asking too much of him. He balked and gave his support to the church.

[32]*Mexico: An Appraisal*, pp. 15-16.

[33]Ibid., p. 15.

[34]"Static and Dynamic Values in the Indigenous Past of America," *Hispanic American Historical Review*, XXIII (Aug. 1943), 388-389.

V

On the question of nationality, there was general agreement among the *indianistas*. But when the immediate problems of the Indian population faced them, they drifted into three ill-defined groups or wings: romanticists, radicals, and moderates.

For the romanticists—the antiquarians, folklorists, artists, and poets —*indianismo* was, in practice, the cult of the lyrical and little else. Having accepted *indianismo* in theory, the romanticists had nothing to offer. Their idealized Indian had scant relation to the flesh-and-blood Indian in the countryside. Their Indian inspired the artist, was eulogized as quaint, furnished material for "scientific investigation," or was displayed in museum cases. Because their interest was sentimental, the romanticists played a theoretical and minor role.

Though the radicals were often equally guilty of stressing the lyrical, their weakness was the impracticality of their social and economic proposals. They called for total reform: confiscation of haciendas, collectivization of land, socialized education. They dealt in wholesale condemnations and categorical imperatives, leaving no room for compromise. With little actual experience in rural affairs, with no clear understanding of the cultural factors involved, they, like the romanticists, had little to offer beyond doctrine. For the radical was an agitator, a dreamer with only a sketch of a program vast and intricate, which would require the careful planning of every detail.

The practical reformers—the Sáenzes and Gamios—were in the moderate wing. They forsook the city to work with Indian groups in the village, saw that the nationality issue was meaningless unless there were tangible benefits for the Indian, and envisaged an agrarian nation with a place for the Indian as well as for the machine. They gradually came to be known as *indigenistas*, and the philosophical, often lyrical, *indianismo* of earlier years gave way to their "scientific" *indigenismo*, a movement concerned primarily with alleviating the socioeconomic plight of the Indian. It was the *indigenistas* who laid out the educational program for the Indian, partly on the basis of Gamio's experiments at San Juan de Teotihuacán.

VI

The task of the practical *indigenistas* was to help the Indian raise his living standard, to make him a part of the national stream of life. Of primary importance was the matter of approach or method, which in turn called for intimate knowledge of Indian characteristics.

From this problem arose the question of what are Indian character-istics, or, more succinctly, "What is an Indian?" The racial classifi-cation—which, in the census of 1921, defined an Indian as one of "more or less pure" blood—proved inadequate: how could one de-cide who was "pure blooded" after four hundred years of racial in-termixing? Further, the Indian question was not one of blood but of the plight of a group or segment of society, declared the *indige-nistas*. So the census of 1930—while still taking race into account—adopted the new socioeconomic definition put forth by the *indige-nistas*.[35] For the Indian, life revolved around Indian things: the planting stick instead of the plow, corn in place of wheat, the *rebozo* or *serape* for the coat, and usually a native language spoken in prefer-ence to Spanish. Racially, he was more "Indian" than Spaniard. In a psychological sense, he was conscious of being Indian, a feeling that had not diminished over the centuries, as Robert Redfield re-ported in *A Village That Chose Progress: Chan Kom Revisited*.[36] By this classification an Indian, merely by a change in economic and intellectual status, became a mestizo.

Reform had to take the characteristics of the Indian into account, insisted the *indigenistas*. A meaningful education had to serve each Indian group according to its needs and thus would effect, paradoxi-cally, a real national unity, by lifting all groups to one plane of civi-lization.[37] The policy of "incorporation" ignored group differences. As the agrarian and political programs had demonstrated, there was little logic in "incorporation." If the rural majority demanded an agrarian program that would break up large landholdings and divide them among the people, many of the Indians did not need such a pro-gram. Unlike his neighbors, the Indian had held on to his tiny plot of land. To benefit him, the agrarian program had to increase the size of his land, improve his agricultural techniques, and encourage co-operative farming.[38] Where matters of political organization were in-volved, the Indian, unlike his apolitical neighbor, had an organization of his own, worthy of respect and consideration, which dated back to the pre-Columbian era, wrote Luis Chávez Orozco.[39] The Indian

[35]Alfonso Caso, "Definición del indio y lo indio," *América indígena*, VIII (Oct. 1948), 237-247; Gamio, *Consideraciones sobre el problema indígena* (Mexico, 1948), pp. 11-15.

[36](Chicago, 1950), p. 74.

[37]Vasconcelos and Gamio, *Aspects of Mexican Civilization*, p. 154.

[38]Sáenz, "Indian Mexico," in Herring and Weinstock, eds. *Renascent Mexico*, p. 176.

[39]*Las instituciones democráticas de los indígenas mexicanos en la época colonial* (Mexico, 1943), pp. 5-11.

considered the politician from outside an invader of the worst sort. Gamio argued that the Indian had been corrupted politically by Western society; and, in fact, the closer he lived to centers of Occidental culture, the more corrupt he was.[40]

According to the *indigenistas*, the formula of the Europeanists not only ignored the characteristics of the Indian but rejected what Gamio called "static and dynamic" values. The "static" values were the long-forgotten higher arts and social practices of the pre-Columbian age, which were once of great significance and could be again. The "dynamic" values were the pre-Columbian practices, tools, and beliefs that still persisted in the modern era.

Among the chief "static" values of the Indian were architecture, sculpture, work in precious metals, his mythology, and an innate sense of democracy. These, in the opinion of Gamio, might be revived because the "mental processes of the Indian" resembled those of his ancestors. By being adapted to modern conditions, these "static" values could be restored to the life of today.[41] The "dynamic" values were found in housing, food, clothing, agriculture, tools, domestic equipment, and, generally speaking, in the material things of indigenous life. There were survivals also in the intellectual concepts of the Indian, in his ethics, his aesthetics, and his religious ideas, and in his interpretations of cosmic phenomena and sickness. Some survivals were of intrinsic worth, even though they might appear degenerate. The useful ones were to be cultivated. Folk arts, now corrupted by the tourist trade, could be restored to their original authentic character. Villages and towns could be laid out as they were before the Conquest, with houses placed on small plots of land surrounded by orchards and cultivated fields—a more hygienic and picturesque plan than the compact block of buildings that the Spaniards introduced.[42]

The *indigenistas* denied, however, that they wanted to return to the planting stick, the medicine man, and the mud hut. As they said, they did not want to "Indianize" Mexico; there was no project to restore pre-Columbian life, for if such an absurd scheme could be carried out, the Indian would be exterminated. But certainly this was not a program to "Europeanize" the Indian, to uproot him from his traditions and his environment. The goal was "Mexicanization" —the catchword—the blending of all strains into a Mexican society

[40]"Static and Dynamic Values," p. 389.

[41]Ibid., pp. 386-387.

[42]Ibid., pp. 391-392.

enriched by the contribution of the Indian. *Indigenistas*, said Gamio, "wish to . . . offer him [the Indian] an harmonious combination of the best . . . of his pre-Hispanic and colonial legacy . . . and the best elements in western culture which may be adaptable to the nature of his particular needs and aspirations."[43] Incorporation was a false god. It not only threatened to change the way of life of the Indian, his tools and techniques, but it ignored all that he stood for. If the Indian was to have status in society, "incorporation" had to be a mutual process.[44] The Indian had to play an important role in the social and economic life of the Republic, for if not, reform was nothing but the plan of the conqueror for a vanquished people whose spirit and way of life he had sworn to destroy. This was the warning of the anthropologist Daniel F. Rubín de la Borbolla.[45]

No matter what the goal was, reconstruction had to start with the reality of the Indian world, declared the *indigenistas*. Should the nation later decide upon industrialization, great care would have to be taken lest the factory system be imposed artificially upon native agrarianism. It would be a national calamity to reject the farm for the factory before either the Indian or the rest of the country was prepared for it. "Production for production's sake . . . [and] a Ford every few seconds had not saved the world."[46] The question, said Celerino Cano, an educator of note, was not how to impose an alien system upon the wreckage of the old but how to integrate the new with the old.[47] Reform, President Cárdenas declared, had to respect the Indian as an individual and to recognize his traditions and sentiments.[48]

The function of the school was to make the modern world intelligible to the Indian—to link the primitive with the modern. For unless this were done, declared the *indigenistas*, the tools of Western civilization could have little impact upon the village. Thus, the curriculum emphasized subjects of immediate value to the community: agriculture, animal husbandry, craftsmanship, rural hygiene, native languages, and academic disciplines geared to local utilitarian needs.

[43]Ibid., pp. 392-393.

[44]Sáenz, "Indian Mexico," in Herring and Weinstock, eds. *Renascent Mexico*, pp. 177-178.

[45]"El problema indígena de México," *Educación*, I (June 1940), p. 97.

[46]Beteta, "Social Forces in Mexican Life," in Herring and Terrill, eds. *The Genius of Mexico*, pp. 35-56.

[47]"El antecedente filosófico-social," *Revista mexicana de educación*, I (Nov. 1940), 261.

[48]*Excelsior*, April 15, 1940.

But according to the *indigenistas*, the purpose was not to perpetuate peasant status; it was to help the Indian to improve his social and economic position. In the teaching of language, the objective was not to keep the Indian ignorant of Spanish but to teach him Spanish through his own language. The *indigenistas* believed that one learned a second language with more facility after having mastered his own.[49] Above all else, the goals of education were to give the individual a sense of his own value, to justify his world to him, and ultimately to erase the myth of inferiority from the national conscience. With these aims in mind, the curriculum stressed the study of the pre-Hispanic heritage, so that the Indian might find inspiration for greatness in the record of his own past.[50]

Unlike the conservative reformers, the *indigenistas* did not look upon education as an answer to all problems. They thought it senseless to hope to build a nation through education. That was for populations united by historic, racial, cultural, and economic bonds, where education bound existing ties more closely. But the Mexicans were not a united people; their differences were too fundamental for education to harmonize.[51] For the *indigenistas*, then, education was only one aspect of a reform program that was entirely social.

Nor would it have been logical otherwise. The *indigenistas* had in mind a larger reform than did the conservatives. To them the school was a political organism, an instrument to use against the *status quo*. The school could never be neutral; it had to take a stand, and, by the reasoning of *indigenismo*, on all issues, particularly socioeconomic ones. It was no accident that the collectivist-minded *indigenistas* found their bible in John Dewey.

VII

Theory was one thing and practice something else, for the *indigenistas* seldom wielded political power. Yet their infrequent moments of glory came at crucial times in the history of rural education: at the start of the national movement in 1921, again in the mid-twenties, and during the reform administration of President Cárdenas.

Their initial opportunity came with Gamio's activity at San Juan

[49] Julio de la Fuente, "Ocho años de experiencia en el medio rural," *Revista mexicana de educación*, I (Aug. 1940), 60.

[50] Gamio, "Static and Dynamic Values," p. 389.

[51] Vasconcelos and Gamio, *Aspects of Mexican Civilization*, pp. 129-131.

de Teotihuacán. There, in one of the exciting experiments in the history of rural education, the anthropologist-educator developed and tested theories that became the guiding principles of *indigenismo*. Gamio's project, begun under President Carranza, received strong support from President Obregón but was discarded by Calles after Gamio's dismissal from the Ministry of Education in 1925.

Another limited opportunity followed almost immediately, when Sáenz replaced Gamio as Calles' undersecretary of education. Sáenz labored valiantly to implement *indigenista* doctrines. Perhaps the salient experiment of the time was the founding of a school for Indians in Mexico City: *La Casa del Estudiante Indígena*. This school had two purposes: to train leaders for Indian communities and to demonstrate to the doubting people of the capital that Indians were human beings with an intellectual capacity equal to their own. But while the students proved their ability easily—much to the astonishment of some residents of the capital—they refused to return home upon graduation. So in the end the parents lost their children to urban centers, and the rural communities did not profit from the experiment. To remedy this failing, *La Casa del Estudiante Indígena* was replaced by a number of similar schools built in rural areas where students could remain in contact with the village. Unfortunately, President Calles and his successors had little sympathy for this idea, and these schools got only what was left of funds and personnel after the needs of other institutions were met. By 1936 they were on the verge of collapse.

There was a final opportunity under President Cárdenas after 1935. His administration—firmly supporting *indigenismo*—improved the quality of Indian schools, multiplied their number, placed neighborhood primary schools under their direction, and organized a Department of Indian Education to supervise them. Then, in a bold departure from past practice, the president organized the autonomous Department of Indian Affairs to handle all Indian problems. Both the Department of Indian Education and the Department of Cultural Missions—the latter a pet of the Ministry of Education—were placed under it. Finally, in another precedent-shattering step, the administration recognized both the Spanish and Indian languages as official for rural schools.

The Cardenista period was the epoch of *indigenismo*. Although the Department of Indian Affairs and some of the policies lived on through the administration of President Avila Camacho, they were never the same again. In 1946 President Alemán, who dissented from the *indigenista* approach, disbanded the department and filled the gap with the *Instituto Nacional Indigenista,* the National Indianist Institute. Shorn of the department's cabinet rank, an orphan at birth, the *Instituto's* program reached only a tiny fraction of the Indian population. To quote the chief of the *Time* news bureau in Mexico, the *Instituto* had less money for its four centers "than the government spends maintaining the capital's fountains."[52]

Indigenismo and *indianismo* were products of their times, the post-revolutionary decade and the world depression of the twenties and thirties. So long as nineteenth-century Europe was strong and prosperous, Mexicans imitated Europe; when World War I and depression destroyed the model and brought chaos to Mexico, Mexicans rejected the outside world. The United States experienced a similar, if somewhat more limited, reaction in the depression years of the New Deal. The WPA artist and writer took inspiration from "American" ways. Both *indigenismo* and *indianismo* were products of an era that believed in government planning, of an era that saw the Soviet experiment accorded world recognition and a planned New Deal launched in the United States.

A swing to conservatism came during the forties and grew strong after 1943. World War II created new problems and made Mexican industrialization almost inevitable. By 1949, when Jesús Silva Herzog was writing that the Revolution was only a matter of historical interest, the *indianismo* of yesterday was a forgotten phenomenon, and *indigenismo* no longer a movement of national significance. Industrialization and conservatism were the keynotes of this age; the agricultural objectives of the Revolution were in disrepute. With industrialization there was no time to worry about the Indian and his special characteristics; the Republic of the future needed technicians and mechanics, not artisans or small farmers. Nor was there much sympathy for the social welfare planning of the depression years. The reforms of the postwar years aimed to create a country able to support industry. All else was secondary.

Both *indianismo* and *indigenismo* had lost their force. Their followers no longer had their revolutionary fervor, and many of their reforms had failed when put to a practical test. The school of the *indigenistas* had faced a dilemma. As designed for life in the village, it was accused of preparing the children of the peasant for the life of the peasant; if its program sought to avoid this charge, it was said to have no practical meaning for the people of the village. In 1940,

[52]Quoted by Selden Rodman, *Mexican Journal: The Conquerors Conquered* (New York, 1958), p. 47.

the last year of the *indigenista* experiment, the problem had been "solved" by making urban and rural curricula fundamentally the same, with some concessions to environment. But according to Ralph Beals the school, having lost contact with rural reality, made no impact on the village.[53] There were other weaknesses. As an ideology, *indianismo* ignored the diversity of the Indian groups. While the *indigenistas* avoided this error, their movement touched only a narrow segment of the rural population: the Indian as defined by the anthropologist. Neither *indianismo* nor *indigenismo* had provided a well-rounded, practical solution to the problems of the typical mid-twentieth-century Mexican.

Yet both made significant contributions. By furnishing a platform for political debate, by raising issues for public airing, they strengthened the cause of reform. They upheld the dignity of the Indian and the value of the village, thus giving recognition to both. The problems of the countryside were brought into national focus. Whatever its failures, the school the *indigenistas* built was closer to reality than any that had ever been designed in Mexico.

[53]*Cherán*, p. 175.

Chapter VIII

THE NOBLE EXPERIMENT

I

EDUCATORS OF INDIANIST LEANINGS had long advocated a special federal agency to work with the Indian people of Mexico. Too much of what had been done previously, they believed, had failed because the characteristics of the Indian were unknown or ignored. What these men envisaged, as Moisés Sáenz declared in his studies of Carapan, was an organization to explore fully the problems of the Indian groups and to recommend programs for them. The autonomous Department of Indian Affairs, the "noble experiment" of President Cárdenas, came in answer to these demands. Although the department was a novel adventure in the history of independent Mexico, its roots were as old as the Conquest.

Inspiration had come from the Spanish crown of the sixteenth century, which, viewing the conquered natives as its wards, established a court for their protection known as the *Juzgado de Indios*. Concerned primarily with agrarian matters, the *Juzgado* was abandoned after independence by the national regimes, which, swayed by the liberal ideology of the era, discarded the distinctions between Indians and Europeans upheld by the famous Laws of the Indies. Now all Mexicans were one, a concept that put the Indian population at the mercy of the better educated and more prosperous creoles and mestizos.

During the Revolution the idea of the *Juzgado* was revived by spokesmen for the Indian who persuaded President Obregón in 1921 to establish a *Procuraduría de Pueblos*, or Attorney's Office for Communities, to represent the peasant in land disputes. In the same year the newly organized Ministry of Public Education founded an Office of Indian Culture and Rural Education to promote and supervise schools for Indians. When this office was discarded in 1924, only the attorneys were left to deal with the problems of the Indian population.

In the opinion of Cárdenas and his Indianist followers, the closing of this office was a mistake. Citing the census of 1930, they pointed out that there were more than two and a half million persons who spoke an Indian language, half of whom knew no other. There were ten states with groups of 50,000 or more Indian-speaking individuals; concentrated chiefly in southern Mexico, from Hidalgo to Chiapas, and in Yucatán, they literally isolated this region from the Spanish-speaking world.[1] But language, as Manuel Gamio, Alfonso Caso, and others had demonstrated, was just one criterion for determining who was Indian; there were cultural and economic characteristics of equal, if not more, importance. On this basis, the Indian population probably exceeded 4 million. Since the close of the colonial era, these millions of individuals had been left to fend for themselves, to their detriment and that of the Republic.

Instead of working with the Indian as a group, federal authorities adopted a program benefiting him as farmer and laborer, as part of the total population of poor and underprivileged.[2] To the Indianists this fell short of what was called for: the Indian had problems unique to himself, problems that demanded an intelligent and coordinated effort from the government. Yet a haphazard plan was followed. Indian schools were built, but their teachers had no knowledge of local languages and customs and were usually unsympathetic to both. When a land program was mapped out, the peculiar needs of the local Indian community were overlooked. In the opinion of the Indianists, this random approach explained the failure of many attempts to help the Indian.

The Department of Indian Affairs was established in January 1936. With this department, whose organization had been advocated by Gamio as far back as 1916, the Indianists hoped to carry out their ideas. Equally important to them, the department was the symbol of a moral crusade long postponed, public recognition of the wrongs done the Indian since time immemorial. Now all was to be corrected. The department would be the conscience of the administration, where the declarations of the president and his associates found expression in practice. Here was the specific step to help the Indian through a program designed for him.

Although falling short of the ministry advocated by Gamio, the department marked a departure from past practices in rural reform. Its function was to promote, unify, and direct the activities of federal and state governments in behalf of the Indian. This was to be done through systematic studies of his economic and social problems

[1]Secretía. de Gob., *Seis años de gobierno . . . 1934-1940*, p. 355.

[2]Sáenz, "Indian Mexico," in Herring and Weinstock, eds. *Renascent Mexico*, p. 175.

and the formulation of specific programs to meet them. The department was also a watchdog, seeing to it that the programs were carried out effectively and that a reasonable percentage of public funds was spent on them. By incorporating the old Attorney's Office for Communities with the department, Cárdenas offered the Indian legal protection. He appointed as head of the department Graciano Sánchez, an agrarian leader of strong Indianist views, whose place was taken in 1939 by Luis Chávez Orozco, a historian of the same school.

The Department of Indian Affairs was received favorably by a majority of those concerned with rural problems. Had Cárdenas accomplished nothing more than establishing this department during his administration, declared the noted sociologist Lucio Mendieta y Núñez, that alone would have assured him a place in Mexican history.[3] These sentiments were echoed by others. Still many Indianists felt that though the department was a step in the right direction, it was not enough; what was called for was a political body of ministerial rank.[4] The more realistic conceded that a department was all that was possible under the circumstances. Any attempt to establish an agency with greater autonomy and authority would have raised howls of protest from the cabinet, which would have jeopardized the entire experiment. It was a case of accepting what was possible under existing conditions.

From the other side of the political fence came cries of alarm. That the creation of a special agency for one segment of the population had established a dangerous precedent was the almost unanimous opinion of supporters of former policy. They saw the department as the result of what they called the "influence of United States Indian policy" upon Mexican thought, maintaining that it copied the reservation system of Washington. By the same token, they asked, why not create a department of white affairs, another for the mestizo, and one for the Negro? In their opinion the administration had accepted the concept inherent in colonial legislation that the Indian was inferior and thus incapable of taking care of himself.[5]

Until 1938 the department had two broad functions. First, it offered legal advice and aid to the Indian. The Attorney's Office became the Indian's spokesman, representing him approximately fifty thousand times between 1935 and 1940 on matters dealing with land,

[3] *Valor económico y social de las razas indígenas de México* (Mexico, 1938), p. 22.

[4] Ramón P. de Negri, "La tragedia biológica y social de nuestros indios," *Excelsior,* Dec. 10, 1936.

[5] Victoriano Anguiano Equihua, *Lázaro Cárdenas: Su feudo y la política nacional* (Mexico, 1951), p. 259.

taxes, rural defense, legal funds, and labor rights.[6] Second, the department undertook to improve the living conditions of the Indian groups. It did this by urging the various branches of government to build hospitals, roads, dams, and schools; by organizing cooperative societies; and by mapping out a program to teach the Indian to speak Spanish. The department sponsored eight Indian congresses, where the Indian came to present his problems and to petition for aid. Cárdenas never missed these meetings, where he listened patiently to the complaints of the Indians. In 1940 the department held an Inter-American Indianist Congress in Pátzcuaro, Michoacán, attended by nine other Western hemisphere republics.

There were also projects for the benefit of specific Indian groups, such as the program for the Otomíes of the state of Hidalgo. Under the sponsorship of the Department of Indian Affairs, federal and local officials launched a program whose aim was to permit the Otomíes in the Mezquital to utilize their resources more effectively. Almost every section of government was assigned some task. The Department of Indian Affairs, using its own staff, helped local authorities to install telephone lines; it built shops and equipped them with hand looms for the wool produced locally; it donated small power plants and corn-grinding machines and established a vocational school. The Ministry of Public Works built roads and helped health officials to construct a hospital. From the officials in the Ministry of Education came schools; the Department of Irrigation built a dam that doubled the amount of land under cultivation. Trees were supplied by the Ministry of Agriculture, and land for fifty-nine villages was provided by agrarian officials. Over 313,000 pesos of credit were furnished local *ejidatarios* by the *Banco Ejidal* by 1940. There was a similar project for the Yaquis of Sonora, who received 500,000 hectares of land, an irrigation system, tractors, farm equipment, and price supports for their wheat crop.[7] The Tarahumaras, the Chamulas, and the Kikapoos won other benefits.

The petroleum question curtailed the department's activities after 1938. Although many of its special projects were continued, its principal concern became the Indian's schooling. This had been its emphasis after the Department of Indian Education, which controlled the *Centros de Educación Indígena* (Centers of Indian Education), and members of the old cultural missions were transferred to the jurisdiction of the Department of Indian Affairs.

[6]Secretía. de Gob., *Seis años de gobierno . . . 1934-1940,* p. 360.

[7]Ibid., pp. 374-381.

The concept of special schools for Indians, as distinct from those for the peasantry in general, dated back to Vasconcelos' brief flirtation with an Office of Indian Culture and Rural Education and, more particularly, to the *Casa del Estudiante Indígena*, the House of the Indian Student, established in Mexico City in 1926. Its founders, Moisés Sáenz and Rafael Ramírez, had two reasons in mind for establishing it. Their principal aim was to "incorporate the Indian" into Mexican life; the *Casa* was to bridge the gap between the primitive village and the world of automobiles and phonographs. In addition, they hoped to demonstrate to all that the Indian could learn Western ways, that he could profit from education. To substantiate this it was necessary to refute a misconception bred by centuries of apathy toward this segment of society, declared George I. Sánchez.[8] Mexicans had to learn that the traditional human beasts of burden had the minds of the city-bred once they received the schooling previously denied them.

Only "racially-pure" Indian boys between the ages of fourteen and eighteen, announced the literature on the *Casa*, would be admitted. Depending on their previous schooling or lack of it, they would spend from four to seven years at the *Casa*. At the end of that time they were to return home to "raise the intellectual level of their brothers." The instruction given was the best that the institutions of that time offered young men of an equal educational level. As a biological experiment the *Casa* was an instant success. By 1927 it had demonstrated what should have been self-evident from the beginning: that given an equal opportunity the Indian was not inferior to the white man. In terms of its other goals, the school was a failure.

Sáenz and Ramírez expected the Indian student to return to his village upon the completion of his studies. The first classes quickly dispelled this dream. To the surprise of everyone, the "incorporated" Indian did not want to go back to his native village. So successful was he in adapting to new ways that he chose to stay in Mexico City or, if he left the capital, to move to another urban center.[9] Hoping to keep the educated Indian in touch with his own people, the Ministry of Education converted the *Casa* into a teacher-training institution in 1928, but to no avail. Life amidst the bright lights of Mexico City wrecked the Indian's sympathy for the simple ways of the village. The Huichol, who arrived in tattered rags, after living with city so-

[8]*Mexico: A Revolution by Education*, p. 152.

[9]Manuel Mesa Andraca, "La casa del estudiante indígena, informe del visitador especial," in Secretía. de Educ. Públ., *Memoria relativa al estado que guarda el ramo de educación pública el 31 de agosto de 1932* (Mexico, 1932), I, 31.

phisticates found that he had little in common with his country cousins; his ties were with a world distinct from that he remembered in the mountains of Nayarit.

The *Casa* failed in other ways. Some policy maker left the selection of students in the hands of governors, congressmen, and senators. When the first group of two hundred students arrived, half were anything but "pure Indians," and among them were the nephews, sons, and godchildren of politicians. Having learned from this experience, officials in Mexico City delegated the selection of students to federal school inspectors, with better results.[10] But the problem was never completely eliminated. From the beginning native parents were reluctant to send their sons to a faraway school from which they rarely returned. Despite the watchdog activity of the Ministry of Education, the school was not an all-Indian institution; there were always non-Indians present. At best the *Casa* was a school for peasants. This turn of events, although hardly anticipated, was a blessing in disguise. By accepting non-Indian students, the *Casa* introduced the Indian to the habits and manners of the average Mexican and repudiated the charges of critics who said that it was an Indian reservation in the style of the United States. Whatever the background of some students, there was never any doubt that a majority were sleeping in beds, using toilets, and brushing their teeth for the first time. Yet, paradoxically, this very fact brought the downfall of the school. By introducing the students to modern ways, the *Casa* alienated them from the village. Also, its location in Mexico City precluded any program in agriculture.

The *Casa* was the one experiment with Indian education that never suffered from a chronic shortage of funds. Over 700,000 pesos were spent on the building alone, and from 1926 to 1932 the yearly budget averaged 181,000 pesos, high for Mexico. Despite this, only 114 students in the normal-school curriculum finished their studies out of a total of 524 enrolled from 1926 to 1932. Approximately 10,000 pesos were spent on every student graduating from the teaching course, from five to eight times the amount spent in a rural normal school. Of the 114 who completed their work, 109 were teaching in rural schools in 1932. Reports on 67 of them in 1931 indicated that 3 were doing excellent work, 40 were doing average work, and 15 were not meeting the requirements of rural teaching; there was no basis for judgment in the case of 9 of them.[11]

[10]Ibid., I, 29.
[11]Ibid., I, 65-66.

Most Mexicans concluded that the *Casa* had demonstrated clearly that "country Indians can be educated to look, act, and think like city-bred mestizos." But almost 2 million pesos were spent in trying to prove an elementary fact to Mexican conservatives, which no amount of money or effort would convince them of.[12] These unexpected results prompted Narciso Bassols to abandon the *Casa del Estudiante Indígena* in favor of the system of *Centros de Educación Indígena*, vocational residence schools for Indians. It was thought that the program of the *Casa* could be carried on more effectively by an agency in close contact with the people that it served. So studies were made, wrote Ramírez, to find some way to integrate the Indians by groups instead of by individuals, in order to determine a method that would not alienate the Indians from their true ideals once they were part of the larger community.[13] This decision of Bassols raised a storm of protest from the partisans of the *Casa*, who declared that Bassols had sabotaged the program of Indian education.

The *Centros de Educación Indígena* had existed side by side with the *Casa* since 1927, when the first of them was established among the Tarahumaras of Yoquivo, Chihuahua. Each focused on the region around it, reflecting local ways and attitudes. They were called *Centros* and not schools because their founders believed that the type of learning they advocated for the Indian sprang from his participation in those activities adapted to him and his region rather than from formal instruction.[14] Situated in the heart of Indian zones, they were also agencies for the cultural incorporation of the people in the surrounding communities. Life at the *Centros*, as well as the equipment and materials provided their students, was simple and rustic, only a step beyond that of the neighborhoods around them. The transition from the backward life of the rural community to the school environment was intended to be a gradual one.

Each *Centro* accepted approximately fifty students, boys and girls ranging from twelve to twenty years of age. There was a faculty of one or two teachers and six vocational instructors, who offered grades one to four and courses that supplemented those of the rural school. Special emphasis was placed on teaching the Indian to speak Spanish. Classwork was so arranged as not to interfere with the social and vocational activities, which were deemed of equal importance. The *Centros* operated on a family pattern; each student member had a

[12]Simpson, p. 294.

[13]Cited in Sánchez, *Mexico: A Revolution by Education*, p. 154.

[14]Ibid., p. 155.

role to play, whether serving in the kitchen, tilling the fields, helping the inhabitants of the local community, or lending a hand with the building of classrooms and annexes. As boarding schools, the *Centros*, unlike the rural schools, were able to guide their students free of the restrictive limitations of the home environment.

One of the *Centros* was in San Gabrielito, Guerrero, in the heart of an Indian zone afflicted with a disease called *mal del pinto*, a peculiar discoloration of the skin. On this tropical plateau bordering the Pacific Ocean, a director and his staff of five teachers established their school with the help of their first students. While health authorities conducted experiments and tests in the treatment of the disease, the students built the school. They made the materials from which it was constructed—adobe bricks for the walls and tiles for the roof—and with their own hands put up the building: a one-story stucco painted white, with a fine red tile roof, writes Katherine M. Cook. There was an apartment for the director on one side and a kitchen in a lean-to at one end. The large room served as a place to eat, to study, and to sleep and as a music room for the school orchestra and band. The students had come to San Gabrielito bringing with them only the clothes on their backs and blankets to sleep on. Their first task was to build beds, each boy making his own, a cot resembling an army cot but with woven matting instead of the canvas covering. The next necessity was a change of clothes, which had to be purchased. To get money with which to buy clothing each student, with the help of the teachers, made articles for sale, a difficult project in a land where handicrafts had poor sales value.

School did not wait for the completion of the building but began at the same time. Along with the construction activity and the making of school equipment—benches, chairs, and other things—were classes in Spanish and the three R's; but agriculture was the heart of the curriculum. The students put into cultivation some thirty hectares of land, which furnished much of their food. Life at San Gabrielito reflected the customs of the countryside. "Housing, food, clothing, and the manner of living" followed a plan "designed to raise prevailing standards," Cook learned, "but gradually and in keeping with the practical possibilities of the resources of the . . . [local] communities."[15] Every effort was made to keep the school from weaning its students away from their native environment.

Bassols' changes did not go beyond closing the *Casa del Estudiante Indígena* and opening new *Centros*. Only slightly concerned with the

[15]Cook, pp. 64-66.

Indian as a group, he devoted little time or effort to the specialized needs of the Indian schools. Left almost on their own, the *Centros* lacked spokesmen in the Ministry of Education. Their neglect was almost inevitable. Because their salaries were poor, they attracted marginal instructors, and by 1935 some of them even lacked farm lands and shops for their students.[16] These deficiencies were not necessarily the product of Bassols' indifference, for most antedated his term in office; on the other hand, he did little to correct them. The Cardenistas, fervent Indianists that they were, determined to eliminate them. First they placed the *Centros* under the Department of Indian Affairs, the spokesman for the Indian. Then, in keeping with the emphasis given agrarian reform, they reorganized the *Centros* as *Escuelas Vocacionales de Agricultura para Indígenas,* Vocational Schools of Agriculture for Indians. Their philosophy was that an education of value to the Indian must stress agriculture for the boys and homemaking for the girls.[17] Finally, the Cardenistas did everything possible to rehabilitate and expand the *Vocacionales.* Buildings were repaired; more schools were established; lands, shops, and equipment were provided; and additional funds were made available for salaries of personnel. By 1940 there were twenty-nine *Vocacionales,* more than double the number in 1933, with 3,000 students, a third of whom were girls. There were five schools for the Náhuatl groups, four for the Mixtecas and Tarahumaras, three for the Otomíes, and two for the Tzeltales and Tzotziles; the others were distributed among nine other groups, ranging from the Yaquis in Sonora to the Mayas in Yucatán.[18]

II

With the departure of Cárdenas from the national scene, leaders less sympathetic to Indianism came into office. More concerned with industry and technical training, they tended to neglect rural problems, particularly those of the Indian.

On the surface there were no radical changes under President Avila Camacho, but a subtle transformation was taking shape. The welfare state of the Cárdenas era was over, declared the architects of national policy, spokesmen for businessmen and industrialists. No longer was

[16]Departamento de Asuntos Indígenas, *Memorias, corresponden a los períodos del 1º de enero al 31 de agosto de 1936 y 1º de septiembre al 31 de agosto de 1937* (Mexico, 1938), p. 14.

[17]*El Nacional,* Dec. 27, 1936.

[18]Secretía. de Gob., *Seis años de gobierno . . . 1934-1940,* p. 364.

the government to feed and clothe the Indian; now it would help him "to help himself." The timid rugged individualism of the Avila Camacho era hardened into fixed policy under his successors. In the opinion of Miguel Alemán, Indianism had converted the Indian into a charity ward of the state;[19] there was no room for this now, nor for the individual approach to the problems of the Indian pioneered by Cárdenas. While Avila Camacho had accepted the "noble experiment," Alemán had no sympathy for it. Upon taking office in late 1946, Alemán disbanded the department, which now became the Office of Indian Affairs of the Ministry of Education. President Ruiz Cortines announced that "the problems of the Indian were but part of the national one," which could be liquidated like any other, without demagoguery or propaganda.[20] Thus the experiment of the Indianists, brought to an end by Alemán, had no chance of revival under Ruiz Cortines or his successor.

In accordance with the importance attached to technical training after 1941 and the de-emphasis of the small farm and the *ejido*, the *Vocacionales* once again became *Centros* in the style of those of the twenties. Now agriculture was only one part of their curriculum, which stressed vocational training in all fields. Lacking the funds with which to support them, the Ministry closed eight of the *Vocacionales*, and when coeducation was banned by constitutional amendment, some became schools for women. There were also changes in the length of their programs. In 1960 all but two of the schools offered only grades four to six, taking students who had completed three years of rural schooling. Meanwhile the staffs of the old cultural missions were replaced by less experienced personnel. The Attorney's Office continued as part of the Office of Indian Affairs, although with less personnel and fewer responsibilities, for the defense of the Indian's rights was no longer a matter of prime consideration in the forties and fifties. Ironically, it was during the decline of policy favorable to the Indian that an attempt was made to give the Department of Indian Affairs secretarial rank, something dear to the heart of Indianists. In the summer of 1942, before the reforms of Alemán emasculated the department, a bill to give it ministerial status was submitted to Congress.[21] A number of prominent leaders gave it their

[19]Letter from Gonzalo Aguirre Beltrán, director of the Office of Indian Affairs, to Manuel Gamio, March 6, 1947, *Boletín indigenista*, VII (March 1947), 40.

[20]Secretía. de Educ. Públ., *Acción educativa del gobierno federal del 1º de diciembre de 1952 al 31 de agosto de 1954* (Mexico, 1954), p. 93.

[21]*Boletín indigenista*, II (June 1942), 19.

backing, but nothing came of the proposal, which was out of step with the thinking of the administration.

Between 1941 and 1958 the department and later the Office of Indian Affairs were in the hands of six different men. Each came with his staff of assistants and a different set of plans. From 1941 to 1946 the chief of Indian Affairs was a prosperous landlord, a political appointee whose ideas were in harmony with the age of Díaz. Throughout his tenure of office there were charges of corruption, graft, and incompetence. Seeking to bring order out of chaos, President Alemán appointed Gonzalo Aguirre Beltrán, scholar and anthropologist, who brought with him Julio de la Fuente, also an able anthropologist, and gave him a major role to play. Indicative of the new scientific spirit was the hiring of anthropologists and other specialists and the founding of a research section. Particular attention was given to raising standards at the *Centros* and to combining their activities with those of the rural schools in their areas. Before much had been done, however, Aguirre Beltrán gave up the struggle. His place was taken by a less prominent figure, who was replaced six months later by someone else. Partly as a result of these changes little was accomplished.

In 1950, Mariano Samayoa, an old revolutionary figure sympathetic to the plight of the Indian but lacking the technical preparation for his post, became the last of Alemán's appointees. He had in mind a series of experimental communities called *Comunidades de Promoción Indígena*, Communities of Indian Improvement, through which he hoped to circumvent a traditional barrier to reform in the Indian community. It was found that, even when young people accepted the need for change, it was frequently impossible for them to act in the face of the hostility of their elders and the traditions of the village. Change took place at a pace set by the recalcitrant elements in the community.

The new head of Indian Affairs expected to surmount this difficulty by moving young couples to new communities under the guidance and supervision of trained leaders. By being isolated in communities where change was the norm, these young people were free to break the shackles that bound their elders to the past. The result would be the incorporation of these communities into the currents of national life. The example set would stimulate the transformation of the villages around them by bringing change through imitation.[22]

Two such experiments were launched by 1955. One was established among the Otomíes at Los Remedios in the Mezquital and an-

[22]Mariano Samayoa, "Comunidades de promoción indígena," *Boletín indigenista*, XI (Sept. 1951), 240, 242, 244.

other at Guachochi in the Tarahumara of Chihuahua. The couples were given land to cultivate, building materials for their homes, and animals to raise. These activities were carried on under the watchful eye of experts in farming and crafts who coordinated their work with that of the schoolteacher, social worker, and nurse. The program in the communities served to initiate the Indians in the ways of living together as citizens. Jointly they resolved their problems of habitation, water service, lighting, order and security, hygiene, and communications. Toward this end, committees of social action and material improvement were formed. As individuals and as a unit, men and women underwent training programs that prepared them for rural life: the women attended classes in homemaking, sewing, cooking, and hygiene, while the men learned about crop rotation, the care of animals, and soil conservation. From the start the idea was to make the village self-sufficient. Both experiments were later abandoned.

As early as 1952 the major educational projects on behalf of the Indian were in the hands of the National Indianist Institute, which President Alemán had established in 1946 as an advisory body on Indian problems to the federal government. Under the able leadership of the distinguished anthropologist Alfonso Caso, the institute assumed many of the activities formerly carried on by the old autonomous Department of Indian Affairs, although on a lesser scale.

Taking a leaf from Gamio's thesis of integral education, the institute developed a number of *Centros Coordinadores Indígenas*, Indian Coordinating Centers, special projects for particular Indian groups. At first the idea was to organize a center for every group, but lack of funds and a shortage of specialized personnel limited them to the leading Indian groups, or to those in dire straits. By 1957 four of them had been organized. There was one in the Tzeltal-Tzotzil region of Chiapas, another among the Tarahumaras of Chihuahua, two in the Mixteca of Oaxaca, and one for the Mazatecos of the Papaloapan basin. These Coordinating Centers carried out work in four principal spheres: communications, economy, health, and education.[23]

What this activity meant to the Indian was illustrated by the program for the Tarahumaras, who lived in one of the most inhospitable regions of Mexico, an uneven land divided by crags and abysses that made communication almost impossible. Approximately 40,000 to 50,000 Tarahumaras (there was no exact figure) lived in an area of

[23]Instituto Nacional Indigenista, "Informe del Instituto Nacional Indigenista: 1955," *Boletín indigenista*, XVI (March 1956), 64.

about 60,000 square kilometers, a demographic density of less than one per square kilometer. A large part of the population was semi-nomadic, living in the lowlands during the winter and moving to the highlands in the summer in search of arable land and climate. Geography had isolated the Tarahumaras from the world and from each other; each family lived where it could plant corn and beans, usually four to five kilometers from its nearest neighbor.

On the average the Tarahumara farmer counted on one good crop every five years. From each hectare he harvested 400 kilograms of corn, one of the lowest yields in Mexico (the national average was 850 kilograms per hectare, low by world standards), or enough food to last him from five to seven months. He consumed his bean harvest in three months. Sometimes he got additional food from his sheep and goats; but they were often more of a liability than an asset, and he could not raise better animals because of the character of the land. So the Indian tempered his hunger by hunting and by gathering fruit. When things got bad, as they often did, he ate lizards, worms, and the bark of oak trees.[24]

Not only did the land of the Tarahumara fail to produce enough for his wants, but he had too little productive land. By 1952 the pace of land redistribution had slowed down perceptibly, despite the fact that nearly 5.5 million hectares were still available for distribution. In addition, the rising population in the state of Chihuahua brought into the area many non-Indians, who were pushing the Tarahumaras off what land they had.[25] In the face of this problem the Tarahumaras were receiving almost no protection from the Office of Indian Affairs, which had closed three of its branches in the zone. In education, the local Indian boarding schools were training men only; the women had no place in their program. A majority of the population had no contact with Spanish; despite this there was no bilingual language program.

At his level of life the Tarahumara offered almost nothing to the national economy. During the year he might buy 15 pesos' worth of goods, of which about 3 pesos filtered into the national economy, compared to the 200 pesos of the average urban laborer.

Paradoxically, however, the region had a history of rural education. Its first schools dated back to the turn of the century, when the

[24]Inst. Nacional Indigenista, "Actividades del Instituto Nacional Indigenista en el Centro Coordinador de la Tarahumara, Chihuahua, México," *Boletín indigenista*, XVI (Dec. 1956), 338, 340.

[25]Inst. Nacional Indigenista, "Sobre el Centro Coordinador Tarahumara de reciente creación," *Boletín indigenista*, XII (Sept. 1952), 258.

Jesuits had established four of them. The Office of Indian Affairs had two boarding schools, a Brigade of Indian Improvement, and two attorneys in Creel and Guachochi. There were also federal and state schools, but not a sufficient number to meet the needs of the population. The program of the National Indianist Institute was designed to unify and coordinate these dispersed efforts of local and national governments, to remedy their deficiencies, and to establish uniform educational methods, beginning with a literacy program in the native languages.

First a survey was made of the region and its problems, and then work was begun at Guachochi, some 220 miles from Parral. The first job was to prepare men and women to teach the Tarahumaras to speak Spanish so that they could attend the local rural schools. This involved establishing a special school for them and then schools for their students. By 1956 there were 531 students in these language schools;[26] 300 earlier students had gone on to local boarding and primary schools by 1954.[27] New rural schools were also built by the federal and state governments under the guidance of the institute, which made them conform to an overall program.

While the school program was being developed, social and economic reforms were being carried out. Some lands were given the Indians (though not enough), but the main emphasis was on improving the lumber industry, the chief source of revenue in the area. Every effort was made to bring the Tarahumaras into the lumber business; trees cut from Indian lands were sold to local lumbermen, who were required to train and use the Tarahumaras in their work. Regulations were passed covering wages and hours in the lumber business, whose owners often exploited the natives by working them long hours for peon wages. The *ejido* at Cusarare was reorganized: the Indians cut their own trees and made and sold the lumber; the institute and the Ministry of Agriculture offered materials and guidance and the *Banco Ejidal* financial aid. In May 1955 a profit of 78,000 pesos was divided among the *ejidatarios*.[28] The institute also established a number of cooperative societies among the Indians in the lumber trade. To develop the region, new roads were built and old ones improved. Four medical centers were established by 1956, each under the direction of a doctor and native nurses, who gave free

[26]Alfonso Caso, "Informe del Instituto Nacional Indigenista: 1956," *Boletín indigenista*, XVII (June 1957), 170.

[27]Inst. Nacional Indigenista, "El Instituto Nacional Indigenista en la región Tarahumara," *Boletín indigenista*, XV (Dec. 1955), 354.

[28]Ibid., p. 356.

service. In addition to the medical centers, a modern clinic was built in Baquiriachi.[29] On a local and small-scale basis, the institute was putting Gamio's theory of integral education into practice.

III

What was the state of Indian education in 1960? A quantitative evaluation was not difficult. The National Indianist Institute had established four Indian Coordinating Centers by 1957, which had organized over a hundred language schools where more than 4,000 individuals were learning the Spanish language.[30] The Office of Indian Affairs had twenty-one Indian boarding schools with 2,824 students. Of the 471 students who completed their work in 1957, 301 returned to their communities; 70 went on to the rural *Normales* and the rest to vocational schools. Besides the schools, the office had twelve Brigades of Indian Improvement—replicas of the cultural missions—which also sponsored twelve homes for preschool-age children. It employed twenty-six attorneys.[31] In addition, the office was taking part in a special program for the Chicontepec zone and in a locally sponsored project for the Otomíes, the *Patrimonio Indígena del Valle del Mezquital.*

Qualitatively an evaluation was more difficult. Obviously the effort fell short of the need. There were approximately two and a half million Indian-speaking Mexicans and another million who spoke Spanish but were Indian in every other way. The combined activity of the Office of Indian Affairs and the National Indianist Institute touched only a fraction of this number. Funds were lacking for a larger program. The budget of the National Indianist Institute was 800,000 pesos; Caso said that forty Indian Coordinating Centers were needed, or ten times 800,000 pesos, so he had become a fund raiser rather than a social scientist, wrote Selden Rodman (p. 52).

The activity of the Office of Indian Affairs was almost exclusively educational in character. With only twenty-one boarding schools, it neglected thousands of possible students. Nor were all of these schools performing well. Some offered more work than others; a few were badly managed; others discriminated against Indians, admitting mestizos preferably and in some cases even expelling Indians in order

[29]Ibid., p. 352.

[30]Caso, "Informe del Instituto Nacional Indigenista," p. 170.

[31]Dirección General de Asuntos Indígenas, "Trabajos de la Dirección General de Asuntos Indígenas," *Boletín indigenista,* XVII (Dec. 1957), 330, 332.

to find a place for the mestizos. This had happened at San Gabrielito, in a school that Katherine M. Cook had described enthusiastically.[32] According to a report of the president of the National Confederation of Indian Youth in 1949, the program of the schools was not always geared to the needs of the rural community. One result was that many of their graduates—80 per cent, he said—were unable to put their knowledge to use in the rural community and so fled to the city. Although the schools were for the Indians, a majority of their instructors spoke only Spanish.[33]

By creating the National Indianist Institute, the Alemán administration had stripped the Office of Indian Affairs of many functions, relegating it to the position of overseer of an ever less-important system of Indian schools. The two agencies often duplicated functions that could have been served better by one wealthier and more powerful body.[34] Finally, the lack of continuity had hurt the educational program for the Indian. The frequent changes of personnel at all levels, especially at the top, and the new programs introduced with each one had created a disjointed effort that made long-range planning difficult.

[32]"Congreso estatal Guerrerense," *Boletín indigenista*, XV (March 1955), 70.

[33]Speech of Onésimo Ríos, *Boletín indigenista*, IX (June 1949), 182.

[34]Opinion of Confederación Nacional de Jóvenes y de Comunidades Indígenas, *El Nacional*, Oct. 19, 1958.

Chapter IX
THE STRUGGLE FOR A UNIVERSAL LANGUAGE

I

MEXICAN RURAL EDUCATION has confronted a multitude of difficulties, but none more formidable than the polyglot picture typical of vast sections of the countryside. When Vasconcelos began to lay the foundations for a system of rural schools in 1921, more than 1 million out of 14 million Mexicans knew no Spanish. They were monolinguals, speaking one of fifty or more Indian languages: Náhuatl, Trique, Mixtec, Otomí, Tarascan, Totonac, and others. Another million or so spoke Spanish but were more at home in their native tongues. There were hundreds of local dialects. Stronghold of the Indian tongues was the southeast, from Tamaulipas south to the Pacific Ocean, west to Michoacán, and east to Guatemala, and in the peninsula of Yucatán, where three out of four persons spoke Maya. But there were language pockets even in the northern states of Sonora, Chihuahua, and Coahuila. They were usually found in isolated rural regions, but some were next door to civilization. On the outskirts of Mexico City a majority of the Otomíes, living in close contact with the conquerors and their descendants since 1522, made almost no use of Spanish. Cut off from the Spanish-speaking population, the Otomíes were outcasts in their native land.

Two decades later the picture had not changed perceptibly, despite 12,000 rural schools built since 1921. There were still 2.5 million people who spoke an Indian tongue, half of whom knew no Spanish whatsoever. Rural education had failed to meet its language challenge; this was a national tragedy. Until newspapers, books, and laws had meaning in the village, there could be no nation and no democracy.

II

That the Indian-speaking millions should learn Spanish was advocated from the time of the Conquest, but how to bring it about was a different matter. On this problem and on the question of why the native tongues survived there is no unanimity of opinion.

Some believe a deliberate effort was made to keep the Indian ignorant of Spanish. According to Luis Cabrera, a spokesman for this view, the rulers of Mexico had tried since 1521 to keep the Indian tongues alive in order to exploit their users. The Spanish missionaries encouraged the Indian to keep his language for fear of losing their influence over him. They made use of the native tongues to explain Christian dogma and translated the catechism into Náhuatl, Tarascan, and Otomí in order to preserve a prestige that would have been lost had they encouraged Spanish. The conquistadors and other landholders of the colonial era and the *hacendados* of independence habitually spoke to their peons and servants in the Indian's own language. In practice, the preservation of the indigenous tongues was a technique of domination.[1]

Men of Cabrera's view proposed to substitute Spanish for the native languages by the simple device of banning the native tongues and forcing the Indian to speak the language of Cervantes. This they would accomplish by using only Spanish in the school and ending the isolation of the native village, on the premise that once in contact with the more energetic Spanish-speaking population the Indian would accept its language and reject his own. To paraphrase Gregorio Torres Quintero (p. 7), father of the rudimentary-school plan of 1911, if the teacher spoke only Spanish in school, his students would have to learn it. Cabrera saw nothing of value in the native tongues. He believed that only "academic snobbisms . . . aim at the preservation and even the purification of the indigenous languages which, as dead tongues could have historical and archaeological interest, but as living languages are ethnic barriers."[2] Others, like Rafael Ramírez, pointed out that the occasional use of the Indian languages in school led to new difficulties. Since the Indian rarely spent more than a year or so in school, relying on his language for any length of time lost to him whatever opportunity he had to learn Spanish. This opinion represented the view of political conservatives, with the exception of men such as Ramírez.[3]

Another group—the bilingualists—had a different view of the issue. While accepting Spanish as the official language of Mexico and recognizing that tradition had much to do with the survival of the native tongues, the bilingualists rejected Cabrera's solution. In their opinion

[1]Cabrera, "The Key to the Mexican Chaos," in Herring and Weinstock, eds. *Renascent Mexico*, p. 17.

[2]Ibid., p. 19.

[3]Ramírez, "La política educativa del nuevo trato hacia los indios," *Revista de educación*, IV (Aug. 1939), 9-10.

it was not merely because of lack of contact that the Indian had not learned Spanish, but because the wrong approach had been pursued since Cortés had stepped on Mexican soil. The error of the missionaries, and of contemporary educators, lay in their attempt to teach Spanish to an Indian who lacked a formal language background of any kind. The answer lay in using the native tongues as a preliminary step to learning Spanish: teach the Indian the grammar of his native tongue, teach him to read and write it, and then superimpose Spanish on this foundation. Having learned grammar in his own language, the individual would be ready to study a foreign language.[4] For the majority of bilingualists the two-language approach was a vehicle for learning Spanish, to be discarded once that goal was achieved for all Mexicans. But a minority of them had other ideas.

To this minority the Indian languages were an asset. Culturally, Mexico gained by the language diversity of its people. Psychologically, the native tongues were a defense, the Indian's protection against the exploiter, and to destroy his language was to place him more completely at the mercy of his enemy.[5] According to the noted ethnologist Carlos Basauri, the Indian tongues could pave the way for an understanding of Spanish language and civilization. By using both languages, the Indian could find the relationship between the psychological entities and symbolisms peculiar to each of them. Without losing sight of the psychological structure of either, he could translate from one to the other. By feeling and thinking in both, he would establish a bond between himself and the Spanish-speaking person.[6]

Bilingualists generally supported a leftist political program. Thus, since the conservatives endorsed the direct approach, language goals assumed political implications that transcended the problems of education.[7]

III

Until the late 1930's the proponents of the direct approach had matters their own way. Since the time of Vasconcelos—himself an advocate of the direct approach—a goal of rural education had been to

[4]Aureliano Esquivel Casas, "Temas de educación indígena, enseñanza de la lengua nacional," *Revista mexicana de educación*, I (Oct. 1940), 213.

[5]Genaro Vásquez quoted in *Excelsior*, Sept. 11, 1935.

[6]Basauri, "El problema del bilingüismo y la educación en México," *Revista de educación*, II (Dec. 1938), 8.

[7]Fuente, "Ocho años de experiencia en el medio rural," p. 60.

root out the indigenous tongues by using only Spanish in the class-room. But this philosophy did not reckon with the problems of the school in the Indian-speaking community. Theory did not work. The average teacher in the Indian-speaking village, speaking only Span-ish, was unable to communicate with his students or their parents. Without training in the native tongues, he was forced to resort to catch-as-catch-can. One teacher in Chiapas was lucky enough to find among his students one who could translate Spanish into the local tongue,[8] a clumsy expedient but more direct than the Cortés-to-Aguilar-to-Doña-Marina-to-Montezuma communication system of the Conquest.

Bilingualists won their opportunity in the Indianist administration of President Cárdenas. Part of the spadework was done by Mariano Silva y Aceves, founder of the Mexican Institute of Linguistic Studies at the National University. Patiently and indefatigably he labored to convince teachers and ethnologists that the way to approach the In-dian was through his own language. Much of the credit also belonged to Luis Chávez Orozco, an educator-historian with an intimate knowledge of the language programs of the colonial era who was equally familiar with the bilingual work of the Soviet Union. Having replaced Graciano Sánchez as head of the Department of Indian Af-fairs in 1939, Chávez Orozco did everything to encourage the ex-periment.

The initial step was taken in 1937, when an international conven-tion of schoolteachers in Mexico City exhorted their governments to follow the bilingual method for the education of the Indian of the Americas. Later a convention of Mexican teachers took up the ques-tion, recommending, after a spirited debate, that instruction for the Indian be carried out through his own language when bilingual teach-ers and suitable textbooks were available. At the meeting Moisés Sáenz urged that hundreds of rural schoolteachers be called in imme-diately and given training in linguistics.[9]

Making a recommendation was one thing; getting under way was something entirely different, for a language program of this type was a pioneer venture. Despite the linguistic work of the colonial period, especially that of the Franciscans, there were no adequate alphabets of the native languages. Those of the friars approximated native sounds with Spanish letters and had numerous weaknesses; they were particularly inaccurate in phonetic translation, for the friars found

[8] Tannenbaum, "Agrarismo, Indianismo, y Nacionalismo," *Hispanic American His-torical Review*, XXIII (Aug. 1943), 400-401.

[9] Townsend, pp. 324-325.

no Spanish equivalent for many Indian sounds. Primers were also lacking; those written by colonial missionaries had been modified until they no longer gave an accurate picture of the ethnic and linguistic units.[10] Finally, there was a shortage of personnel for the job; only a few bilingual teachers were available, and they had no formal training in the Indian tongues.

Partly to gratify the president, the Tarascan language of Michoacán was the choice for the pioneer bilingual venture. The experiment was in the hands of the Department of Indian Affairs and the Department of Anthropology of the National Polytechnic Institute, which called in Morris Swadesh, an authority on linguistics from the University of Wisconsin and a student of Edward Sapir, and put him in charge of the technical supervision.

Once the Department of Indian Affairs and the anthropologists had gotten the work under way, Chávez Orozco in May 1939, on orders from Cárdenas, invited linguists, ethnologists, and anthropologists from the National University, the National Polytechnic Institute, the Ministry of Education, and other organizations to participate in what was called the First Assembly of Philologists and Linguists. Swadesh led the discussions at the sessions, which brought forth plans for literacy campaigns in several Indian languages, of which the Tarascan was one. Out of this assembly also came the Council of Indian Languages, a technical body of experts whose views have influenced literacy activity to date.

Of first importance was the question of method. Under the system adopted by the assembly, the Indians were to learn to read and write their native tongues first, under the supervision of bilingual native teachers; then, still using their own language, they were to learn the fundamentals. Spanish was to be introduced gradually from the beginning; once the students mastered it, it was to be the language of the school.[11]

Through this system an answer was sought for a major difficulty that had plagued attempts to teach Spanish to the Indian through the direct approach. The chief stumbling block in the past was the inability of the Indian to make out the meaning of words on paper. He was told that written Spanish represented the sounds made by man; however, the sounds were not forming the words he spoke daily but those he heard foreigners speak, which he did not understand. "It was

[10]Basauri, "El estudio de las lenguas autóctonas, base de pedagogía indígena," *Revista de educación*, I (Aug. 1937), 22.

[11]Ignacio M. del Castillo, "La alfabetización en lenguas indígenas: El proyecto tarasco," *América indígena*, V (April 1945), 146.

as if the reader of this book had not learnt to read, first of all in English or . . . whatever was his mother tongue; but had to do so in Arabic," a language and writing "full of ideas and ways of looking at things which were completely strange to him."[12]

Once method was fixed, the next question was to find a linguistic formula that could be applied in teaching an Indian language. Planning revolved around the formation of a general alphabet, from which letters could be selected for the alphabets of fifty or more separate languages and which could be applied by country schoolteachers. Every combination taken from the mother alphabet had to be the essence of simplicity, employing only signs that were indispensable. Uniformity among the particular alphabets was called for to avoid typographical errors and phonetic difficulties for teachers and students. The formula had to be flexible, permitting the use of letters in different senses in the various languages, so long as their values were similar and good usage was observed. To make it possible for the illiterate person to go from his own language to Spanish, the universal or mother alphabet had to provide characters resembling those of the Spanish alphabet.[13]

The complexity of the native languages offers proof of the tremendous challenge presented in writing the alphabet. Totonac demanded signs for seventeen consonants and seven vowels. In Mixtec there were an equal number of vowels and consonants; in addition signs for "tones" were required, for Mixtec was a tonal language, with three levels of tone or pitches. Otomí needed signs for approximately twenty-two consonants and nine vowels and for six additional consonantal signs for the Spanish words that formed a part of this language. Chinantec, the most perplexing of the native tongues, depended on thirty or so consonant sounds, eleven vowels (which could be nasalized), three diphthongs, and three different tones. Vowels and consonants were long or short. There was a "glottal stop" and "nasal inspiration."[14]

The assembly wrote an alphabet for the Tarascan program based on the principle of "one sound, one sign," though not precluding the use of two letters to represent one sound. From this universal alphabet others could be devised for any Indian language by making certain changes. Dots and dashes above and below the letters were held to

[12]John B. Trend, *Mexico, a New Spain with Old Friends* (Cambridge, Eng., 1940), p. 134.

[13]Ibid., p. 135.

[14]Ibid., p. 129.

a minimum. Only lower-case lettering was permitted, to make reading as simple as possible. Primers also were devised for teaching the alphabet. Each primer in one set had eight words of one or two syllables. On every page some of the words were repeated, and new words were gradually added using some of the same syllables. Three different letters were on the first page; new letters were introduced on the following. Thus the students learned to recognize words and, by comparing similar ones, to recognize syllables. A second set of primers relied on pictures to illustrate the syllables. It was found that children worked best with the picture primers, while adults preferred the other type, for the child memorized and the adult reasoned.[15]

With Swadesh in charge, the program was officially designated the Tarascan Project. Among the technical experts on the staff at Paracho, a small lumber town where headquarters were established in Michoacán, was Maxwell D. Lathrop, of the Summer Institute of Linguistics of the University of Oklahoma, a Protestant organization whose members had been working with the Indian tongues since 1935 and which since 1939 has been of inestimable aid to the linguistic program.

At Paracho the work began with the preparation of twenty native bilingual teachers, who were recruited from among the students of both sexes at the normal school in Morelia, the schools for Indians in Erongarícuaro and Morelia, and a school for the children of army enlisted personnel in Pátzcuaro. They were given an intensive course in the use of the alphabet and primers and then assigned to one of four "literacy centers" that were directed by members of the staff. Each center held day classes for children, adult night classes, and classes in homes for those unable to come to the centers. A small printing press was later installed in Paracho, which published material for the project and got out a small weekly newspaper in Tarascan that was distributed in the villages on market day.

From the beginning the results were encouraging. According to Ignacio M. del Castillo, a member of the staff at Paracho, the language experiment stirred new interest among the Tarascan-speaking people, who were astonished to learn that their own language, like Spanish, could be written on paper. Then, wrote Castillo, "we understood what it means to the Indian to learn in his native language!" One startling fact had been demonstrated by 1940: by using the bilingual method the Indian could learn to read and write speedily. Children and adults learned to read in from fifteen to twenty days and to

[15]Ignacio M. del Castillo, "La alfabetización en lenguas indígenas," pp. 147, 149.

write in ten to fifteen days more. In short, an illiterate required only from thirty to forty-five days to pick up the rudiments of reading and writing with the bilingual system.[16]

Despite the success achieved, the administration of President Avila Camacho abandoned the project. Lack of funds was the reason given. Outsiders placed the blame elsewhere. Some singled out extremists in the Catholic Church, who viewed with alarm the participation of Protestants in the program. For others the explanation lay in the growing criticism of the experiment from conservatives influential in the new government to whom the activity in Michoacán was nothing but an imitation of the language plan of the Soviet Union. Whatever the reasons, the project was abandoned.

I V

Thereafter, the Tarascan experiment languished until Torres Bodet replaced Véjar Vásquez, whose lack of sympathy for the bilingual method was public knowledge.[17] At the urging of Alfonso Caso, then director of the Office of Higher Education and Scientific Research, Torres Bodet asked various members of the Council of Indian Languages to draw up an evaluation of the bilingual system. Their report stressed the failure of the direct approach and called attention to the success of the Tarascan Project and of similar experiments in the United States and the Soviet Union. Won over to this point of view, Torres Bodet then requested the council to draw up a teaching plan following the bilingual idea, which became part of the national literacy crusade.

According to the plan submitted by the council in 1944, the language that a person knows best is learned as a child; it is less difficult for him to learn to read and write it than a foreign tongue or one he knows imperfectly. The denial of these simple facts had undermined education in the past. Confronted with a language barrier, the rural school had undertaken three things at one time: to teach the Indian to speak Spanish, to teach him to read and write it, and to give him an elementary education. In the hands of a Spanish-speaking teacher the job was too big: the Indian did not learn Spanish, and education fell by the wayside. Instead of spending his time with the three R's and other basic requirements, the teacher had to emphasize the teach-

16Ibid., pp. 147-149.
17Kirk, p. 150.

ing of Spanish, but he failed even in this task because he did not know the local language.[18]

The council's plan would succeed by putting the job of language teaching in the hands of native bilingual instructors known as *alfabetizadores*, who were to give special one-year preprimary school language classes where the Indian would learn to read and write his own language first and then Spanish. Once having learned Spanish, the pupil would move on to the rural school, which, free of the language question, would be able to concentrate on education.

Four languages were chosen for the initial activity of the Institute for Indian Literacy, the bureau in charge of the program. The Maya of Yucatán, the Náhuatl of Morelos and the Puebla mountain region, and the Otomí of Hidalgo were selected on the basis of their importance: they were spoken by large segments of the population; their users had the highest index of monolinguality; and, because of the size of their respective regions, the people who spoke them played a major role in the life of the Republic. Tarascan, the fourth language, was chosen because of the work done in it already. As conditions became favorable, the program would include other linguistic groups.[19]

Preparation of material was the next hurdle. The first step was to reduce languages to writing in an alphabet that lessened the stumbling blocks in learning to read and write, first in a native tongue and then in Spanish. This done, primers must be prepared, which would give elementary data on diet, hygiene, and crops.

Difficulties began with the alphabet. Náhuatl and Maya had long literary traditions and their own alphabets; there was also an alphabet in Tarascan; but with Otomí the preparation had to start almost from scratch. For all the languages the council had urged using the universal alphabet of the Tarascan Project, which represented each sound by one sign. This proved impossible; neither the universal nor the Indian alphabets could be used. The former employed signs foreign to Spanish, not available in type, and difficult to draw by hand, while the others had numerous inconsistencies. In the end four alphabets were designed. For each the formula consisted in representing the native sounds that were similar to those in Spanish with the signs of the Indian languages, but in such a way as to avoid confusion. For example, the Spanish *j* was used to represent the aspiration that by tradition and by the rules of philology is written with *h*; the *k* was

[18]Instituto de Alfabetización Indígena, "El Instituto de Alfabetización en Lenguas Indígenas," *Boletín indigenista*, V (June 1945), 162, 164, 166.

[19]Ibid., p. 172.

used to represent the voiceless velar occlusive sound that in Spanish is formed also with *c* or with *qu*.

Writing primers, the next hurdle, raised important questions. Was the Indian ultimately to learn the language of Cervantes or the local Spanish dialect? How many sections did the text need? Was there any relationship between language sounds and the organization of the lessons? How was the text to emphasize local characteristics in order to facilitate language learning?

The question of style was resolved on practical grounds. Any language was valid that served a social function; the goal was to give quickly a rudimentary knowledge of Spanish to persons who did not speak it, which was to be done by following the lines of least resistance. Ultimately each regional dialect was respected. The objective was to encourage the Indian-speaking person to read and write, first his native tongue and then Spanish, without regard to classical forms that purists considered proper. Spanish terms introduced into the Indian languages for the sake of convenience were treated as native ones; local Spanish terms and phrases were adopted even when incorrect grammatically. Every group would learn the Spanish spoken locally. A grammatical command of Spanish was beyond the scope of the campaign.[20]

At first the primers were divided into three sections: Spanish, Indian, and bilingual. After further study this system of organization was discarded on the theory that Spanish was a foreign language to the monolingual Indian and that the translation method of learning a new language was totally inadequate for him. The way to practical results was through oral instruction in the language to be mastered.[21] Thus only two sections were used: one with the Indian language, for the teaching of reading and writing; and another in Spanish, to be used after oral instruction in it, during which the Indian learned to express himself simply in Spanish. The technique was to give by word of mouth a basic amount of everyday Spanish, relating it to local phenomena so that students would understand without translating.

The other questions proved less difficult. It was decided to teach sounds in the order of the frequency with which they occurred in each language. The question of how to emphasize local characteristics in the text was solved quite by accident. Among the teachers selected for the program was one who proved to be a remarkable artist, who could dramatize local color in drawings. What he left un-

[20]Secretía. de Educ. Públ., *La obra educativa en el sexenio, 1940-1946*, pp. 139-142.

[21]Inst. de Alfabetización Indígena, "Actividades del Instituto de Alfabetización Indígena," *Boletín indigenista*, V (Dec. 1945), 402.

done was finished by other artists with the aid of ethnologists and other experts.[22]

There were three stages in the teacher-training program. First, the institute selected fifty teachers, bilingual natives who had completed their normal-school studies, and brought them to Mexico City. There the teachers—seven from Morelos, eleven from Puebla, eleven from Hidalgo, ten from Michoacán, eight from Yucatán, and three from Campeche—were put through intensive courses in language study and on the use of the materials prepared for the program. In the second stage, each teacher returned to his native region to select and train ten more individuals from the bilingual population who had completed six years of primary school. This done, there were fifty master instructors and five hundred *alfabetizadores* available for the program—the final stage.

Laying the framework for the literacy drive was the contribution of the Avila Camacho administration; the crusade itself was that of the Alemán regime. While the Ministry of Education under Ruiz Cortines accepted the language program in theory, it eventually disbanded the Institute for Indian Literacy, although carrying on similar activity until 1957 through the *Patrimonio Indígena del Valle del Mezquital*, an intersecretarial effort. By 1958 the burden had been shouldered by the National Indianist Institute at its Indian Coordinating Centers.

The bulk of the work of the Institute for Indian Literacy—and the most exciting phase—was done in the years from 1948 to 1950. All of the programs but the Náhuatl, which never got started, were under way. Of the three, the Tarascan was the most successful, partly because of the experience of the past in the zone, but also because of the character of the Tarascans, traditionally much more willing to accept innovation than the Otomíes or the Mayas. Close to 2,000 Tarascan students had taken examinations by 1949; results demonstrated that a majority had learned to read and write their own language and were learning Spanish.[23] For the three projects—Tarascan, Maya, and Otomí—10,240 individuals, school-age children and adults, had taken the language course between 1948 and 1950, of which 4,461 had successfully completed it.[24] By 1955 there were 209 literacy centers, of which more than half were in the Maya region of the Yu-

---

[22]Secretía. de Educ. Públ., *La obra educativa en el sexenio, 1940-1946*, pp. 141-142.

[23]Angélica Castro, "El Instituto de Alfabetización para Indígenas Monolíngües," *Boletín indigenista*, IX (March 1949), 74.

[24]Angélica Castro, "El Instituto de Alfabetización para Indígenas Monolíngües," *Boletín indigenista*, XI (March 1951), 68.

catán peninsula.[25] These were abandoned for lack of funds by 1956.

When the National Indianist Institute entered the language field, it brought with it a new concept. The Institute for Indian Literacy had operated almost exclusively as a language body, only incidentally concerned with economic and social problems. The National Indianist Institute departed from this ivory-tower approach by making language teaching and learning an integral part of the reforms at its Indian Coordinating Centers in Chiapas, Oaxaca, Veracruz, and Chihuahua. From the need to combine language teaching with reform came the "cultural promoter," whose function was to teach reading and writing in the Indian and Spanish languages and to encourage local participation and acceptance of the program of community transformation of the institute. Language learning and teaching had become part of the total effort to transform the backward rural community.[26]

V

A beginning has now been made in the struggle to bring the national language to Mexicans who either did not know it or made scant use of it, and much has been learned about the character of the problem.

No matter what the theory, it was the practical method that paid dividends in the village. If the literacy effort achieved some success, it was because the language people stressed practice over theory, as the rural school had not. Limited in funds and personnel, they did not waste energy on subjects meaningless to the Indian.

No substitute for good teaching was found. Regardless of his linguistic ability, a teacher failed if he lacked the ability to communicate with his students. In the final analysis those who struggled to teach the Indian to read and write—and succeeded—were teachers and not linguists or students of linguistics. If the language instructor was to succeed, his teaching had to answer today's needs. And successful teaching was a slow and arduous task, for the Indian learned slowly, not because of poor intelligence, but because his experience was limited.[27]

Without question, the inferior position of the woman in the Indian

[25]Secretía. de Educ. Públ., *Acción educativa del gobierno federal, 1954-1955* (Mexico, 1955), p. 95.

[26]Carlos Antonio Castro, "La lingüística en el centro coordinador Tzeltal-Tzotzil," *América indígena*, XVI (April 1956), 153-154.

[27]Angélica Castro, "Mesa redonda sobre el problema del analfabetismo," *Boletín indigenista*, XIII (Sept. 1953), 248.

household encouraged the persistence of the indigenous tongues in the rural community. Relegated to a secondary role and confined to a narrow domestic sphere, she was isolated from every force of modern life and especially from the school. Set apart from the currents of the twentieth century, she kept alive the indigenous tongues by passing them on to her children. An effective literacy program had to devise ways to break the shackles that bound women to domestic slavery and to bring them into contact with the modern world. Until this was done, a powerful enemy of the literacy program was left free to combat the effort.[28]

Since activities in much of the rural scene were conducted without Spanish, one of the perplexing problems was to induce those who learned Spanish to use it after they left school. This involved more than providing reading matter—books, readers, and newspapers—for the Indian. The problem was to make him want to read. After all, of what use was a reading and speaking knowledge of Spanish to the individual in the Indian-speaking community, whose wants were elementary and could be filled without the use of Spanish? What the government had to recognize was that illiteracy was as much an economic question as an educational one. It could not be solved without economic reforms long needed in the rural scene. The recent activity of the National Indianist Institute had recognized this simple fact: when life is a struggle for survival, education is of secondary importance. Under rural economic conditions there is too often no time for education, either for the children or the adults.

Rural poverty particularly affected the literacy effort in school enrollment and attendance. Absence or truancy from school was a serious problem in the rural villages, where children were looked upon as economic units. During the first two years of the literacy effort, over 60 per cent of its students abandoned it before the end of the term. Fewer dropped out in later years, but poor attendance and enrollment were major handicaps until the end. The Institute for Indian Literacy never found a solution to this problem, which sprang from forces beyond the scope of language learning.

Due to the widespread poverty, the literacy effort gained ground only in those areas where the standard of living was high enough for people to want to raise their cultural sights. The literacy program, therefore, had to stress economic reforms for the community, and this called for more funds and a broad approach. As was observed by Angélica Castro, director of the training center in the Mezquital,

---

[28]Carlos Antonio Castro, "La lingüística en . . . Tzeltal-Tzotzil," p. 150.

where the Indian was involved, reform was expensive.[29] Aside from human material, which was excellent but offered nothing but goodwill, there was nothing in the Indian community; everything had to be imported, from the teacher trained at government expense to the books, pencils, primers, and readers. But these were useless without the irrigation, plows, and animals and the agricultural credit that government had to provide in order to make literacy useful.

The literacy program required money, but funds were limited. The income of the Ministry of Education was channeled into agencies backed by pressure groups. The Indian had no lobbyist, and literacy got what was left after the capital and the cities got their share. The Institute for Indian Literacy was another federal bureau, living from day to day hoping that somehow funds would be found to expand its work. Its poverty had a direct effect upon its personnel. In 1953 the salary of the language teachers in the Mezquital was 60 pesos a month, and while this amount was increased to 280 pesos by 1956, the teacher in the old-type rural school, who had many of the same functions and almost the same educational background, earned 550 pesos or nearly double the amount.[30] This salary inequality was a serious handicap to the literacy effort.

At the planning level there was need for more participation of Indian personnel. Some steps were taken in this direction. By 1956, much of the Tarascan and Otomí programs was handled by natives, who prepared and selected the material and directed their colleagues in the program. But laudable as these efforts were, there was need to relinquish more of the program to native personnel. No one understands Indian problems as well as an Indian.[31]

Finally, despite notable results, the literacy program was not universally approved. Many rural schoolteachers rejected the method in the beginning, and, while the majority later accepted it, a recalcitrant minority was never won over. Outside the teaching profession, some in influential positions continued to agitate for the one-language approach of the Vasconcelos era. Still others criticized the program because it did not continue to emphasize the Indian tongues during all six years of elementary education.[32] In rural Mexico, where there was

[29]"El Instituto de Alfabetización," *Boletín indigenista*, XI (March 1951), 72.

[30]Juan Comas, "Informe con motivo de la visita realizada al Patrimonio Indígena del Valle del Mezquital," *Boletín indigenista*, XVI (Dec. 1956), 348, 350.

[31]Angélica Castro, "El Instituto de Alfabetización," *Boletín indigenista*, XI (March 1951), 72.

[32]Esquivel Casas, "El problema de las escuelas de las comunidades indígenas," *El Nacional*, April 21, 1949.

almost universal support of the program, a few opposed it because they suspected that it was an attempt to keep them ignorant of Spanish.

Like the educational picture in general, the language situation has hopeful and gloomy aspects. On the gloomy side, census figures indicate a growing Indian-speaking population. According to semi-official sources, which are prone to underestimate unfavorable statistics, there are more persons speaking an Indian language today than in 1921.[33] From this angle the language experiment does not look promising. But there is a bright side. While the number of Indian-speaking persons has multiplied, the number of individuals speaking only an Indian language has diminished by nearly 450,000 between 1940 and 1950. Similar trends are reflected in the individual states, although there are exceptions. Oaxaca had 30,000 more monolinguals in 1950 than ten years before. And among the states with dense mono-lingual populations, the percentage of change between the two census dates is insignificant.

Despite this confusing and incomplete statistical picture, there is reason for concluding that progress has been made. The bilingual stage that is developing represents a distinct advance over the time when the Indian spoke only his native tongue. Of course the change for the better cannot be credited entirely to the limited language programs; the improvements in communications, and particularly road building, are probably responsible for much of the decrease in mono-linguality. On the basis of figures for 1950 and the limited language work undertaken to date there can be no accurate appraisal of the bilingual ideal, yet the bilingualists believe that they have found a solution to the language barrier that has plagued Mexico for more than four hundred years.

[33]Miguel León-Portilla, "Panorama de la población indígena de México," *América indígena*, XIX (Jan. 1959), 61.

Chapter X

BETWEEN DOGMA AND DOCTRINE

I

Paradoxes characterize Mexico, none more baffling than the specter of religious controversy that hovers over the rural school. Without rural schools of its own for more than three centuries, the church has blocked efforts to build them, contesting reform doctrines with dogma. Bitter and frequently tragic, persistent and ubiquitous, this conflict has gripped Mexico periodically since 1917.

Scene of this bitter struggle is a land where nearly all Mexicans call themselves Catholic. According to the census of 1910, out of a population of 15,160,369 Mexicans, 99.16 per cent were Catholics.[1] If the census of 1950 is correct, there were then only 330,111 Protestants in Mexico.[2] Not only were Mexicans Catholic, but some of the fathers of the rural school had paid homage to the church's role in Mexican history. To quote José Vasconcelos, "the free and ardent proselytism of the missionary" had both a civilizing and democratic impact on society; by making everyone brothers in God, Christianity represented "the most powerful ratification of democratic doctrines."[3] Christian faith, he concluded, had brought the American Indian from cannibalism to civilization.[4]

Why a religious controversy in a nominally Catholic land? There is no simple answer, nor can the issue be understood in the light of the American experience. The laws against clerical schools, the ban on church ownership of property, and scores of similar restrictions were a Mexican development, wrote Ernest Gruening. These restrictions would not have been tolerated in the United States, but Mexican history and the entire picture were different.[5] What makes this conflict unique?

[1]Depto. de la Estadística Nacional, *Resumen del censo general . . . de 1921*, p. 102.

[2]Dirección General de Estadística, *Anuario estadístico de los Estados Unidos Mexicanos, 1957* (Mexico, 1959), p. 45.

[3]Vasconcelos and Gamio, *Aspects of Mexican Civilization*, p. 47.

[4]*La raza cósmica*, p. 12.

[5]*Mexico and Its Heritage*, p. 281.

II

One thesis advanced is that only by eliminating religion from the discussion will there be a clear picture of the basic factors involved, to cite George I. Sánchez, an American Catholic of Mexican-Spanish descent.[6] Or as Ramón Beteta argues, there was no religious question in Mexican history, since the struggle was not about religion but over the opposition of the church to the blueprints of the state.[7] According to a president of the Mexican Chamber of Commerce, the conservatives and reactionaries had cloaked themselves with the mantle of religion, and a political and economic struggle was seen by a befuddled world as a religious question.[8] Even President Plutarco Elías Calles, whose policies fanned the conflict, declared that he respected all creeds, the clergy of all faiths, and believers, so long as their ministers did not flout the laws by meddling in political questions or serve the powerful who exploited the poor.[9]

That much of this explanation is valid, there is little doubt. Yet this answer, which so many experts have accepted, overlooks a multitude of problems and ignores the fundamental character of the Revolution, especially of its educational policies. The upheaval of 1910 had a number of clear, if poorly defined, goals. One of them was the destruction of the *status quo*, which the church had helped to build. To achieve these goals the Revolution forged a variety of weapons, one of which was the rural school. As Beteta acknowledged, the reforms promised in the 1910 Revolution would not materialize unless its ideas were taught the children. To abandon the school to its enemies would jeopardize the success of the Revolution. He recognized frankly that when a country experienced sweeping change its pedagogical aspect would receive special attention. With every revolution there was planted the seed of educational reform. History recorded no social upheaval that had not brought the transformation of the school with it. All revolutionists, he concluded, recognized that a regime spawned by revolution perished if the people were not ready to improve and defend the new system. To prepare them for this challenge was the function of the revolutionary school.[10]

---

[6]*Mexico: A Revolution by Education*, p. 167.

[7]*Economic and Social Program of Mexico (A Controversy)* (Mexico, 1935), p. 140.

[8]José Miguel Bejarano, "La controversia que ha colocado a México ante el tribunal del mundo es una manifestación superficial de luchas políticas locales," in Luis C. Balderrama, *El clero y el gobierno de México* (Mexico, 1927), I, 285.

[9]Murray, trans. and ed. *Mexico before the World*, p. 59.

[10]*Economic and Social Program*, p. 202.

By stressing education and by making the school a federal monopoly, the reformers created a religious issue. For the Catholic Church has viewed education as one of its prerogatives, fighting vigorously the secularization of the public schools, writes Leo Pfeffer, whose *Church, State, and Freedom* discusses the issue in the United States.[11] According to the encyclical of Pope Pius XI on the *Christian Education of Youth*, "education belongs preeminently to the Church."[12] For the church, only one school is acceptable: the Catholic school, where the clergy watches over every phase of education, not merely religious instruction but every branch of learning, regulating the entire organization of the school, its teachers, syllabuses, and textbooks.[13] Nothing in the doctrine of Catholicism visualizes the teaching of religion independently of other subjects; religion is not just a branch of the curriculum or simple instruction; no matter what else the school may teach, its ultimate objective is the reverence and praise of God. Everything else is secondary. There can be no neutral or lay school, Pius XI affirmed, for such a school cannot live in practice, since "it is bound to become irreligious."[14]

Catholic attitudes on education reflect a basic difference from Protestantism. Catholicism, fundamentally, lacks that hunger for universal literacy so implicit in Protestantism and Judaism. Being Bible-centered, these creeds have demanded literate congregations able to read the Bible. By contrast, Catholicism has always been priest-centered, stressing the need for church attendance and the memorization of prayers over Bible reading. Throughout the Middle Ages literacy was restricted almost exclusively to priests and monks. Not until recently has the church encouraged lay study of the Bible. This difference, Pfeffer writes (p. 293), helps explain why "public responsibility for universal education," common to "Judea before the rise of the Catholic Church, is not again . . . found until the 1647 statute of Calvinist Massachusetts."

Although the Catholic Church now recognizes the merit of literacy, it has not acknowledged the ability of the state to provide suitable schools for Catholic children. Because of the intransigent attitude of the secularists who dictate the tone of instruction in the average community, runs the Catholic argument, the public school will never care adequately for the moral side of a Catholic child's education.

---

[11] (Boston, 1953), p. 293.

[12] (New York, 1936), p. 4.

[13] Ibid., pp. 7, 27.

[14] Ibid., p. 26.

This conviction has driven Catholic fathers and mothers to fight for Catholic schools, since an education for good citizenship, which the secularists advocate, does not fulfill the goals of Catholic education, whose aim is the perfection of a supernatural dimension to life.[15]

In the United States, a multiplicity of competing and jealous Protestant sects, all fearful of the Catholic Church, and the fact that the Catholic Church has occupied a minority position caused a different relationship to develop between church and school. The church demanded the right to bring Catholic dogma into the public schools for the instruction of children of Catholic parents; failing to achieve this it asked for public funds for the maintenance of Catholic schools. Whether out of loyalty to the principle of the separation of church and state or because of their antagonism to Catholicism, Protestants rejected both demands. From this came "the secularization of public education."[16]

The establishment of a public school system was a major victory for the supporters of the modern state. As Pfeffer writes (p. 288), "If we do not have a secular public school we cannot have a secular state: for the separation of church and state means the separation of church and state schools." This is the heart of the Mexican question. No matter how presented, the Mexican conflict was a struggle between the civil power and a church whose tenets included the claim that education belonged to it. Regardless of the economic and political factors involved, the religious issue is there. Whether it is the least or the most important issue is debatable; for, as indicated already, the school controversy involves a multitude of questions.

The issue is old, dating back to the Conquest, when crown and church triumphed. One imposed its economic and political system by force of arms; the other subjugated by persuasion and other means. Since the fall of Tenochtitlán, when the Spanish crown granted the church special privileges in return for its support, there have been quarrels between secular and ecclesiastical authorities. In 1767 the crown expelled the powerful Jesuit order from America, and one reason for this action was the Jesuits' monopoly of higher education. The struggle grew more acute after independence when the infant Republic fought to assert its preeminence over the church. One of the prerogatives given the church by the crown was the control of education in New Spain, which the Republic eventually coveted, to the anger of the clergy.

[15]Neil G. McCluskey, *Catholic Viewpoint on Education* (Garden City, N. Y., 1959), p. 71.

[16]Pfeffer, pp. 287-288.

Yet the church did not establish a system of public education, particularly in the villages. Since the close of the sixteenth century the representatives of the church had played a very minor role in rural life, notwithstanding the thousands of churches dotting the countryside. Seldom did priests make the village their home, preferring to stay in the cities and towns, from which they came to attend feast days and local celebrations in the villages. Without a rural clergy, the villagers carried on their religious life far from prayer books and literacy. They buried their dead, performed marriages, and worshiped God in their own way.

Despite the absence of a rural clergy and the lack of parochial schools, Catholicism, as interpreted by the peasants, prospered in the villages. The Mexicans in the tiny hamlets were zealous Catholics. Yet in the absence of parochial schools the peasants had only a limited grasp of Christian theology. To gain converts the early friars had planted Catholicism on the ruins of the old theology, taking pains to combine the two. They built their churches on the sites of the ancient places of worship and made Catholic festivals fall on the days dedicated to the pagan ideals. With this pragmatic decision, wise at the time, the friars won the Indians but failed to uproot old beliefs. Ancient temples of worship were razed, and their stones built new altars, but the pagan cults did not die. As the years passed and the missionaries relaxed their vigil, the Indian fashioned a new faith, wrote Moisés Sáenz: "He evolved a religion without theology, a mixture of the new Christianity with his own paganism, rich in meaning."[17] To quote Manuel Gamio, "the exterior and attractive modalities of Catholicism" were incorporated into the mythology, and there rose "a strange hybrid of superstition and idolatrous religious concepts, very far in essence from the principles of Roman Catholicism."[18] Parochial schools might have prevented this, but there were none in the villages.

By overlooking theological impurities, the church won the village. To cite Genaro Vásquez, the everyday life of the Mexicans was filled by the church; it was an essential part of life, occupying the Mexicans continually within the churches and outside of them. There were local religious festivals, saints' days and birthdays, and public ceremonies and sermons that dictated the daily activity of the Mexicans.[19] This religiosity made the church a formidable foe of the

[17]"The Genius of Mexican Life," in Herring and Terrill, eds. *The Genius of Mexico,* p. 10.

[18]Vasconcelos and Gamio, *Aspects of Mexican Civilization,* p. 111.

[19]*Excelsior,* Sept. 11, 1935.

school in the village where, deprived of a rural clergy, it represented a social and spiritual way of life under attack by the school. When the school endeavored to modify local customs and practices, often based on religious traditions, the community rose to defend them, not so much out of loyalty to the church as out of resentment at attacks on native ways frequently transcending the history of Catholicism in the region.

Formed during three centuries of colonial rule, the Mexican church was foreign and medieval, exercising both political and economic power. Usually friendly to Spanish interests, its hierarchy sided with colonial rulers, supporting the crown against the patriot priests who died fighting for Mexican independence. By opposing Hidalgo, Morelos, and other priests of similar views, the hierarchy lost a golden opportunity to win lasting support among the Mexicans. Having abandoned Hidalgo and his supporters, who often advocated reforms antagonistic to ruling groups, the hierarchy accepted an alliance with the dictator Antonio López de Santa Anna, spokesman for neocolonial groups after independence. Santa Anna crushed the reforms of the 1830's and ruled for nearly three decades, during which Mexico suffered internal chaos and defeats by Texas and the United States. There is no blacker period in Mexican history. When Benito Juárez ousted Santa Anna and introduced modern ways to Mexico in the 1850's, the church rulers rebelled, calling on Europe for aid and supporting the Napoleonic scheme to put Maximilian on a Mexican throne. Defeated again, the leadership of the church befriended Porfirio Díaz, ally of foreigner and *hacendado*, who managed Mexico with an iron fist. When he fell, the church hierarchy opposed his conquerors. A century after independence the church was still seeking "to convert itself into a temporal power in rivalry to the State," trying, wrote Victoriano Huerta's minister of education Jorge Vera Estañol, "to reestablish the theocratic régime of the middle ages."[20]

With the coming of independence, and particularly after *La Reforma*, a wave of nationalism began to sweep over Mexico. The Revolution was its culmination. The enemy was the church, a Spanish institution transported to America by the Conquest, imposed on the Indian, and tied intimately to the role of Spain in America. Even after independence a large percentage of the clergy was foreign born, coming mainly from Spain. In 1916 nearly all of the bishops had been educated in Rome. Few in the hierarchy paid homage to

[20]*Carranza and His Bolshevik Regime*, p. 25.

Mexico. Even Maximilian had to reprimand the Mexican bishops for their lack of patriotism.[21] Much of the legislation of the Revolution was nationalistic and antiforeign. The registration of the clergy, for example, condemned by Catholics everywhere, was part of the attempt to eliminate foreign influences from the national scene. Clerical ties with outsiders whose views were antagonistic to the Revolution menaced Mexico. This was particularly so of education, where clerical schools openly attacked the reformers. To cite Luis C. Balderrama, the United States employed its schools to Americanize the immigrant; before the adoption of Article 3 of the Constitution, Mexico's schools made the Mexican a foreigner.[22]

Western in origin, the church represented European thinking. A reflection of rampant nationalism, the Revolution created a native ideology. *Indianismo*, part of this ideological revolt, judged the activity of the church a failure. The missionaries had erred, wrote Sáenz.[23] The Conquest, and especially the coming of Catholicism, according to the Indianists, debased the magnificent cultures of the pre-Columbian world, uprooting deities that had inspired the ancient Mexicans. Kind or not, the new gods of the Spaniards, meditated Gamio, "no longer provoked the powerful responses of human life to nature, nor offered majestic and objective creative themes." To use an illustration, Mexican art, powerful before the Conquest, became "entangled in semi-abstract concepts and colorless contemplation of anonymous personages" during the colonial years.[24]

With the rural school as its focus, the Indianists offered a program of their own that would eliminate the church from the Mexican rural scene. Aside from material reforms, to paraphrase Sáenz, the architect, the program stressed disinterested and noneconomic activity. The popular arts, utilitarian in a sense but aesthetically gratifying in another, were given a prominent place; oral tradition was stressed, and the theater became the scene for the dramatization of local legends; everything was done to give free reign to the imagination. Symbolism in literature and the plastic arts was emphasized, and games and sports of all types were promoted. With this activity, wrote Sáenz, the religious needs of the Mexicans were satisfied and the religious question settled by substitution and reorientation instead of through suppression and persecution. While the program was in the making, caution would be exercised in dealing with religion, but

[21]González Roa, p. 91.
[22]*El clero y el gobierno de México*, I, 28-29.
[23]*Carapan: Bosquejo de una experiencia*, p. 323.
[24]Vasconcelos and Gamio, *Aspects of Mexican Civilization*, p. 114.

obviously priests and ministers had to be eliminated, even though the churches would stay open and the peasants would be allowed to worship. Nothing would be done to eliminate religious festivals, if properly carried out, but the celebrations would be taken over eventually by secular authorities and related to contemporary social and economic needs. The social scientists of the Revolution would do what the missionaries of the colonial era had done: preserve the rites but change the meaning of the cult.[25]

Indianist proposals and allegations were anathema to the church. While acknowledging a pre-Columbian world, Catholics branded *indianismo* "extreme nationalism, a narrow atavistic nationalism." Holding up the Aztecs for worship made no sense whatsoever, explained a spokesman for the Mexican hierarchy, for never had there lived a more bloodthirsty and cruel people. Indianism had gone astray by eulogizing myth and not fact, inviting a "relapse into old barbarism."[26] The origins of modern Mexico were in Europe, not in America. Because of its roots the church was an enemy of nationalism, the Indianists retorted, labeling it a foreign power dedicated to the welfare of the white man in Mexico. Since the Indianists figured prominently in the program of rural education, the church was often a target of school policy.

Anticlericalism was another factor in the school controversy. Mexicans, and particularly the planners of the new schools, former disciples of the Positivist professors in the teacher-training institutions of the old regime, had long fallen under the influence of the anticlerical traditions of France and Spain. Having worshiped at the shrine of the Enlightenment, they raised the banner of anticlericalism to new heights in the Constitution of 1917. Mexican anticlericalism developed features of its own, bitter, uncompromising, and negative, characteristics that Carleton Beals has described in a story about Dwight Morrow and Diego Rivera, the mural painter who at the request of Vasconcelos painted the frescoes in the Ministry of Education.

Morrow had commissioned Rivera to paint a fresco in Cortés' palace in Cuernavaca. A famous anticlerical, Rivera always depicted the priests as brutal men, lashing Indians and gathering gold. With Morrow's commission in his pocket, Rivera began to paint his clerics. When he learned what Rivera was up to, Morrow, thoroughly alarmed, went to visit the artist, for he had no desire to fan the fires

---

[25]Sáenz, *Carapan: Bosquejo de una experiencia,* pp. 329-330.

[26]R. A. McGowan, "The Catholic Attitude toward the Social and Educational Program of the Mexican Government," in Beteta, ed. *Economic and Social Program,* p. 134.

of the religious conflict then raging in Mexico. Diego was on the scaffolding, brush in hand.

Morrow extolled the unfinished fresco, then said, "Don Diego, these are pretty mean-looking priests."

"Mm," grumbled Diego, without laying down his brush or turning around.

"Don't you think you could paint a nice-looking priest for a change?"

"Mm," growled Diego.

But Morrow persisted. "Haven't you ever seen one?"

"Nope," grumbled Diego. "Never."

On the following day, however, Diego appeared at the Morrow house in Cuernavaca. "I've just read of one," he told Morrow excitedly.

So "Diego changed his plans." On "one of the doorway panels he painted a picture of the famous Bartolomé de las Casas, who spent his life laboring in behalf of the Indians and protecting them from feudal abuses." On the opposite panel "Diego put the fires of the Inquisition."[27]

Anticlerical sentiments painted by Rivera on wall and canvas were exploited by politicians. Faced with insurmountable problems and having promised the world to their followers, scores of politicians eventually fell back upon the church issue, which they manipulated in order to postpone reforms and to camouflage failures or changes of policy. Calles was a master at this. There is reason to suspect that much of the anticlerical campaign of the twenties and early thirties, which frequently centered around the schools, was directly fomented by him. Confronted by dangers from abroad and at home and unable or unwilling to carry out the reforms envisaged by the Revolution, he revived the religious question. By raising the Jacobin banner of the nineteenth-century liberals, Calles distracted the attention of the agrarian and labor sectors from his failure to improve their lot, particularly after he had decided that reform was dangerous. Fighting the rebellions that broke out furnished countless military officers, whose inactivity posed a danger to Calles, with the opportunity to enrich themselves with property stolen from Catholics foolish enough to support hopeless and ill-advised adventures.[28]

[27]Carleton Beals, *Glass Houses: Ten Years of Free-Lancing* (Philadelphia, 1938), pp. 311-312.

[28]Virginia Prewett, *Reportage on Mexico* (New York, 1941), p. 70; John W. F. Dulles, *Yesterday in Mexico: A Chronicle of the Revolution, 1919-1936* (Austin, Tex., 1961), p. 311.

Looking back over the currents of thought that dominated Mexican thinking in the twenties and thirties, one concludes that the conflict was inevitable. The Catholic Church was conservative, representing the *status quo*. The Revolution, radical in thought and action, called for immediate reforms in behalf of peasants and workers. Throughout the nineteenth century, and particularly under Díaz, the church had sided with the old oligarchy. On the haciendas, wrote Emilio Portes Gil, there were always chapels where the peasants, their wives, and their children arrived on bended knee "to hear the voice of the priest," hoping to find relief from their suffering in this world with "the delights of the next."[29] On economic and social matters the church favored its old allies, even after the Revolution had defeated Díaz. The Constitution of 1917 defined the social obligations of property holders, insisting on the right of the state to regulate property for the benefit of the majority. Private property, declared the church, was sacred, "inalienable and indivisible." Its doctrine was evolution, not revolution. If there was to be land reform, the church wanted landlords compensated for the property taken from them. It had no faith in the overnight distribution of land, advocating instead a gradual program in behalf of tenants and laborers who were seldom equipped to farm the land. Reform had to come "in a normal manner, step by step, without great transitions and without advances attempted before the people are ready for them."[30]

Reformers rejected this logic. Suppose that the owners had acquired the land by chicanery and violence, by taking advantage of their political privileges or the Indian's ignorance, asked Ramón Beteta. Was this justice? Why offer the *hacendados* full compensation for lands that they had valued below the market price in order to evade paying their share of the public tax, he queried. Without economic change, which called for breaking up the great estates, there was no way out and no place for education, declared the reformers. Against the system of peonage even the remarkable child was helpless. Once out of school and back in a hostile environment he forgot everything he was taught, Beteta pointed out. Economic planning had to come simultaneously with the schooling of the community, children as well as adults; otherwise the school disrupted the rhythm of life without developing the community as a whole.[31]

[29]*The Mexican Schools and the Peasantry*, pp. 9-10.

[30]McGowan, "The Catholic Attitude," in Beteta, ed. *Economic and Social Program*, pp. 108, 120, 110.

[31]*Economic and Social Program*, pp. 142, 208.

III

Recent controversy has focused on Article 3 of the Constitution of 1917. As the blueprint of the Revolution, the Constitution written at Querétaro symbolized militant reform. Seeking the destruction of the hacienda system, it advocated land redistribution, anathema to conservatives. Many of its signers—schoolteachers, professional men, lawyers, journalists, and military officers whose fathers had followed the banners of *La Reforma*—came from provinces dominated by the clergy. Like the Juaristas of 1857, whose blind acceptance of French Jacobin principles was almost pathetic, their hatred of clerical power was fanatic.[32] Regardless of what else was accomplished at Querétaro, they were determined to end clerical domination. To bring this about and to raise living standards, economic and social reforms were called for. Chief among them was public education.

A committee dominated by the fiery General Francisco J. Mújica, a Michoacán radical representing left-wing groups at Querétaro, drafted Article 3. Tacitly shared by Mújica and his colleagues was the conviction that "it was just and proper to restrict the exercise of natural rights when they threatened the development of society." One such right was the freedom of the clergy to have schools. Any impartial student of Mexican history, the committee reported, recognized that the clergy, worshiping Rome above Mexico, was the "vicious and tenacious enemy of our liberties." By rejecting patriotism and selfless service for ambition and power, the clergy had forfeited all rights. Contemporary clerical designs on education were merely part of the old plot to usurp the prerogatives of the Republic. Then and now this ambitious scheme threatened the future of Mexico and for that reason should be suppressed by stripping the clergy of the means to carry it out. To do this it was imperative that ministers be barred from any role in primary education.

Having disposed of clerical demands, the committee proceeded to condemn the teachings of the church. By dealing with abstract ideas beyond the grasp of the child's mentality, it concluded, religious education stunted psychological growth and warped the mind, just as the wrong physical exercises damaged the human body. Viewed from another angle, religious instruction hindered the development of a vigorous society. By capturing the child's mind without being understood by him, religious ideas fanned the flames of fanaticism, making reform difficult if not impossible.[33] No matter how the ques-

[32]Palavicini, I, 144.
[33]Ibid., I, 221-222.

tion was interpreted, religious instruction had to stop at the gates of the primary school.

Two drafts of Article 3 were written by the committee. Embodying the anticlerical spirit of Querétaro, both rejected the recommendations of Venustiano Carranza, who wished to move slowly against the church. Yet so strong were the anticlerical features of the first draft that it was withdrawn after heated debate in the general assembly, and a second one was submitted a few days later. Although not as openly anticlerical as its predecessor, the second draft was no victory for moderation. A majority of the delegates voted for it, but Carranza and his allies, among whom figured leading moderates, opposed it.

Unlike the reformers of 1857, who accepted church schools, the men of Querétaro banned them. All primary instruction, public and private, would be lay and open to all. "No religious corporation or minister of any cult could establish or direct schools of primary instruction. Private schools could be established only with the approval and supervision of Federal authorities."[34] As Beteta later confessed, this restricted the freedom to teach, a "natural right" beloved by minds conditioned by the ideals of the French Revolution. Notwithstanding this, Mexican leaders believed that some elements, among them the clergy, had abused this liberty, to the detriment of the masses.[35] What the Constitutionalists did was to make the school a political weapon for their views. With the school in their hands the future was assured, declared Mújica.

Yet the draft of 1917 did not go far enough for the radicals at Querétaro, who advocated substituting the term "rational" for "lay"; rather than a "neutral" school, they demanded one actively engaged in what they called the war against error, which meant the teachings of the church.[36] Defeated in 1917—although the committee assured them that "lay" did not imply that the school refrained from taking sides—the radicals won a second struggle in 1934. With the coming of hard times and the growing popularity of left-wing programs, many patterned after those of the Soviet Union, the thirties offered a propitious climate for change. The collectivist doctrines of the world of the Great Depression, moreover, often had no place for God. The economic disaster of the time had forced millions to find their own salvation. Salvation had become something everyone did

[34]Ibid., I, 264-265.

[35]Beteta, ed. *Economic and Social Program*, p. 160.

[36]Palavicini, I, 226, 225.

for himself; the all-powerful and benevolent Christ seemed only a legend to millions who prayed for salvation and did not find it. Disillusioned and embittered by their lack of progress, many Mexicans embraced the panaceas of the day, among which was the idea of a socialist school. A century of anticlericalism had prepared public opinion to accept this concept.

Changing the 1917 version of Article 3 began in 1932. While specifying the lay character of primary schooling, the article said nothing about secondary education. By 1932 scores of secondary schools were in the hands of ecclesiastics, who used them to combat the teachings of the primary schools, according to many critics. To remedy this, Narciso Bassols obtained a special presidential decree stating that schooling on the secondary level must be lay in character, too.[37] Using this beginning as a springboard, others—notably the delegations to the PNR (*Partido Nacional Revolucionario*) convention in 1933 from Tabasco and Veracruz, representing the rabidly anticlerical governor of Tabasco, Tomás Garrido Canabal—proceeded to go beyond what Bassols called for, advocating the complete revision of Article 3, which eventually became part of the Six-Year Plan of the National Revolutionary Party.[38]

The 1917 version of the article, wrote Alberto Bremauntz, a leading spokesman for the radicals of the Depression era, had a loophole. Though the clerics had lost their battle, nothing was done to give the school a precise orientation. Lacking this, the school's usefulness to the Revolution was minimal; for laicism had continued to yield young men and women little concerned with getting at the root of problems. A school equipped to prepare the coming generations to support and affirm its doctrines was what the Revolution must have.[39] With this in mind, Bremauntz and other leftist intellectuals, teachers, students, and politicians waged a struggle for the revision of the article, which they achieved by capturing a majority of the PNR convention of 1933.

What they recommended and the PNR approved was the controversial "socialist" amendment accepted by Congress in 1934. Primary and secondary schools fell under federal jurisdiction; private schools had to accept the ideas, textbooks, and nonreligious attitude of the public schools; and church schools were banned. This was just the

---

[37]Millán, p. 53.

[38]Partido Nacional Rev., *Plan sexenal . . . 1934-1939*, p. 2.

[39]*La educación socialista en México (antecedentes y fundamentos de la reforma de 1934)* (Mexico, 1943), p. 4.

beginning. For the "neutral" school of the past a "socialist" school was substituted, the militant enemy of the church. The negative principle of yesteryear did not go far enough, announced Beteta. "The Church had a certain philosophy of life, well defined economic ideas and well-known methods." Were the Republic to survive, it "should, likewise, establish and teach its ideology, preach and defend the economic ideas of the Revolution and forbid the breeding of a class" that had coveted personal privilege at the expense of the public welfare since independence.[40]

The school, declared the men of 1933, was a social institution of the state, which would see to it that it stayed in the hands of those for whom it was established. No subject would be taught without the approval of the state, the "direct representative of the people." Teaching was a privilege granted to those who obeyed the laws. Besides excluding all religious training, education provided "true, scientific, and rational answers," in order that students might have "an exact and positive concept of the world surrounding them, and of the society in which they live." These stipulations would guarantee the "social mission" of the school. The men of 1933 also provided for close federal supervision of private schools—of their "social orientation" and pedagogy, their "socialistic and nonreligious" nature, the preparation of their teachers and directors, and their sanitary conditions. In the final analysis, what they had in mind was the gradual elimination of private education so that by 1940 there would be one system of schools "directed and controlled by the State."[41]

With these revisions, promised Portes Gil, there would come "sentiments and ideas of human fraternity, and [the] moral and economic rehabilitation of the society of today." By working hand in glove with Revolutionary laws, particularly Articles 27 and 123 of the Constitution of 1917, the revisions encouraged students and teachers to build a healthier society, where inequalities were a thing of the past.[42] To cite Ignacio García Téllez, briefly chief of education under Cárdenas, by accepting socialism the Revolution fulfilled the promise to equate the "social function of education" with the "social function of property."[43]

---

[40]Beteta, ed. *Economic and Social Program*, p. 164.

[41]Ramírez, "The Six-Year Plan in Education," in Herring and Weinstock, eds. *Renascent Mexico*, pp. 131-133.

[42]Quoted by Charles S. Macfarland, *Chaos in Mexico: The Conflict of Church and State* (New York, 1935), pp. 85-86.

[43]Quoted in ibid., p. 81.

I V

Almost nothing was done by federal authorities to enforce the religious statutes of Article 3 until 1926. Church schools functioned openly. Both Obregón and Vasconcelos accepted them, explaining that there were not enough public school facilities for all Mexican children. Church instruction was preferable to none, Obregón confessed to Ernest Gruening.[44] But in 1926, either because Calles decided to raise the religious issue (as the church claimed) or because of the activity of the church (to cite the other side), the Ministry of Education clamped down on the private schools. Credit was denied studies made in private schools not "incorporated" by the Ministry, which closed the lyceums and universities to their graduates. Schools that wanted their studies validated had to petition for "incorporation," accepting federal vigilance and official textbooks and pledging to exclude all religious orders and priests from their activity.[45]

By coincidence, or by design, other anticlerical measures were taken at about the same time. Ecclesiastical properties held in violation of the Constitution were confiscated, among them schools. Much to the anger of Vasconcelos, Sáenz and other Protestants won important posts in the Ministry of Education, and Protestant textbooks found their way into the schools. Catholics charged that "readers for the children in the primary grades included lessons filled with hatred of religion," which pitted "the Church . . . against the poor . . . in city and country."[46] Dewey's teachings, emphasizing the experimental method, were resented by Catholics and nationalists alike—by Catholics for what they called the attack on faith and by nationalists because Dewey was a foreigner and, particularly, an American.

Federal school legislation in 1917, the amendments of 1934, and their enforcement brought the wrath of the clergy upon the leaders of the Republic. Archbishop José Mora y del Río, condemning what he called the anti-Catholic measures taken since 1917, rejected Article 3 and added that Articles 5, 27, and 130, covering property rights and church questions, were equally unacceptable. "Under no circumstances can we abandon this criterion without treason to our faith and to our religion," he declared.[47] When the amendments of the thirties were announced, the apostolic delegate Leopoldo Ruiz y Flores, writ-

[44]*Mexico and Its Heritage*, p. 220.

[45]Beteta, ed. *Economic and Social Program*, p. 162.

[46]McGowan, "The Catholic Attitude," in Beteta, ed. *Economic and Social Program*, p. 126.

[47]Quoted by Macfarland, p. 131.

ing from exile in San Antonio, Texas, called them a war against all religion. He warned that there were rights above "any Constitution, rights which the latter [state] should respect and uphold, such as religious rights, the right to educate one's children, the right to life, the right of private property and all other natural rights. *Any law,*" he told Catholics, *"impairing those rights is unjust and null and void."*[48] Until there was a change in Article 3, the apostolic delegate stressed, it was *"illicit* for any Catholic person to establish or support any schools or to send their children to those already existing, whether they be official schools or privately-supported."[49]

Among conservatives, moderates, and even former officials of the Ministry of Public Education, the church had supporters. They believed that the legislation had gone too far. In the opinion of Vasconcelos the Constitution of 1917 denied the right to transmit religion from one generation to the next. Enemies of the Latin world and friends of the United States, he believed, had taken revenge on the church for its support of Huerta. So much beyond the laws of *La Reforma* did those of 1917 go that even Carranza had balked, preferring to allow them to gather dust rather than to enforce them.[50] These conservatives, and particularly the moderates, were not necessarily friends of the church, although they accepted Catholicism as part of Mexico and a force for union. Political liberties, in their opinion, could not be brushed aside lightly; the consequences would be disastrous. If man had a natural right to think and believe as he wished, then the laws had to guarantee the liberty of teaching, even though this gave schools to those who rejected the principle.[51] Instead of placing obstacles before parochial schools, public officials should favor them, for Mexico needed schools. Nor could superstition be combated by suppressing schools; ignorance was not a shield against fanaticism. By suppressing parochial schools, wrote Vera Estañol (p. 52), public authorities wasted the educative power of the church, which could furnish a civic, moral, and sound nationality. To quote Octavio Véjar Vásquez, "without the sign of the cross behind it," there was "no education."[52]

Most neutral observers, among them many Protestants, agreed that the legislation of the thirties was extreme or ill-defined. As Ambas-

[48]Quoted by Portes Gil, *The Conflict between the Civil Power and the Clergy* (Mexico, 1935), p. 120.

[49]Quoted by Beteta, ed. *Economic and Social Program,* p. 190.

[50]Vasconcelos, *Breve historia de México,* 5th ed. (Mexico, 1944), pp. 504-505.

[51]Palavicini, I, 229.

[52]Quoted by Kneller, p. 55.

sador Josephus Daniels wrote, there was an ambiguity in the 1934 version of Article 3 that led to a variety of interpretations. Much of the choice rested with the teachers.[53] The phrase "socialist school," reported Verna Carleton Millán, had stirred a fratricidal warfare that divided the nation when peace and unity were most needed by all reformers. Calling the school socialistic had played havoc with education, she concluded: teachers grumbled or rebelled; there was bitter controversy in the press and agitation in classroom and public forum. Although a decision to change the name for the time being would be considered an immediate triumph for the reaction, Millán (p. 236) believed "it fundamentally important that this be done."

Still the allegations against the church cannot be dismissed lightly. For the church had rejected the reform program, particularly education. "I recall how deeply impressed I was in 1922 when José Vasconcelos, with his characteristic enthusiasm, presented the plans of the Federal Department of Education," reminisced Charles S. Macfarland (p. 77). "They were constructive, and Vasconcelos expressed no sense of opposition to the Church schools at that time," recognizing that Mexico needed them. What he regretted "so far as the Church was concerned, was . . . its tendency to attack the system of public schools." Gruening recalled that Vasconcelos had welcomed parochial schools; but he condemned using them to destroy public schools. Too often the government established a public school, and then a clerical school opened next door. The clerics, who wielded great influence among the people, urged the parents to withdraw their children from the public school, which closed for lack of students. Some time later the parochial school shut its doors, and the children were left without a school.[54] Sáenz confessed that he had heard of only two priests who befriended the school in the rural village. "Experience," he declared, "has taught us simply to take this hostility for granted."[55]

Clerical resentment did not stop with indifference, passive resistance, and vocal denunciations. From 1926 to 1929, and again from 1932 to 1937, the church openly opposed public authority. Unable to get the laws rescinded, the clergy called for a national economic boycott in 1926, asking all Catholics to buy only what was absolutely necessary and to keep their children out of school. Later all churches were closed by the hierarchy. When Bassols put the secondary

[53]*Shirt-Sleeve Diplomat* (Chapel Hill, N. C., 1947), p. 135.

[54]*Mexico and Its Heritage*, p. 221.

[55]Quoted in ibid.

schools under federal jurisdiction, the church called for a boycott of them. School attendance fell off considerably; not until 1935 was it near normal again. Accusing Bassols of advocating sex education, clerically supported groups forced his resignation. Though no public school offered a course on sex education, Millán wrote (p. 55), clergy and Catholics began "a whispering campaign"; nothing Bassols and his supporters did stopped the lies and half-truths that raised a wave of public hysteria. When the clerically minded Véjar Vásquez replaced Luis Sánchez Pontón in 1941, he carried out with clerical blessings a purge of liberals.

Climax of the clerical protest was the *cristero* uprising of 1927, which broke out anew in 1932 and fanned the hatred of the *sinarquistas* in the late thirties. After Calles had clamped down on the clergy, scores of armed bands raised the standard of revolt. Shouting "Long live Christ King," peasants battled peasants, schools were burned, and teachers (and priests) were beaten and even murdered. Although the church denied any connection with the rebels, individual priests fraternized with them, frequently providing moral support and leadership. Nor did the hierarchy discourage the uprisings. From Rome the bishop of Durango cabled his Catholic brethren that though the church had not provoked the rebellion, "now that the movement exists, [and] pacific means having been exhausted," there was nothing to do but support it. Addressing himself "to our Catholic sons . . . [with] arms in defense of their social and religious rights . . . we . . . say to you: be at peace in your consciences and receive our benedictions."[56]

A truce was arranged by Dwight Morrow in 1929, who brought the clergy and President Portes Gil together. All seemed settled; then Bassols' dicta and a papal encyclical calling for action in contravention of the truce reopened the question. With the encyclical came new *cristero* activity, which the socialist amendment fanned to fever pitch. Fanatical mobs again sacked schools and killed teachers (and priests). In Atoyac, Jalisco, enraged peasants fell upon a teacher and his wife for preaching socialism.[57] A woman teacher was killed and her body hacked to pieces by an infuriated mob in Jalancingo, Veracruz.[58] In Ciudad González, Guanajuato, sixteen persons died and twenty-five were injured in a clash between clerical groups and local militia. A cultural mission had stopped in the plaza in front of the

[56]Quoted by Macfarland, p. 132.

[57]*Excelsior*, Sept. 18, 1935.

[58]*Excelsior*, Nov. 24, 1935.

local church. The priest, forewarned of its arrival, encouraged his parishioners to attack it. After weapons were brandished by the priest-incited mob, the cultural mission called upon the local agrarian militia. The outcome was a small-scale battle settled only with the intervention of federal troops and the personal visit of President Cárdenas who, from the altar of the temple, denounced the priest as an agitator.[59] Similar outrages against teachers were committed in nearly every part of Mexico.

By 1935 even the traditionally Catholic newspaper *Excelsior* conceded that rural teachers faced grave perils. In a cartoon titled "A rural teacher, placid and free of worry, on his way to school," *Excelsior* (November 30, 1935) pictured a teacher heavily armed with rifle, pistol, knife, and machete walking nervously to school. Fearful for their lives, many teachers stayed away from school, refusing to teach where they were not wanted. A mass demonstration of some 10,000 teachers in Mexico City asking for federal protection and carrying banners that accused the clergy of joining the *hacendados* in an unholy alliance against education eventually prompted Cárdenas to order the army to defend all rural teachers. A few days later the Ministry of War made arms available to them. Despite this, hundreds of teachers suffered persecution in rural villages, and others lost their schools.

With the outbreak of Franco's rebellion in Spain and the rise of Hitler and Mussolini in the late thirties, the religious issue became entangled with international currents. As Franco's troops advanced, clerical groups in Mexico renewed their offensive, despite efforts of moderates to find a way out of the muddle. While the older *cristeros* eventually conceded defeat, their sons and neighbors took their places. These were the *sinarquistas*, clerical fanatics with international ties. Offspring of ultraconservatives, *sinarquismo* represented a hatred of all left-wing ideas, rejected *La Reforma* and the Revolution, and resurrected the grandeurs of colonial Mexico when church and state were one. Stressing blind devotion and martyrdom, the ideology of *sinarquismo* glorified the cult of Franco's *hispanidad*, holding sway particularly among families linked to the *cristero* revolt. To many observers, *sinarquismo* had much in common with the Spanish Falange and the militant Fascism of totalitarian Europe.

Like the *cristeros* before them, the *sinarquistas* announced that they would not rest until God and church had their rightful place in education. Vilifying the public schools and calling on parents not

[59]Townsend, p. 134.

to send their children to them, they terrorized teachers, often driving them from the villages. Their sabotage of public education was strikingly successful. When Nathan Whetten, an American sociologist, came to a village in Puebla where three out of four persons did not read or write, just 29 of the 371 school-age children were in the classrooms. Local *sinarquistas* had frightened parents by pinning the Communist tag on the teachers. Rather than expose their children to godless men, they preferred to keep them in ignorance.[60] John Collier, another American scholar, estimated that 250,000 Indian peasants were *sinarquistas*.

V

Despite the activity of the *sinarquistas*, peace between church and state loomed as a distinct possibility by 1940. Two developments had made this possible. Faced with international complications, Cárdenas had veered away from his radical program by 1938; and the church, led by more enlightened men, had recognized the need for moderation and compromise. As the conservative leaders of the forties and fifties turned their backs on militant reform, there was little to fight over, for the church was regaining many traditional prerogatives.

Sensing the need for moderation and hoping to win the support of middle groups in his struggle with Calles, Cárdenas began to look for a way out of the religious controversy. To calm the hierarchy and insure his position, he replaced his priest-baiting cabinet chief, Garrido Canabal, whom Calles had appointed, with Saturnino Cedillo, the Catholic boss of San Luis Potosí. Striving to end the conflict over education, Cárdenas ordered teachers to exclude all "anti-religious propaganda from the classrooms." His declaration was published in newspapers throughout Mexico and in the official journals of the Ministry of Education, which delighted in publishing diatribes against the church.[61] By 1938, Betty Kirk reported, there was "open co-operation between Church and State," despite sporadic *sinarquista* trouble. Manuel Avila Camacho, who followed Cárdenas in office, publicly proclaimed that he was a practicing Catholic, "convinced that religious liberty is necessary for the life of Mexico."[62] His successors were equally inclined to accept the *rapprochement*. Mexico's President Adolfo López Mateos (elected in 1958) spoke on the same platform with a priest, something unheard of twenty years earlier.

[60]Whetten, pp. 494-495.
[61]Townsend, p. 135.
[62]Kirk, pp. 132-133.

Mutual tolerance demanded concessions on both sides. Beginning with Archbishop Luis M. Martínez, whose endorsement of the expropriation of the foreign oil companies in 1938 won him national goodwill, there was greater ecclesiastical awareness of Mexico's problems. Although Avila Camacho eventually suppressed with force the *sinarquistas*, there was no public outcry from the upper clergy, even though scores of local priests were involved. On their part, federal authorities offered concessions, too. Cárdenas ended the persecution of the church. Bowing before Catholic opinion, Avila Camacho replaced his leftist minister of education, Sánchez Pontón, with Véjar Vásquez, the staunch defender of the church. Moderates or conservatives have held the office since then. Concurrently the more controversial features of Article 3 were eliminated. Coeducation was banned in 1942 and the socialist amendment dropped in 1945. While the clergy still objected to federal legislation banning parochial schools, it managed to run some eighty of them in Mexico City alone in 1950.[63]

Unfortunately, the church had not done much to further rural education. That it could do something, if willing, no one doubted. When determined to help, a priest could do much in the village. "Will you believe, professor," a rural teacher confessed to Rafael Ramírez, "that in our region the priests are beginning to use the pulpit to support our campaign [against alcoholism]? And how well they do it, and how efficacious their sermons are!"[64] In the mountains of Chihuahua the Tarahumara Indians were learning to speak, read, and write Spanish through the activity of Jesuit missionaries. Recently the church supported Catholic "agricultural weeks" in various parts of Mexico, where the peasants learned to use modern farming techniques. After the church-sponsored farm week in Tepoztlán, Morelos, *El Universal* on January 13, 1951, quoted the Catholic archbishop as saying that "to work for the peasants is to labor for the fatherland," a task he found extremely rewarding since so much of Mexico farmed for a living. After all, he recalled, this was only in keeping with the social objectives of Pope Leo XIII in his encyclical *Rerum novarum*, which antedated the Revolution by nearly four decades. But this was sporadic cooperation.

Although nearly everyone recognized that Mexico needed schools, the church attitude on education differed radically from that of the Republic. In 1962 the church had still not recognized that public

[63]Kneller, p. 55.

[64]Ramírez, "The Anti-Alcoholic Campaign," in Herring and Terrill, eds. *The Genius of Mexico*, p. 204.

schools were in Mexico to stay. Parochial schools were being used to supplant public schools rather than to fill the void. If public schools were to survive in Mexico, controls had to remain on the Catholic educational effort. Any rupture of the wall separating church and public schools would destroy what had been achieved since 1857. Recent federal aid to privately supported teacher-training schools, where the church plays a major role, for example, had hurt public institutions.

A new problem threatens to complicate matters. Mexico's growing population cannot be ignored much longer. Unless means are found to feed, clothe, and educate the millions of Mexicans born every year, some method of limiting population growth is called for. Yet, so far as the Catholic Church is concerned, birth control—outside of the rhythm system, nearly impossible for use in backward rural areas—is unacceptable. If the federal authorities eventually move in the direction of population limitation, the rural school will have to prepare the way, and this will reopen the ancient clash between the secular and ecclesiastical powers.

Chapter XI

ASSETS AND LIABILITIES

I

By 1962 FULLY FOUR DECADES HAD PASSED since Mexico began its heralded crusade for rural education, that cherished promise of the Revolution. The tumult and shouting and the frenzied activity of the early years were a matter of history. Successive administrations had altered policy, reversing trends and discarding yesterday's ideas. Some changes were marked, others merely modified older patterns. Broadly speaking, these twists and turns represented three cycles. There was the pioneer era of the twenties, when northerners built schools around the haciendas and ranchos. Men from the central zone, speaking for the collectivist panaceas of their time and the *ejido* traditions of ancient Mexico, won control in the thirties. Since World War II a new group of businessmen and industrialists, who symbolized the rise of middle-class Mexico, has dictated policy.

A philosopher turned reformer, José Vasconcelos baptized the rural school, trying to adapt classical learning to rural needs. By 1925 his formula had given way to John Dewey's school of learning by doing, which Moisés Sáenz and Rafael Ramírez, professional educators of the Columbia school, adapted to local needs. While Vasconcelos and his successors did not overlook economics, they stressed the cultural and social wants of the individual over the community. A Mexico of small farms, of haciendas, and, to a lesser extent, of *ejidos* was the basis of their rural school, a school reflecting the mild reforms of the twenties, a compromise between the promises of the radicals and the realities of the moment. Like the politics of the era, the second cycle plunged the school headlong into the miasma of collectivism. Discarding the hacienda, the men of this era cherished the *ejido* and enshrined the community. For Narciso Bassols, Lázaro Cárdenas, and the Ramírez of the thirties, learning revolved around a pragmatic program for the group and not the individual. Seeking the economic redemption of the peasant, the architects of the time called on the teacher to take up the banners of change, demanding

195

militant champions of agrarian reform. After the war the Republic's leaders rejected the farm for the factory and discarded the socialistic objectives of the thirties. Although strongly in favor of a sound agriculture, the industrialists put their faith in large, privately owned, mechanized farms and neglected the *ejido*. In place of a curriculum that identified it with the general economic and social reforms of the day, the rural school had a modified version of the urban school's learning for the sake of learning, a program more divorced from immediate needs than ever before. The focus was on the individual rather than on the welfare of the group.

II

In the wake of years of labor by men of ideals, even ardent believers in contemporary Mexican progress admitted that all was not well on the educational scene. Not only was the chronic shortage of schools and teachers still there and growing worse daily, but also there was evidence that something was wrong with Mexico's educational panacea. Despite what had been said before, President Adolfo López Mateos confessed, the battle had not been won on the school front. Rather than emerging victorious, Mexico had tasted defeat, particularly in the village where millions had no schools. Unless Mexicans awakened from the lethargy that gripped them, they would be overwhelmed by the crisis, he warned. Equally outspoken, Jaime Torres Bodet, again minister of education, admonished that emergency measures were called for, that procrastination and halfhearted efforts would merely invite disaster.[1] Victory would not come, other public officials stressed, without thousands of additional schools and a thorough revamping of current ideological and economic foundations.

What politicians were now publicly admitting, others had perceived before. During the late forties and throughout the fifties, reformers had warned that Mexico's educational program lagged, that the rural school was not living up to its intent. Others, Luis Chávez Orozco among them, had castigated scholars from the United States, who had written glowingly of the contemporary schoolhouse, for not having perceived that the school was no longer that of yesteryear. If the school in the city was the victim of neglect, the rural school had suffered even more, the Senate learned late in 1958.[2] Not having

[1] *Novedades*, Aug. 22, 1959.
[2] *El Nacional*, Dec. 24, 1958.

faced the challenge steadily since 1941—this was Mexico's mistake, affirmed Oscar Vera, a Chilean pedagogue. As in other Latin American countries, he pointed out, there was a wide gap between what was on paper and reality.

By placing Mexico's crisis in the context of the world scene, some perspective of its magnitude could be seen. According to Victor Gallo Martínez, chief of the Office of In-Service Training of Teachers, there were between 500 and 550 million school-age children in the world, half of whom were in classrooms. Of the nations in 1959, twenty-nine had 85 per cent of their children (between five and fifteen years of age) in school; twenty-three others had 50 to 85 per cent, and forty-four others had less than half. On the basis of official Mexican statistics, Mexico had 50.7 per cent of its school-age group in the classroom, putting it just above the lowest bracket. Other statistics cited by Gallo Martínez show that from 1952 to 1957 Mexico had an average school-age population between six and twelve years of age of 6,742,495. Of this number, an average of 3,827,-238 registered annually for federal, state, and municipal primary schools during these years.[3] Each year 2,915,257 children of school age had no school to attend. Unofficial calculations, however, were much higher. Scores of estimates placed the number of children without schools at 4 million. Of the 88,850 inhabited places in 1958, to quote Vicente Lombardo Toledano, approximately 50,000 had no schools.[4] If these estimates were correct, they put Mexico on the bottom rung of countries in the educational scale employed by Gallo Martínez.

Even the official prognosis had dire implications for Mexico. If the statistics of Gallo Martínez are accepted, Mexico required 65,795 additional teachers and 23,880 schools to take care of the nearly 3 million children without schools. These figures were calculated on the national average of 138 students per school and 42 for the individual teacher.[5] But the run-of-the-mill rural school did not measure up even to these figures, and 80 per cent of the primary schools were in rural communities. If the unofficial estimate of 4 million children without schools was accepted, Mexico required an additional 25,857 teachers and 7,862 schools above Gallo Martínez' figures.

Not only was there urgent need for more schools and teachers, but he educational picture was unbalanced geographically. As always,

---

[3]*Estructura económica de la educación mexicana* (Mexico, 1959), I, 8, 27.

[4]*Una ojeada a la crisis de la educación en México* (Mexico, 1958), p. 35.

[5]Gallo Martínez, I, 27.

the Federal District was favored, having nearly 85 per cent of its children registered for primary school. After the Federal District came the northern states, which could have solved many of their difficulties with more local effort. Many of the southern states, rural in character and frequently densely populated with Indian-speaking groups, faced critical shortages of schools and teachers. By official estimates, Guerrero, Oaxaca, and Chiapas, with the largest percentages of primary school-age populations, had less than 44 per cent of their children in classrooms. Nearly two thirds of the primary-school children were out of school in Chiapas.[6] These were among the most under-developed of Mexican provinces. The other states fell between the extremes of north and south, although some of the central and coastal states, Colima for example, ranked with the bottom group.

Geographic inequalities were complicated by the existence of thousands of tiny rural communities, pinpoints on the map cut off from the world around them. Few of them had schools, and there were none in sight for them. Federal regulations promised schools to communities with more than twenty school-age children; in practice there were usually at least thirty children in a community before a school would be placed there. This left the tiny villages out of the picture. Lowering the number required to qualify for a school, as some proposed, would not have helped, for the federal government had already failed to provide them for the villages covered by the legislation. Leaving the tiny hamlets out of the program neglected the most backward elements, the ones in dire necessity, and in particular the Indian-speaking groups.[7] Since the grade school was the chief institution of learning and the only one available to nearly all of rural Mexico, its absence boded disaster for the future. Isolated from the halls of learning, the great mass of rural people had no contact with the attitudes, skills, and information demanded by modern nations.

All of these figures, estimates, and implications were turned topsy-turvy by the growth of the Mexican population. Mexico had less than 15 million souls in 1921 (a decline of 1 million from 1910), fewer than 20 million in 1940, but around 35 million in 1960. Not only was the population multiplying rapidly in recent years; it was growing at the highest rate in the world.[8] There were approximately 1 million more Mexicans each year.[9] While this population increase, as Ramón

[6]Ibid., I, 30.

[7]*El Nacional*, Jan. 10, 1959.

[8]Antonio Enríquez Savignac, "Un problema," *El Universal*, Aug. 11, 1959.

[9]*Excelsior*, Sept. 2, 1958.

Beteta surmised, reflected better standards of health and improved living conditions, it posed a gigantic educational problem.[10] Every twelve months, the Senate was told by officials of the Ministry of Education, there were an additional half-million children without classrooms.[11] At this rate the schools faced defeat unless some miracle remedy was discovered, either to halt the population boom or to find ways and means to keep them growing at a pace with the people.

Getting the school population to register for class was one problem; keeping the students in the classroom was another. On a national average, out of every hundred students who entered the first grade, only thirteen finished the sixth. Another one fourth completed less than two years. Of those finishing six years only 2 per cent, Manuel Gómez Morín, chief of the conservative *Partido de Acción Nacional* (PAN), charged, had the possibility of entering a secondary or vocational school.[12] Among those who finished any one year of primary school, few went on to the next grade. During 1952-1957, Gallo Martínez reported, more than 30 per cent of the school group failed their final examinations. If dropouts were added to this figure, just 60 per cent of the school registration completed the year and passed on to the next grade. Put in different terms, four out of every ten pupils either dropped out or failed their studies. (These figures covered only children up to twelve years of age. Mexican law required schooling to age fourteen.) Calculated in monetary losses, the federal government, states, and municipalities were wasting nearly 160 million pesos annually on failures and dropouts, more than a fourth of what they spent on primary education in 1957.[13]

On the rural front, dropouts and failures represented a calamity. School casualties were unbelievably high in rural municipalities. In San Luis Acatlán, Guerrero, for instance, out of a total school-age population of 8,184 in 1958, just 20 completed the sixth grade; of the 1,385 who registered for classes, 973 received promotions at the end of the year. Of the 9,818 children of school age in Chiconautla, Mexico, 8,001 registered for classes, 7,459 attended, 5,408 went on to the next grade, but only 117 finished six years. In Teotihuacán, Mexico, just a few miles out of Mexico City, where the ancient Mexicans had erected the pyramids to the sun and moon, 97 pupils completed six years of schooling out of a registration of 3,128. Of a school-age

[10]*Pensamiento y dinámica de la revolución*, p. 246.

[11]*El Nacional*, Nov. 13, 1958.

[12]*Excelsior*, Dec. 4, 1958.

[13]Gallo Martínez, I, 26.

group of 4,497 in Comalapa, Chiapas, 46 finished the sixth grade; 2,570 had registered for school. Umán, Yucatán, reported 28 pupils completing the sixth grade, out of a school population of 3,430; nearly 1,000 pupils had dropped classes during the year. Moving northward, in Jiquilpan, Michoacán, birthplace of Lázaro Cárdenas, 2,686 students finished the rural-school year out of a school-age group of 8,500; of those finishing, 133 completed the sixth grade. In Magdalena, Sonora, a municipality in a border state, 17 students completed the sixth grade, out of a registration of 1,719.[14]

Nearly all explanations for this large number of dropouts and failures, experts agreed, could be traced to one overriding cause: the poverty of the countryside.[15] With some exceptions, the municipalities and provinces plagued by these failings represented the most underdeveloped regions of Mexico. As an editorial in *El Nacional* (December 18, 1952) emphasized, parents in these areas simply could not afford to send their offspring to school. They were needed at home to help support the family, a condition made worse by the inability of the father to provide them with the clothes, textbooks, and materials required for school. The child who completed his schooling was the exceptional case. This situation would persist until the breadwinner had an adequate income, George F. Kneller warned (p. 86).

Other factors aggravated the harm done by poverty. Sickness and disease in rural Mexico cut into school attendance and performance. Millions of youngsters lived on minimal diets, which impaired their health, drained their energy, and limited their capacity for study. As Narciso Bassols wisely recognized, a hungry Indian makes a poor scholar. In addition, there were the frequent civil and religious festivals in the communities, which kept the children out of school for days on end; nearly half of the school calendar was wasted in this way or on unexpected closings of the school. Limited classroom space and a scarcity of teachers kept others at home. Also, poor teachers discouraged attendance. The isolation of countless villages cut additional school-age groups off from neighboring schools. Parental indifference to the value of learning worsened the picture.[16]

Failures at the grade-school level had a detrimental effect on national literacy goals. In spite of fifteen years of each-one-teach-one programs, the number of persons unable to read and write in 1960 was higher than ever before. The schools had not kept pace with the

[14]Data furnished by the Secretaría de Educación Pública.

[15]José Flores Magón, "El problema más grave de México continúa siendo el de la educación del pueblo," *El Nacional*, Nov. 11, 1958.

[16]Gallo Martínez, I, 34.

problem, Chávez Orozco declared. If half of the school-age children were not in school and hundreds of thousands failed their classroom examinations, Mexico would never master the alphabet. While officials in Mexico City placed illiteracy at 35 per cent, there was ample reason to believe that this figure was too low. Even top officials of the each-one-teach-one campaign privately conceded that 45 per cent was a more accurate figure. Illiteracy in the predominantly rural provinces ran much higher.[17] Chiapas had nearly twice as many illiterates as persons able to read and write; Guerrero had more than twice as many. More than six out of every ten natives of Hidalgo were illiterate. For the 421,289 individuals who knew how to read and write in Oaxaca, 715,840 did not.[18] If literacy was taken as an index of modernization and cultural growth—and it was by the Ministry of Education—then Mexico had reason for alarm.

Glaring deficiencies had appeared elsewhere. From a small and compact organization the Ministry of Education had developed into a colossus. With it had come an unwieldly bureaucracy. Critics believed that the Ministry had grown beyond the ability of one man to supervise. Many former advocates of centralization now called for greater local autonomy. Another group of critics felt that the leadership in the Ministry had declined in recent years.[19] Teachers in particular lamented that no teacher had risen to command the Ministry, which they believed called for a man with a background in education. Recent heads had represented nearly every other profession. Nor had honesty always won converts among the leadership of the house that Vasconcelos built on Calle Argentina; corruption at the top filtered down to the rank and file. This was not to deny that scores of able and honest officials labored until far into the night with the dedication of Sáenz and Ramírez.

A particular weakness lay at the supervisory level. A system of inspectors over the schools in the provinces had long been established. These inspectors, whose forerunners were Vasconcelos' missionaries, were the link between Mexico City and the village school, often carrying the responsibility for the success or failure of the school on their shoulders. Former teachers themselves, these men had won victories where their teachers had failed. Mario Aguilera Dorante, chief of the Republic's provincial primary schools, himself a former missionary and inspector and one of the selfless leaders in the Ministry

[17] New York *Times,* Jan. 18, 1959.

[18] Dir. Gral. de Estadística, *Anuario estadístico de los Estados Unidos Mexicanos,* 1957, p. 48.

[19] Mendoza Rivera, "Honda crisis," p. 247.

of Education, recounts innumerable episodes of victory snatched
from defeat by some able inspector who arrived just when the village
had decided not to finish the school or had rejected some program.
These early inspectors were largely responsible for the success of the
rural school in the twenties and thirties. Without them even the
Sáenzes and Ramírezes would have failed. Unhappily for Mexico,
these crusading figures disappeared from the scene with the passing
of the Cárdenas regime. The inspectors had changed greatly from
the men of former years, Aguilera Dorante emphasized. Although
there were able men left, a majority were not doing their job. Rather
than combat the unhealthy conditions they were supposed to eliminate, many inspectors had succumbed to temptation, refusing to
leave urban offices for the discomforts of the rural village, journeying
out to the countryside only occasionally, and even joining hands with
the local *acaparador*. The victims of their neglect were the teachers,
who needed guidance and encouragement from the top.

Various ills sabotaged the activity of the Republic's inspectors.
Scores had grown old in a job that still called for a man with the ability to ride a horse all day and arrive fresh in a village where inspiration and leadership were needed. A third of the inspectors were between fifty-five and sixty-five years of age, and nearly 40 per cent
were between ages forty-six and fifty-five. Young and enthusiastic
leaders had occupied these posts in the twenties and thirties, until the
rise of the teachers' syndicates elevated seniority above ability. By
1962 age rather than youth, opportunism instead of selfless dedication to ideals, dominated the ranks of the inspectors. A large number
of those selected were cronies of political officeholders, lacking the
background for the job. Errors in appointments were aggravated by
the practice of sending men from the region they knew best to
strange zones where they had to learn their duties in a hit-and-miss
manner. Most of them were overworked, having as many as five hundred teachers to supervise. Like those under them, the inspectors were
poorly paid, often earning less than secondary schoolteachers in the
cities.

Equally harmful to the total picture were the gyrations school policy had taken since 1921. In the early years emphasis had been given
to changing the environment rather than to combating illiteracy.
Even Vasconcelos and the conservatives recognized the wisdom of
this view. "Reading, writing, arithmetic, and the other branches of
knowledge," wrote Jorge Vera Estañol (p. 36), were "not ends in
themselves but, rather, means towards reaching . . . economic, civic
and moral ends." Despite some shifts of emphasis, this was the philos-

ophy of the rural school until the forties, when the school fell back on the routine and practice of bookwork and memorization. During the regime of Avila Camacho, the banners of the School of Action and Manuel Gamio's integral education fell by the wayside.[20] "When I visit the village," confessed Rafael Ramírez to a conference of teachers in 1945, "hoping to find our rural school, to stop and speak with it, it is difficult to locate it." Something had happened to it, he concluded. If he asked the neighbors about it, "Ah yes," he was told, "you are speaking of that school that the people built themselves in order to learn from it how to live better. It has been a long time since we have seen it, but now that you remind us of it, we can tell you that it was wonderful and good." When "I looked at the agenda for this meeting," Ramírez continued, "I was painfully surprised to learn that even our leaders had not reserved for our rural school that special place to which it had a right, but had included it with all of the others."[21]

Ramírez' lament was a simple one. Rather than a school attuned to the daily necessities of the rural population, two thirds of Mexico, the school had become a poor imitation of the urban classroom, out of touch with reality, divorced from the land, race, and economic character of the rural community.[22] Unless the school was prepared to aid the peasant to raise his level of life, however, it would find little support or sympathy in the village. The peasant had scant respect for the school of the three R's, for his life in the village demanded technical skills rather than book culture.[23] As Kneller recognized (p. 99), Mexico's education had to be terminal, not a preparation for higher learning, but rather a place to master the indispensable skills for developing productive attitudes and techniques.

By rejecting these principles, in practice if not completely in theory, the concept of school leadership had also perished. Implicit in this view was the acceptance of the school as a political institution. As Luis Alvarez Barret has written, the Mexican school could not remain an impartial observer, concerned only with principles in the abstract sense. The school, he said, had to wage a militant battle in behalf of those it would benefit, for its obligation was to prepare men

[20]Pedro de Alba, "Prólogo," in García Ruiz, *Hombres y rutas de México*, p. xiii.

[21]Sindicato Nacional de Trabajadores de la Educación, *Conferencia pedagógica*, p. 241.

[22]Carlos Villarriel Castillo, "Consideraciones sociológicas sobre la educación en México," *El Nacional*, Nov. 24, 1958.

[23]Isidro Castillo, "Actitud del magisterio," *Problemas educativos de México*, I (May 1958), 25.

to live better. This put the school in conflict with the exploiters of the village. If the school was to serve the people, as the Ministry of Education proclaimed, Alvarez Barret persisted, then it could not hide from the economic, social, and political struggles raging in rural Mexico.[24] By 1960 this concept of Alvarez Barret had fallen from grace. To the new leaders the good school stayed free of political questions and left economic difficulties to others.[25]

Vacillation had come at another point. At Carapan, Sáenz recognized that lack of perseverance was undermining much of what the school had set out to do. When it came to formulating *proyectos*, blueprints of grandiose works, Mexicans excelled, but these efforts never got very far, he confessed.[26] School policy had often failed, not for want of a workable plan but in the absence of tenacity of purpose. Vasconcelos' legislation had provided the foundations for a sound program, which the changes of 1934 and the forties had only weakened. By 1960 much of Article 3 lay inoperative or forgotten. In the twenties and thirties federal policy had stressed primary education, on the assumption that the needs of the majority were greater. Without eliminating the need for primary schools, the architects of the forties and fifties favored professional schools and particularly the technical demands of industry. Out of the varied educational experiments had come a multitude of patterns often in conflict with each other, which the Ministry never equalized or coordinated.[27] By the forties methodology had superseded content in a school that once prided itself on its freedom from traditional practices.[28]

In addition, schools varied a great deal; some were excellent, and others offered next to nothing. As Henrik F. Infield and Koka Freier observed in *People in Ejidos*, the good schools looked alive even during vacation time. "Although the school stood empty," they wrote of one such school, "there were no signs of neglect. The classrooms were clean and friendly, with solid, comfortable desks and benches, and the usual maps and pictures on the white washed walls." This school accommodated all of the children on the local *ejido* and some from a neighboring community.[29] They contrasted this scene with

[24]"La función política de la escuela," *Revista mexicana de educación*, I (Aug. 1940), 12-14.

[25]José Angel Ceniceros, *Nuestra constitución política y la educación mexicana* (Mexico, 1955), p. 38.

[26]*Carapan: Bosquejo de una experiencia*, p. 303.

[27]Kneller, p. 83.

[28]Vicente Lombardo Toledano, *Una ojeada a la crisis*, p. 18.

[29]*People in Ejidos: A Visit to the Cooperative Farms of Mexico* (New York, 1954), p. 109.

that of a school in the Mezquital where, despite the impressiveness of the outside, the classroom "looked unfinished and dilapidated. The floor was of clay, the paint on the walls and the ceiling had peeled off long ago leaving ugly blotches here and there." There was dust and dirt everywhere. Furniture and decorations consisted of a crude anatomic drawing, a map of Mexico, and "a heavy, crazily-slanted sheet of wallboard which, supported by two uneven rough-hewn wooden horses, obviously served as a desk." Three old and tattered books represented the library.[30] Few observers denied that the school of the Mezquital, rather than the model on the *ejido* described by Infield and Freier, characterized a majority of the Republic's schools in 1962. This and similar schools would teach their pupils very little.

Poor physical conditions, teacher and community apathy, weakness of leadership, and flabbiness of ideals and goals handicapped learning in the classroom, particularly since a majority of rural schools offered only two or three grades of work. Schooling in the primary grades was divided into three cycles of two years each. The main content of the total program was included in each, amplified or intensified from one cycle to another, giving the child a terminal education after two, four, or six years. Since most rural schools had three grades or less, their pupils completed one cycle at best.[31] On this basis, the schools had changed little from the twenties; the pressure of time still confined their students to a cursory glance at the three R's. There were about twenty children in the first grade, ten in the second, and fifteen in grades three to six, where these grades were available. Most rural schools had only one classroom and one teacher, so classes were large and varied and difficult to teach. Little effort was made to separate the students by aptitude and ages, particularly since attendance was irregular. Schools of this type did not always prepare their students well. A conversation between Infield and Freier and a group of youths between fourteen and fifteen years of age tells the story. All of the children had been to school, but when asked if they knew how to read and write, their answer was an embarrassed: "Muy poco"—very little, or not at all. Infield and Freier asked the brighter ones why this was so. "We start going to school only at eleven," they replied, "and we quit soon. It's for three years only, that's all there is."[32]

This failure of the rural school threatened the future of reform in Mexico. Leadership was indispensable; only individuals who visu-

[30]Ibid., pp. 41-42.
[31]"Panorama educacional," *Excelsior*, Dec. 8, 1958.
[32]Infield and Freier, p. 104.

alized a new future could offer it. The average peasant lived in the past and saw only the present; there was no different tomorrow for him. The progress of the rural community, and particularly the success or failure of the *ejido*, to cite the testimony of Infield and Freier (p. 122), "depended, at least within certain limits, not only on external factors, but on the presence or absence of congenial leadership." In judging two *ejidos* in the Laguna, located in the same area, with similar lands and resources and populated by the same kind of people, one successful and the other characterized by "apathy, inefficiency, and unrelieved want," Infield and Freier (p. 113) concluded that among the several factors explaining these differences, the decisive one was "leadership or the lack of it." The prosperous *ejido* had it; the other did not. Able leadership required training and preparation that, judging from the difficulties that plagued the small village *ejidos*, the rural school was not providing.

III

Two overriding difficulties lay behind Mexico's crisis in rural education. One was the insufficiency of the federal budget; national income never covered all of the Republic's needs. Equally old and traditional was the backwardness of the rural scene. These two factors, above all others, helped to explain Mexico's current predicament.

Almost every Mexican ruler since 1921 had allotted an increasing amount of the public revenue to schools. From 21.9 million pesos in 1923 the school budget had swelled to nearly 1.5 billion by 1959. Despite this respectable increase, however, the gains had not kept pace with spending.[33] Recent budgets, although mounting in pesos, indicate a decline in relation to total national spending, particularly during the years of Miguel Alemán. Vasconcelos' expenditures for 1923 represented a larger percentage of the total than did Alemán's in 1950. School funds, in addition, were used for other purposes; the Miguel Alemán hospital in Mexico City was constructed with school money, to cite a case in point.[34] Cárdenas' ideal of setting aside one fifth of the national revenue for education, which many felt was a minimum, had not been achieved since the years 1936 and 1937. While gross per capita expenditures had gone up, from 57 cents in 1910 to 20.70 pesos for primary schools alone in 1957, benefits were minimized by the rising cost of living and a chronic inflation. The

[33]*El Nacional*, Nov. 4, 1958.
[34]*El Nacional*, Nov. 18, 1952.

devaluation of the peso in Alemán's time curtailed its buying power even more. What this meant was that money earmarked for schools had not matched needs. Between 1952 and 1957 average yearly expenditures represented 58.28 per cent of what was needed.[35]

Monetary deficiencies on the rural school front were equally apparent. Approximately 80 per cent of the public elementary schools, with almost half of the national enrollment, were rural. About 70 per cent were federal, the states and municipalities controlled another 24 per cent, and the rest were supported either by private groups or jointly by private and public funds. Unequivocally, the grade schools represented the leading activity numerically of the federal program in education. More persons depended upon the central government for their primary schooling than for any other type. In the face of this, rural education had consistently gotten the smallest share of the public funds. To illustrate this point: of the money given the Ministry in 1925 only a third, 10 million pesos, went to rural education.[36] Money for all primary schools, rural and urban, represented one fifth of the national school budget in 1958.[37] José Luis Martínez, a member of the Chamber of Deputies from Jalisco, declared that the sum set aside for 1959 represented a third of what was required.[38]

Compared to what schools of other types received, the disproportion was striking. Higher education in 1954 had nearly half of the school budget.[39] Between 1952 and 1957, Gallo Martínez reports (I, 40), primary schools in the Federal District received more than a fourth of the funds earmarked for primary education in the entire Republic. At the secondary level the disproportion was even more striking. Next favored were the provinces nearest the capital, although this was not always so. Though tremendous sums were devoted to rural services, as Robert E. Scott stressed (p. 71), in relation to what was needed, much more was spent in urban areas and on industrial programs. Rural Mexico, he concluded, represented the "classical example of the ineffectual position in the political process of large numbers of unaware, unorganized, and unintegrated people in competition with much smaller but politically acute and organized groups."

[35]Gallo Martínez, I, 40.

[36]Gruening, "Emerging Mexico," p. 685.

[37]*Excelsior*, Sept. 3, 1959.

[38]*El Nacional*, Dec. 28, 1958.

[39]Domingo Tirado Benedí, *Problemas de la educación mexicana* (Mexico, 1955), p. 55.

Confronted with the rising demands imposed upon it by the fifties, the Ministry's effort had lagged behind needs. Pleading financial inability to keep abreast of the worsening picture, officials in Mexico City had concentrated on keeping the situation from getting completely out of hand. Nothing was done to eliminate basic deficiencies. Guillermo Ibarra, senator from Sonora, acknowledged that each year the resources of the federal branch were less able to satisfy new demands. Much of the problem, he indicated, rose out of the growing population.[40] Already touched upon in relation to other questions, this population explosion was particularly vexing in monetary terms. Like all developing and underdeveloped countries, Mexico had a large percentage of children compared to older groups. Children in the school years represented more than one fourth of the population of the Republic. (France and Sweden had less than one fifth of their population in this category.) School costs, therefore, were proportionately higher in underdeveloped countries like Mexico, which were less able to cope with them. Unable to keep pace with the growing population, Mexico had a larger number of schoolless children each year. By 1964—to stress the implications of this dilemma—Mexico will have 10 million children of school age, 2 million more than in 1960.

Inequalities and deficiencies on the educational scene would persist, admonished Torres Bodet, until every Mexican accepted his share of the responsibility. No matter how urgent was the cooperation of private individuals and groups, however, the burden of education had to rest with the government of Mexico. Public education was a social responsibility, as the Constitution stated specifically. Abdicating this responsibility held grave perils for the future of the Republic, the Senate was warned by Celerino Cano, a prominent educator.[41] Accepting it, on the other hand, called for increased funds. Where would the money come from? It could not be raised without wholesale changes on the national and local scene and sacrifices on the part of those who had contributed almost nothing until now.

A beginning, observers felt, could be made by a wiser use of funds available. Something like three fourths of the 1959 school budget went to teachers' salaries; less than 6 per cent covered expansion of facilities; equipment, supplies, and maintenance got an additional 4 per cent; administrative expenses ate up the rest. The monetary pie, declared Torres Bodet, was cut poorly, allowing little room for ex-

[40]*El Nacional*, Oct. 22, 1958.
[41]*El Nacional*, Nov. 11, 1958.

pansion.[42] Politics permitting, changes were possible, nonetheless. At least 3,000 teachers, officials in the Ministry conceded, were on commissions, drawing salaries unrelated to teaching. Many of them had received their commissions, scholarships to do nothing in some cases, through the influence of union leaders. By putting these teachers back in the classroom, the Ministry would have solved the teacher shortage in the capital and other urban centers and released funds for rural programs. Torres Bodet attempted to revoke these commissions in 1959, but syndical pressures sabotaged his good intentions. At the administrative level, the Ministry was top-heavy. This bureaucracy, the greatest in Mexico, was badly in need of pruning. Reorganization was not a new suggestion; many had offered it before. Nothing had been done, among other reasons, because the unions fought it and because any savings would have brought congressional slashes of the school budget. Inertia was another barrier. So many diverse groups were involved, all with interests at stake, that nothing moved. Changes in building practices would also have helped. Instead of showplaces for the tourists and the middle class, smaller and less expensive schools were called for.

Savings were possible on another front. In 1959 Defense had a budget nearly half that of schools, in a country where the army was a luxury. This was not a new problem but one dating back to Vasconcelos and before him. Vast sums were spent on weapons, munitions, and equipment that could buy books and supplies, now the responsibility of impoverished parents. If half of the money set aside for the military had been spent on schools and teachers' salaries, Mexico could have taken a giant stride toward extricating itself from its educational predicament.

Dividing the financial burden of the rural schools equitably among the provinces would have helped, too. Instead, the lion's share of the costs fell upon the shoulders of the central government. Of the 20.70 pesos spent per capita on all primary schools in 1957, the federal share was 12.09 pesos. For their part, the provinces contributed 4.55 pesos on the average. Semiofficial sources gave another 2.16 pesos, and private enterprise 1.90 pesos. There were no stipulations, however, as to what share of the cost should fall upon the individual states. Some, therefore, gave very little. Hidalgo contributed 1.49 per cent of its budget; Aguascalientes, 5.29 per cent; Campeche, 4.08 per cent. Yucatán, on the other hand, offered 27.30 per cent, yet faced a chronic deficiency of schools for lack of funds.[43] Economic underdevelop-

[42]*El Nacional,* Dec. 7, 1958.
[43]Gallo Martínez, I, 48, 44-45.

ment was the explanation. Yucatán did not have the income required by its educational needs and would not have until wealthier provinces faced their responsibilities, releasing federal funds for the poorer states.

The new landed gentry, and the wealthy in general, were equally guilty of shirking their responsibilities. Numerous congressmen called for the enforcement of Article 123, almost inoperative since the days of Bassols and Cárdenas.[44] Thousands of business and agricultural corporations had failed to establish schools for the children of their workers. Others suggested enlarging the geographical scope of educational responsibility beyond the three-kilometer radius marked out by the legislation. In return for the various tax concessions, subsidies, and special tariffs offered business and large-scale agriculture since World War II, the additional price demanded of them was small by comparison. While the Republic's school structure faced disaster, a new class of rich had won fabulous profits, paying almost nothing in income taxes. It was time, critics alleged, for effective income tax legislation based on ability to pay. There was no better place to use the additional revenue than on public services, of which education was one. Since countless wealthy Mexicans purchased millions in luxury goods, it seemed sensible to tax these products, as the United States did. Mexico had a special development bank for industry: why not establish a similar one for education, asked Cano.[45]

Budget reforms, fiscal changes, and the enforcement of existing legislation would help temporarily. Meeting the difficulties head on called for a reappraisal of the total economic picture and particularly of agrarian policy. Mexico, despite its mushrooming cities and new factories, was still predominantly a rural country. Social problems, as Howard Cline recognized (p. 73), were fundamentally rural problems. Of the approximately 35 million Mexicans in 1960, two thirds lived in villages. More than half of the economically active population farmed for a living, raised livestock, or fished the lakes and coastal waters; an estimated 3 million artisans labored at least part time at the same crafts that had amazed the Spanish conquerors. A bare 1.2 million of the economically active population was employed in industry. Despite some gains during recent years, the benefits of industrialization had not trickled down to these rural groups. A majority of them lived as before. As Selden Rodman noted, the prosperity of the towns merely magnified the rural poverty around them.

[44]*El Nacional*, Oct. 22, 1958.
[45]*El Nacional*, Nov. 4, 1958.

Mexico's unbalanced economic structure, which sabotaged the efforts of the rural school, threatened even the world of the industrialists. Approximately half of the population farmed for a living but received only one fifth of the national income; 86 per cent of the population earned less than 300 pesos a month, 44 per cent less than 100 pesos. About a third of the population ate no wheat bread, wore homemade sandals, or went barefoot. Candles, alcoholic drinks, and fireworks were the staples of the Indian community. Countless communities had no hardware stores, no furniture stores, no places selling books, shoes, radios, implements, or drugs. What passed for village grocery stores carried salt, sugar, matches, rice, cigarettes, soap, canned salmon, chilies, and candy. Items of clothing for sale on the market consisted mainly of straw hats, *rebozos*, thread, buttons, ribbon, and earrings.[46] These were the symbols of a village economy that lived from day to day; poverty was its trademark. The *bracero* movement offered stark testimony that all was not well. If the lure of adventure had taken some Mexicans north, poverty and the lack of opportunity drove millions of others into Texas and California in search of what Mexico denied them. "When before in history," asked Carleton Beals, "has such a vast exodus occurred from a country with a labor shortage, an ever-expanding industry and the earmarks of prosperity?"[47]

Rural poverty, starkly manifested in the almost nonexistent purchasing power of the peasantry, undermined the entire economic structure. Mexico's new industries needed markets. Not finding buyers at home, they turned to foreign trade and particularly to the United States. This, Beals emphasized (p. 134), was dangerous and unhealthy, making Mexico's prosperity nearly wholly dependent upon conditions in the United States. To correct this situation, to have a virile and autonomous native industry, protested Jesús Silva Herzog, it was imperative that the peasant have buying power.[48] There could be no sound industrial development, added Antonio Díaz Soto y Gama, without prosperous small farms and *ejidos*. Recent administrations, he lamented, had neglected this elementary fact. Manufacturers had received encouragement of every type, including abundant credit; but the needs of the small farmer had been generally overlooked. While prices of domestic manufactured products rose, rural income did not. Díaz Soto y Gama concluded that much industrial

[46]Townsend, p. 323.

[47]"Mexico's Bonanza," *American Mercury*, LXXXVIII (Jan. 1959), 133.

[48]*El agrarismo mexicano*, p. 572.

expansion rested on the shoulders of those least able to support it.[49] These allegations, with some modifications, were repeated by scores of other observers of the rural scene, among them the chief of López Mateo's national Agrarian Department.[50]

If these views were justified, how could this picture be corrected? Silva Herzog offered two remedies, inextricably bound to each other. Before anything else was done, it was necessary to eliminate the evils that still plagued the rural scene; effective legislation and economic reforms were essential. The difficulties would not be overcome, however, without enlightened and trained farmers able, through a dynamic program of rural education, to take advantage of the reforms. The remedies suggested were not novel but were based on principles harking back to the Revolution. Cárdenas had built his program around them. The new landed gentry, which had risen to prominence with Alemán's revision of Article 27 in 1946, had simply overlooked them, Silva Herzog declared.[51] Like the *hacendados* of old, the new landowners were blind to the inequalities around them. Seeking to expand their holdings, they had done little to correct the mistakes of past policies, which had divided the great estates into microscopic personal plots that offered their owners marginal rewards. Burdened with small, unproductive pieces of land and denied the credit and leadership that might have provided the tools, fertilizers, and techniques necessary to eliminate antiquated farming methods on many of these lands, the average peasant struggled on as before.[52]

Partly responsible for this picture was the failure of leaders in Mexico to furnish an effective educational program. Without the knowledge, techniques, and leadership required to transform the peasant into an efficient farmer, even the good lands remained unproductive. Yet, as Frank Tannenbaum recognized, there could be no effective rural school so long as the peasants lacked land. Its feasibility and its success, he asserted, depended upon the village having land. "In other words," he wrote, "the fulfillment of the educational program of the Revolution will depend upon the fulfillment of the agrarian program. The first becomes impossible without the second and the second becomes only half useful if it lacks a school." Only a school reflecting community needs, however, could "make its *ejido* serve those broad

[49]"Necesario equilíbrio entre la agricultura y la industria," *El Universal*, Dec. 17, 1958.

[50]Teodoro Hernández, "El problema agrario obligado antecedente de la industrialización," *El Universal*, April 26, 1959.

[51]*Excelsior*, Aug. 5, 1959.

[52]Antonio Gazol Santafé, "El crédito al campo," *El Nacional*, Feb. 1, 1959.

ends which lie embedded in the Revolution itself," he added. "They are both parts of the same aspirations, the rejuvenation of the rural community."[53] As Ramón Beteta had stated back in the thirties, no matter how new the school or how modern the teaching methods, they were wasted "unless our masses have the necessary economic means and the free time to avail themselves of the new educational facilities."[54] It was equally self-evident that the rural school would bring no cultural growth to communities that lived on the margin of life and death. Nor would democratic principles, so much a part of the propaganda of recent Mexican leadership, thrive under the conditions that characterized rural Mexico in 1962.

Failure to recognize this relationship explained the collapse of much of what the rural school had attempted previously. Bassols and Cárdenas had seen this connection clearly; failure to implement it fully had limited the success of their school. Recent administrations, however, had virtually ignored it. If the present *ejidos* were a disappointment to some, part of the blame rested with a policy that shunned furnishing credit and encouragement, and even schools, to them. According to Bernardo Cobos, a schoolteacher member of the Mexican Confederation of Workers (CTM), there were fewer schools on the *ejidos* in 1958 than two decades before.[55] Because of a policy that de-emphasized the practical side of learning, thousands of school farms lay idle or were cultivated by private groups. Amidst the rising cost of living little had been done by rural schoolmasters to help the peasants organize themselves into cooperatives. There was almost no other defense against the *acaparador* or the evils that afflicted farmers on lands too small for the individual purchase of modern equipment or supplies.[56] The cooperative had floundered in the thirties, but there was nothing wrong with the idea that sensible and understanding leadership would not eliminate. Perhaps, too, it was the hopelessness of rural life that helped to explain the failure of parents and communities to take advantage of what schooling Mexico offered. If the average schoolmaster had been assigned a responsible role in bringing about basic change in the community, he might not have deserted his calling for other pursuits.

Mexico's difficulties on the rural scene would not be solved overnight or simply with more money and new legislation. To change age-

[53]*Peace by Revolution*, p. 303.

[54]*Economic and Social Program*, p. 210.

[55]*El Nacional*, Nov. 13, 1958.

[56]Luis Chávez Orozco, "¿Más agrarismo o mayor equidad con el campesino?" *Excelsior*, July 1, 1959.

old habits required goodwill, dedicated and wise effort, and time. The average peasant, even more than his neighbors in the cities and towns, had not learned the value of persistence and cooperation. Centuries of suffering had inured him to his own hardships and to those of others. "He can see his neighbors or even close relatives in dire want without lifting a hand to help them," wrote William Cameron Townsend (p. 156), a Protestant missionary with years of experience on the Mexican scene. Attitudes of this type made the *ejido*, the cooperative, and reform in general difficult to implant successfully. On the political side, the training of the peasant to handle his political affairs raised countless obstacles. Despite the legends of community spirit in rural Mexico, it was an uphill battle to get the peasant to participate in community affairs. Some clever individual managed usually to surround himself with a faction and then proceeded to rule the disorganized and uninterested majority. Indifference frustrated even the best of intentions, as Townsend's account (p. 327) of Cárdenas' well-meaning gift of livestock to the village of Tetelcingo underlines. Cárdenas had sent pigs, and his spokesmen had raffled them off. One winner refused a sow because it was too big. Another took his home, but the sow died unexpectedly, and no one could explain why. A few days later the neighborhood was invited to a feast, where pork was served. The schoolteachers took the rejected sow home, but it died when the caretaker forgot to feed it during their vacation. Still one boar survived, and now there are better pigs in the community.

This was not to deny the possibility of transforming rural attitudes and customs. Much had been accomplished already in this direction. What was clearly implied was that initial leadership in behalf of change and the subsequent close supervision necessary had to come from the world outside of the village. Since the school was representative of the outside world in the community, much of the responsibility for leadership lay with it. But the school alone could not provide the essential impetus. Encouragement from the top was needed, encouragement that would not materialize until privileged groups had developed a sense of social responsibility. Without minimizing other barriers, perhaps the indifference of society to the plight of the countryside was the greatest hurdle confronting the rural school. On patriotic holidays spellbinding orators extolled the virtues of ancient Mexico and the qualities of Juárez and Zapata, announcing that they were of Indian descent. Once the day was over, the village was forgotten. During the war Cárdenas, then chief of national defense, accused authorities of drafting only the sons of peasants into the army.

In Oaxaca there were rumors that only Indians were taken by the military. Numberless municipalities compelled the peasants to work for them, despite provisions in the Constitution forbidding this sort of labor. During recent literacy campaigns housewives in Mexico City refused to teach their servants to read and write on the grounds that the servants had no need for literacy. Newsreels depicting the suffering of war-torn Europe were the topic of conversation at fashionable bars and country clubs; few of the patrons concerned themselves with poverty and starvation in the Mezquital. Before an economic and social system could make the rural school effective, this indifference had to disappear.

To revive the faith of the people in their rural school was also imperative. This would be done by making it of use to them. New agrarian reforms were necessary in order to do this. A beginning, to cite Silva Herzog, would be to revise Alemán's legislation, once again opening large tracts of privately owned land to expropriation, particularly in the new irrigation districts where a few influential friends of former presidents had taken over.[57] Modifications in past patterns of land distribution had to come, too, lest mistakes be repeated. To avoid breaking up the land into plots too small to farm efficiently, Silva Herzog suggested creating more of the collective *ejidos* established by Cárdenas in the Laguna and elsewhere; these had prospered while others had failed. Where the land was kept together in large tracts, modern agricultural practices were feasible.[58] Unless the farmer sold his products on the regional or national market, which he could not do without roads, no amount of land would benefit him. Even fertile lands required water for irrigation and healthy farmers to till the soil. These came with a system of small, inexpensive-to-build dams and rural medical facilities. Some of these things were being provided, but many of the benefits had not reached the small village, where the needs were greatest.

I V

Despite past mistakes and the lack of vision of recent years, the picture was not hopeless. Much had been accomplished since Vasconcelos' crusade of the early twenties. Only a handful of schools served the villages of the sixteenth century. There were virtually no schools in 1820 or under Porfirio Díaz. But in 1960 more than 20,000 federal

[57]*El agrarismo mexicano*, p. 573.

[58]Ibid., p. 572.

rural schools, with more than 2 million students and thousands of teachers, existed in addition to state and municipal rural schools. To say that they were often poorly equipped, understaffed, and neglected did not negate their existence and functioning. Strong inroads had been made on illiteracy. Schools of agriculture, as well as centers to train teachers for the rural schools, had been established. Peasants sent their children to these schools; before 1910 virtually all schools had been closed to such children. An Office of Indian Affairs (although somewhat crippled), a National Indianist Institute, and schools for Indians represented forward steps in providing education for the peasants.

Intangible benefits also could be enumerated. Much of the land distribution of the thirties would not have taken place without the activity of thousands of rural teachers who urged the people to petition for land and then saw to it that they received it. Land brought other benefits. There were the emotional rewards that came with freedom from the *hacendado*, the self-respect that was won even when the soil itself represented marginal economic advantages. Having a school in the village, even a poor one, furnished testimony that life had changed since the days of Díaz, that learning was not the prerogative of the white man and his descendants. These and many other benefits were often more important than material victories. To a great extent, the rural school had made them possible.

Nor was yesterday's reform spirit entirely a matter of history. Within the Ministry an able coterie of twenty to thirty men, grown old in the service of their country's schools, kept intact some of the idealism and perception of the Sáenzes, Ramírezes, and Bassolses and imbued younger men with them. Both President López Mateos and his minister of education, Jaime Torres Bodet, had publicly recognized that a crisis existed on the school front and that emergency measures were called for. An intensive school-building program was under way, and new normal schools were on the drafting boards. Perhaps, as the belated recognition that the small farmer had not shared the fruits of progress indicated, the neglect of rural education was coming to an end. So long as there were thousands of teachers dedicated to their profession, optimism was justified; for the young Mexicans sitting at their feet embodied the hopes of tomorrow.

BIBLIOGRAPHY

OFFICIAL PUBLICATIONS

Departamento de Asuntos Indígenas. *Memorias, corresponden a los períodos del 1º de enero al 31 de agosto de 1936 y 1º de septiembre al 31 de agosto de 1937.* Mexico, 1938.

———. *Memoria . . . 1941-1942.* Mexico, 1942.

———. *Memoria . . . 1942-1943.* Mexico, 1943.

———. *Memoria . . . 1943-1944.* Mexico, 1944.

———. *Memoria . . . 1944-1945.* Mexico, 1945.

———. *Memoria . . . 1945-1946 y síntesis de su labor en el sexenio 1940-1946.* Mexico, 1946.

Departamento de Enseñanza Agrícola. *Escuelas prácticas de agricultura.* Mexico, 1946.

Departamento de la Estadística Nacional. *Resumen del censo general de habitantes de 30 de noviembre de 1921.* Mexico, 1928.

Dirección General de Asuntos Indígenas. *Reglamentos, instrucciones y disposiciones técnicas y administrativas.* Mexico, 1958.

———. "Trabajos de la Dirección General de Asuntos Indígenas," *Boletín indigenista*, XVII (Dec. 1957).

Dirección General de Enseñanza Normal. *Seis años de labor educativa . . . 1952-1958.* Mexico, 1958.

Dirección General de Estadística. *Anuario estadístico de los Estados Unidos Mexicanos, 1957.* Mexico, 1959.

———. *Quinto censo de población 15 de mayo de 1930: Resumen general.* Mexico, 1934.

———. *6º censo de población 1940: Resumen general.* Mexico, 1943.

Instituto de Alfabetización Indígena. "Actividades del Instituto de Alfabetización Indígena," *Boletín indigenista*, V (Dec. 1945).

———. "El Instituto de Alfabetización en Lenguas Indígenas," ibid., V (June 1945).

Instituto Federal de Capacitación del Magisterio. *Capacitación de los maestros en servicio no titulados.* Mexico, 1959.

Instituto Nacional Indigenista. "Actividades del Instituto Nacional Indigenista en el Centro Coordinador de la Tarahumara, Chihuahua, México," *Boletín indigenista*, XVI (Dec. 1956).

———. "Informe del Instituto Nacional Indigenista: 1955," ibid., XVI (March 1956).

———. "El Instituto Nacional Indigenista en la región Tarahumara," ibid., XV (Dec. 1955).

———. "Sobre el Centro Coordinador Tarahumara de reciente creación," ibid., XII (Sept. 1952).

Partido de la Revolución Mexicana. *Segundo plan sexenal, 1941-1946.* Mexico, 1940.

Partido Nacional Revolucionario. *Plan sexenal de gobierno del Partido Nacional Revolucionario, 1934-1939.* Mexico, 1934.

Secretaría de Educación Pública. *Acción educativa del gobierno federal del 1º de diciembre de 1952 al 31 de agosto de 1954.* Mexico, 1954.

———. *Acción educativa del gobierno federal, 1954-1955.* Mexico, 1955.

———. "Dimensiones y contorno del analfabetismo en México," *Escuela nueva*, I, No. 5 (Oct. 10, 1955).

———. *La educación pública en México, desde el 1º de diciembre de 1934 hasta el 3º de noviembre de 1940.* 3 vols. Mexico, 1941.

———. *La educación rural mexicana y sus proyecciones.* Mexico, 1954.

———. *El esfuerzo educativo en México: La obra del gobierno federal en el ramo de educación pública durante la administración del presidente Plutarco Elías Calles (1924-1928).* 2 vols. Mexico, 1928.

———. *Ley de emergencia que establece la campaña nacional contra el analfabetismo.* Mexico, 1944.

———. *Memoria que indica el estado que guarda el ramo de educación pública el 31 de agosto de 1931.* Mexico, 1931.

———. *Memoria relativa al estado que guarda el ramo de educación pública el 31 de agosto de 1932.* 2 vols. Mexico, 1932.

———. *Memoria relativa al estado que guarda el ramo de educación pública el 31 de agosto de 1933.* 2 vols. Mexico, 1933.

———. *Memoria . . . 1947.* Mexico, 1947.

———. *Memoria . . . 1947-1948.* Mexico, 1948.

———. *Memoria . . . 1948-1949.* Mexico, 1949.

———. *Memoria . . . 1949-1950.* Mexico, 1950.

———. *Las misiones culturales en 1927.* Mexico, 1928.

———. *La obra educativa en el sexenio, 1940-1946.* Mexico, 1946.

———. *6 años de labor educativo: Memoria de la Dirección General de Alfabetización y Educación Extraescolar.* Mexico, 1958.

Secretaría de Gobernación. *Seis años de gobierno al servicio de México, 1934-1940.* Mexico, 1940.

Universidad Nacional de México. *El movimiento educativo en México.* Mexico, 1922.

ARTICLES

Aguirre Beltrán, Gonzalo. Letter to Manuel Gamio, March 6, 1947, *Boletín indigenista*, VII (March 1947).

Alvarez Barret, Luis. "La función política de la escuela," *Revista mexicana de educación*, I (Aug. 1940).

Basauri, Carlos. "El estudio de las lenguas autóctonas, base de pedagogía indígena," *Revista de educación,* I (Aug. 1937).

———. "El problema del bilingüismo y la educación en México," ibid., II (Dec. 1938).

Beals, Carleton. "The Calles Plan," *New Republic,* LXVIII (Sept. 2, 1931).

———. "Mexico's Bonanza," *American Mercury,* LXXXVIII (Jan. 1959).

Bremauntz, Alberto. "Como se hizo la reforma legal implantando la educación socialista," *Revista mexicana de educación,* I (Nov. 1940).

Calverton, Victor F. "Red Rule in Mexico's Schools," *Current History,* XLIII (Dec. 1935).

Calvillo Madrigal, Salvador. "Política agraria," *El Nacional,* Dec. 17, 1952.

Cano, Celerino. "El antecedente filosófico-social," *Revista mexicana de educación,* I (Nov. 1940).

Caso, Alfonso. "Definición del indio y lo indio," *América indígena,* VIII (Oct. 1948).

———. "Informe del Instituto Nacional Indigenista: 1956," *Boletín indigenista,* XVII (June 1957).

Castillo, Ignacio M. del. "La alfabetización en lenguas indígenas: El proyecto tarasco," *América indígena,* V (April 1945).

Castillo, Isidro. "Actitud del magisterio," *Problemas educativos de México,* I (May 1958).

Castillo Penado, Rubén. "Las misiones culturales de México," *Escuela nueva,* I, No. 1 (June 1955).

Castro, Angélica. "El Instituto de Alfabetización para Indígenas Monolíngües," *Boletín indigenista,* IX (March 1949).

———. "El Instituto de Alfabetización para Indígenas Monolíngües," ibid., XI (March 1951).

———. "Mesa redonda sobre el problema del analfabetismo," ibid., XIII (Sept. 1953).

Castro, Carlos Antonio, "La lingüística en el centro coordinador Tzeltal-Tzotzil," *América indígena,* XVI (April 1956).

Chávez Orozco, Luis. "¿Más agrarismo o mayor equidad con el campesino?" *Excelsior,* July 1, 1959.

Comas, Juan. "Informe con motivo de la visita realizada al Patrimonio Indígena del Valle del Mezquital," *Boletín indigenista,* XVI (Dec. 1956).

Díaz Cárdenas, León. "Crítica panorámica y sintética de las actividades educativas en el pasado sexenio," *Revista mexicana de educación,* I (Nov. 1940).

Díaz Soto y Gama, Antonio. "Necesario equilíbrio entre la agricultura y la industria," *El Universal,* Dec. 17, 1958.

Enríquez Savignac, Antonio. "Un problema," *El Universal,* Aug. 11, 1959.

Esquivel Casas, Aureliano. "El problema de las escuelas de las comunidades indígenas," *El Nacional,* April 21, 1949.

————. "Temas de educación indígena, enseñanza de la lengua nacional," *Revista mexicana de educación,* I (Oct. 1940).

Flores Magón, José. "El problema más grave de México continúa siendo el de la educación del pueblo," *El Nacional,* Nov. 11, 1958.

Fuente, Julio de la. "Ocho años de experiencia en el medio rural," *Revista mexicana de educación,* I (Aug. 1940).

Galarza, Ernesto. "New Molds for Latin American Youth," in *Some Educational and Anthropological Aspects of Latin America,* University of Texas Latin-American Studies, No. 5 (Austin, Tex., 1948).

Gamio, Manuel. "Las pretendidas razas inferiores," *El Universal,* March 4, 1921.

————. "Static and Dynamic Values in the Indigenous Past of America," *Hispanic American Historical Review,* XXIII (Aug. 1943).

García Ruiz, Ramón. "Sugestiones para la enseñanza de la geografía en la escuela primaria," *Revista mexicana de educación,* I (Aug. 1940).

Gazol Santafé, Antonio. "El crédito al campo," *El Nacional,* Feb. 1, 1959.

Gruening, Ernest H. "Emerging Mexico," *Nation,* CXX (June 10, 1925).

————. "The New Era in Mexico," *Century Magazine,* CIX (March 1925).

Hernández, Teodoro. "El problema agrario obligado antecedente de la industrialización," *El Universal,* April 26, 1959.

León-Portilla, Miguel. "Panorama de la población indígena de México," *América indígena,* XIX (Jan. 1959).

Lobato, Ernesto. "La burocracia mexicana," *Problemas de México,* I (Oct. 1, 1958).

Lombardo Toledano, Humberto. "Proyecto de reorganización de la Secretaría de Educación Pública," *Revista mexicana de educación,* I (Dec. 1940).

López Rosada, Diego G., and Juan Noyola Vásquez. "Los salarios reales en México, 1939-1950," *El trimestre económico,* XVIII (April-June 1951).

Mendoza Rivera, Ignacio. "Honda crisis de la educación en México," *Problemas de México,* I (Oct. 1, 1958).

Morales Jiménez, Alberto. "Las escuelas rudimentarias: Antecedentes de la escuela rural," *Revista mexicana de educación,* I (Nov. 1940).

Mújica Montoya, Emilio. "Los salarios en la economía nacional," *Investigación económica,* XVI, No. 4 (1956).

Negri, Ramón P. de. "La tragedia biológica y social de nuestros indios," *Excelsior*, Dec. 10, 1936.

Ramírez, Rafael. "La política educativa del nuevo trato hacia los indios," *Revista de educación*, IV (Aug. 1939).

Ramírez Altamirano, Alfonso. "La unificación y coordinación de los sistemas educativos," *Revista mexicana de educación*, I (Dec. 1940).

Redfield, Robert. "The Indian in Mexico," *Annals of the American Academy of Political and Social Science*, CCVIII (March 1940).

Román Díaz de León, Manuel. "Miseria y analfabetismo," *El Nacional*, Oct. 17, 1953.

Rubín de la Borbolla, Daniel F. "El problema indígena de México," *Educación*, I (June 1940).

Salas Anzures, Miguel. "Las nuevas formas socio-políticas y el programa de la escuela rural," *El Nacional*, March 29, 1948.

Samayoa, Mariano. "Comunidades de promoción indígena," *Boletín indigenista*, XI (Sept. 1951).

Sánchez, George I. "Education," *Annals of the American Academy of Political and Social Science*, CCVIII (March 1940).

———. "Education in Mexico," in Arthur Henry Moehlman and Joseph S. Roucek, eds. *Comparative Education* (New York, 1951).

Santos Valdés, José. "El artículo tercero constitucional," *Magisterio: Revista de orientación pedagógica*, I (April 1959).

Schaeffer, Wendel Karl Gordon. "El control del aparato jurídico y de los sindicatos de burócratas," *Problemas de México*, I (Oct. 1, 1958).

Silva Herzog, Jesús. "La revolución mexicana ya es un hecho histórico," *Cuadernos americanos*, XLVII (Sept.-Oct. 1949).

Sindicato Nacional de Trabajadores de la Educación. "El problema de la educación extraescolar," *Problemas educativos de México*, I (April 1958).

Tannenbaum, Frank. "Agrarismo, Indianismo, y Nacionalismo," *Hispanic American Historical Review*, XXIII (Aug. 1943).

———. "The Miracle School," *Century Magazine*, CVI (Aug. 1923).

Uhl, Alexander H. "The 19th Century Comes to Mexico," *New Republic*, CXVI (May 5, 1947).

Villarriel Castillo, Carlos. "Consideraciones sociológicas sobre la educación en México," *El Nacional*, Nov. 24, 1958.

BOOKS

Alvarez Barret, Luis. *La obra educativa de don Rafael Ramírez*. Mexico, 1959.

Anguiano Equihua, Victoriano. *Lázaro Cárdenas: Su feudo y la política nacional*. Mexico, 1951.

Ateneo Nacional Agronómico. *Problemas agrícolas actuales.* Mexico, 1955.

Bailey, Helen Miller. *Santa Cruz of the Etla Hills.* Gainesville, Fla., 1958.

Balderrama, Luis C. *El clero y el gobierno de México.* 2 vols. Mexico, 1927.

Barranco, Manuel. *Mexico: Its Educational Problems—Suggestions for Their Solution.* New York, 1915.

Beals, Carleton. *Glass Houses: Ten Years of Free-Lancing.* Philadelphia, 1938.

————. *Mexican Maze.* Philadelphia, 1931.

————. *Porfirio Díaz: Dictator of Mexico.* Philadelphia, 1932.

Beals, Ralph L. *Cherán: A Sierra Tarascan Village.* Washington, D. C., 1946.

Beteta, Ramón, ed. *Economic and Social Program of Mexico (A Controversy).* Mexico, 1935.

————. *Pensamiento y dinámica de la revolución mexicana: Antología de documentos políticosociales.* Mexico, 1950.

Bremauntz, Alberto. *La educación socialista en México (antecedentes y fundamentos de la reforma de 1934).* Mexico, 1943.

Cabrera, Luis. *Veinte años después.* 3rd ed. Mexico, 1938.

Caso, Antonio. *México (apuntamientos de cultura patria).* Mexico, 1943.

Ceniceros, José Angel. *Educación y mexicanidad.* Mexico, 1958.

————. *Nuestra constitución política y la educación mexicana.* Mexico, 1955.

Chávez Orozco, Luis. *La escuela mexicana y la sociedad mexicana.* Mexico, 1940.

————. *Las instituciones democráticas de los indígenas mexicanos en la época colonial.* Mexico, 1943.

Cline, Howard F. *The United States and Mexico.* Cambridge, Mass., 1953.

Cook, Katherine M. *The House of the People: An Account of Mexico's New Schools of Action.* Washington, D. C., 1932.

Correa, Eduardo J. *El balance del Avila Camachismo.* Mexico, 1946.

————. *El balance del Cardenismo.* Mexico, 1941.

Crawford, William Rex. *A Century of Latin-American Thought.* Cambridge, Mass., 1944.

Cumberland, Charles C. *Mexican Revolution, Genesis under Madero.* Austin, Tex., 1952.

Daniels, Josephus. *Shirt-Sleeve Diplomat.* Chapel Hill, N. C., 1947.

Dewey, John. *Impressions of Soviet Russia and the Revolutionary World: Mexico—China—Turkey.* New York, 1929.

Dulles, John W. F. *Yesterday in Mexico: A Chronicle of the Revolution, 1919-1936.* Austin, Tex., 1961.

Flandrau, Charles M. *Viva Mexico!* New York, 1917.

Gallo Martínez, Victor. *Estructura económica de la educación mexicana.* 2 vols. Mexico, 1959.

Gamio, Manuel. *Consideraciones sobre el problema indígena.* Mexico, 1948.

————. *Forjando patria (pro nacionalismo).* Mexico, 1916.

García Romero, Luis. *La enseñanza del alfabeto, un deber.* Mexico, 1944.

García Ruiz, Ramón. *Hombres y rutas de México.* Guadalajara, Mexico, 1953.

García Téllez, Ignacio. *Socialización de la cultura: Seis meses de acción educativa.* Mexico, 1935.

Gaxiola, Francisco J. *El presidente Rodríguez (1932-1934).* Mexico, 1938.

Geisert, Harold L. *Population Problems in Mexico and Central America.* Washington, D. C., 1959.

Gill, Tom. *Land Hunger in Mexico.* Washington, D. C., 1951.

González Navarro, Moisés. *El porfiriato: La vida social,* in *Historia moderna de México,* ed. Daniel Cosío Villegas [Vol. V]. Mexico, 1957.

González Roa, Fernando. *The Mexican People and Their Detractors.* New York, [1916].

Gruening, Ernest H. *Mexico and Its Heritage.* New York, 1928.

Gunther, John. *Inside Latin America.* New York, 1941.

Herring, Hubert C., and Katharine Terrill, eds. *The Genius of Mexico.* New York, 1931.

————, and Herbert Weinstock, eds. *Renascent Mexico.* New York, 1935.

Hübner, Manuel E. *México en marcha.* Santiago, Chile, 1936.

Hughes, Lloyd H. *The Mexican Cultural Mission Programme.* Paris, 1950.

Infield, Henrik F., and Koka Freier. *People in Ejidos: A Visit to the Co-operative Farms of Mexico.* New York, 1954.

Johnson, John J. *Political Change in Latin America: The Emergence of the Middle Sectors.* Stanford, Calif., 1958.

Johnston, Marjorie C. *Education in Mexico.* Washington, D. C., 1956.

Kirk, Betty. *Covering the Mexican Front: The Battle of Europe versus America.* Norman, Okla., 1942.

Kluckhohn, Frank L. *The Mexican Challenge.* New York, 1939.

Kneller, George F. *The Education of the Mexican Nation.* New York, 1951.

Lewis, Oscar. *Five Families: Mexican Case Studies in the Culture of Poverty.* New York, 1959.

————. *México desde 1940.* Mexico, 1958.

Lombardo Toledano, Vicente. *Una ojeada a la crisis de la educación en México.* Mexico, 1958.

McBride, George M. *The Land Systems of Mexico.* New York, 1923.

McCluskey, Neil G. *Catholic Viewpoint on Education.* Garden City, N. Y., 1959.

Macfarland, Charles S. *Chaos in Mexico: The Conflict of Church and State.* New York, 1935.

Magdaleno, Mauricio. *Narciso Bassols: Notas para una fisonomía política.* Mexico, 1934.

Mejía Zúñiga, Raúl. *Moisés Sáenz: Educador de Mexico.* Mexico, 1956.

Méndez Bravo, Alberto. *La escuela rural mejicana.* Santiago, Chile, 1929.

Mendieta y Núñez, Lucio. *Valor económico y social de las razas indígenas de México.* Mexico, 1938.

Millán, Verna Carleton. *Mexico Reborn.* Boston, 1939.

Mosk, Sanford A. *Industrial Revolution in Mexico.* Berkeley, Calif., 1950.

Murray, Robert Hammond, trans. and ed. *Mexico before the World: Public Documents and Addresses of Plutarco Elías Calles.* New York, 1927.

Palavicini, Félix F. *Historia de la constitución de 1917.* 2 vols. Mexico, 1938.

Pani, Alberto J. *Una encuesta sobre educación popular.* Mexico, 1918.

———. *La higiene en México.* Mexico, 1916.

———. *Mi contribución al nuevo régimen (1910-1933).* Mexico, 1936.

———. *On the Road to Democracy,* trans. J. Palomo Rincón. Mexico, 1918.

Partido Comunista. *Hacia una educación al servicio del pueblo.* Mexico, 1938.

Pfeffer, Leo. *Church, State, and Freedom.* Boston, 1953.

Pius XI, Pope. *Christian Education of Youth.* New York, 1936.

Portes Gil, Emilio. *The Conflict between the Civil Power and the Clergy.* Mexico, 1935.

———. *The Mexican Schools and the Peasantry.* Mexico, 1936.

Prewett, Virginia. *Reportage on Mexico.* New York, 1941.

Puig Casauranc, José M. *De nuestro México: Cosas sociales y aspectos políticos.* Mexico, 1926.

———. *Galatea rebelde a varios Pigmaliones: De Obregón a Cárdenas (antecedentes del fenómeno mexicano actual) (1938).* Mexico, 1938.

Ramos, Samuel. *Veinte años de educación en México.* Mexico, 1941.

Redfield, Robert. *Tepoztlán, a Mexican Village.* Chicago, 1930.

———. *A Village That Chose Progress: Chan Kom Revisited.* Chicago, 1950.

Rodman, Selden. *Mexican Journal: The Conquerors Conquered.* New York, 1958.

Rodríguez, Abelardo L. *A que debe tender el plan de los seis años.* Mexico, 1933.

Sáenz, Moisés. *Carapan: Bosquejo de una experiencia.* Lima, Peru, 1936.

———. *Mexico: An Appraisal and a Forecast.* New York, 1929.

———. *Reseña de la educación pública en México en 1927.* Mexico, 1928.

———, and Herbert I. Priestley. *Some Mexican Problems.* Chicago, 1926.

Sánchez, George I. *Mexico: A Revolution by Education.* New York, 1936.

Scott, Robert E. *Mexican Government in Transition.* Urbana, Ill., 1959.

Senior, Clarence O. *Democracy Comes to a Cotton Kingdom: The Story of Mexico's La Laguna.* Mexico, 1940.

———. *Land Reform and Democracy.* Gainesville, Fla., 1958.

Silva Herzog, Jesús. *El agrarismo mexicano y la reforma agraria: Exposición y crítica.* Mexico, 1959.

———. *La revolución mexicana en crisis.* Mexico, 1944.

Simpson, Eyler N. *The Ejido: Mexico's Way Out.* Chapel Hill, N. C., 1937.

Sindicato Nacional de Trabajadores de la Educación. *Conferencia pedagógica.* Mexico, 1945.

Smith, Francis Hopkinson. *A White Umbrella in Mexico.* Boston, 1889.

Tannenbaum, Frank. *Mexico: The Struggle for Peace and Bread.* New York, 1950.

———. *Peace by Revolution: An Interpretation of Mexico.* New York, 1933.

Tirado Benedí, Domingo. *Problemas de la educación mexicana.* Mexico, 1955.

Torres Bodet, Jaime. *Educación mexicana: Discursos, entrevistas, mensajes.* Mexico, 1944.

Torres Quintero, Gregorio. *La instrucción rudimentaria en la república.* Mexico, 1913.

Townsend, William Cameron. *Lázaro Cárdenas, Mexican Democrat.* Ann Arbor, Mich., 1952.

Trend, John B. *Mexico, a New Spain with Old Friends.* Cambridge, Eng., 1940.

Tucker, William P. *The Mexican Government Today.* Minneapolis, Minn., 1957.

Turner, John K. *Barbarous Mexico.* Chicago, 1910.

Tweedie, Ethel B. *Mexico As I Saw It.* New York, 1901.

Vaillant, George C. *Aztecs of Mexico: Origin, Rise and Fall of the Aztec Nation.* Garden City, N. Y., 1941.

Vasconcelos, José, and Manuel Gamio. *Aspects of Mexican Civilization.* Chicago, 1926.

———. *Breve historia de México.* 5th ed. Mexico, 1944.

———. *El desastre: Tercera parte de Ulises criollo, continuación de La tormenta.* Mexico, 1938.

———. *La raza cósmica: Misión de la raza iberoamericana, Argentina y Brazil.* Mexico, 1948.

Vera Estañol, Jorge. *Carranza and His Bolshevik Regime.* Los Angeles, 1920.

Weyl, Nathaniel, and Sylvia Weyl. *The Reconquest of Mexico: The Years of Lázaro Cárdenas.* London, 1939.

Whetten, Nathan L. *Rural Mexico.* Chicago, 1948.

NEWSPAPERS AND PERIODICALS

Files of the following were consulted:

El Demócrata	*Novedades*
Excelsior	*El Popular*
El Nacional	*Tiempo*
New York *Times*	*El Universal*

UNPUBLISHED MATERIALS

Bassols, Narciso, to Moisés Sáenz. Mexico City, Feb. 4, 1933. Unpublished letter in private collection.

Castro, Angélica. "Experiencia con la utilización de la lengua indígena en la enseñanza en el Valle del Mezquital." Unpublished manuscript. Mexico, 1958.

INDEX

Acaparadores, 57, 63, 202, 213
Actopan, Hidalgo, 93
Agrarian Department, 56, 212
Agrarian program. *See* Land
Agriculture: collective farms, xiii, 53, 63, 69 (*see also* Collectivism); cooperatives, xiii, 47, 48, 57, 63, 100, 155, 213, 214; description of conditions, 12, 16-17, 22, 71; agricultural schools, 51, 99, 104-117. *See also Ejidos;* Hacienda system
Agronomists, 95, 97, 98, 106, 109
Aguascalientes (state), 16, 209
Aguilera Dorante, Mario, 201, 202
Aguirre Beltrán, Gonzalo, 152
Alemán, Miguel: characteristics of his administration, 68, 70, 71, 120; land policies, 68, 69, 212, 215; biographical note, 70; literacy program, 82, 168; school-building program, 84, 85, 86; educational expenditures, 122, 206-207; policies regarding Indians, 139, 151, 152, 153, 157
Alfabetizadores, 166, 168
Almazán, Juan Andreu, 74, 77
Alvarez Barret, Luis, 102, 114, 203-204
Anticlericalism. *See* Catholic Church: anticlericalism
Arrequín, Enrique, 73, 74
Articles of the Constitution. *See* Constitution of 1917
Assembly of Philologists and Linguists, 162
Ateneo de la Juventud, 26
Attorney's Office for Communities (*Procuraduría de Pueblos*), 142, 144, 151, 155
Avila Camacho, Manuel: political career, 61, 70, 71, 77; land policies, 68, 70, 71; educational appointments, 72, 73, 75, 76; educational policies and program, 77, 78, 79, 85, 86, 122, 203; actions affecting unions, 120; policies regarding Indians, 139, 150-151; literacy programs, 165, 168; actions in church-state conflict, 192, 193
Azcualtipan, Hidalgo, 92
Aztecs, 10, 11, 180
Azuela, Mariano, 123

Bajío of Guanajuato, 16
Balderrama, Luis C., cited, 179
Banco Ejidal, 53, 145, 155. *See also Ejidos: ejidal* banks

Baquiriachi, Chihuahua, 156
Basauri, Carlos, 160
Bassols, Narciso: career summarized, 50-52; educational views, 50-52, 75, 106, 108, 195, 200; developments in rural education, 59, 64, 78, 97, 99, 100-101, 103, 110-111, 112-113, 118; differences with teachers' unions, 119; changes in Indian schools, 148, 149-150; school-church conflict, 185, 189-190; mentioned, 54, 55, 72, 74, 86, 114, 128, 210, 213
Beals, Carleton, cited, 180, 211
Beals, Ralph L., cited, 130, 141
Belmar, Francisco, 20
Bergsonism, 128
Beteta, Ramón, 132, 174, 182, 184, 186, 198-199, 213
Birth control, 18, 51-52, 194. *See also* Population
Bonilla, Guillermo, 101-102, 103
Braceros, 67, 211
Bremauntz, Alberto, 79, 185
Brigades of Indian Improvement, 155, 156
Bureau of Anthropology, 29

Cabrera, Luis, cited, 13, 53, 127, 159
Calle Argentina, 35, 37, 60, 72, 74, 75, 76, 201. *See also* Ministry of Public Education
Calles, Plutarco Elías: political career, 25, 26, 45, 46, 47, 50, 52-53, 118; involved in church-state conflict, 32, 174, 181, 187, 190, 192; education under, 43, 44, 59, 71, 78, 139; relationships with Cárdenas, 52-53, 192; mentioned, 29, 38, 51
Campeche (state), 15, 114, 209
Campesinas (Escuelas Regionales Campesinas), 110-113, 114
Cano, Celerino, 137, 208, 210
Capitalism, 25, 47, 49
Carapan, Michoacán, 55, 142, 204
Cárdenas, Lázaro: political career, 48, 61, 62, 66, 70, 74, 77; policies regarding Indians, 48, 53, 54, 138, 139, 142, 144, 145, 150, 151, 161, 162; rural programs, 52-55, 57-58, 66, 101, 191, 212, 213, 214, 215; educational policies and programs, 52-55, 57-58, 80, 86, 101, 112, 117, 119, 191, 195, 202, 212, 213; land policies and programs, 53, 56-57, 62, 64, 68, 69, 101; attitude toward

religion, 61, 191, 192, 193; literacy program, 81, 82, 83, 161, 162; cooperation with unions, 119, 120; educational expenditures, 122, 206; mentioned, 72, 87, 186, 200, 210

Cardenistas, 81, 86, 112, 114, 139, 150

Carranza, Venustiano, 20, 21, 25, 32, 35, 40, 139, 184, 188

Casa del Estudiante Indígena (House of the Indian Student), 139, 146-148, 149

Casa del Pueblo (House of the People), 37, 46

Caso, Alfonso, 143, 153, 156, 165

Castillo, Ignacio M. del, 164

Castro, Angélica, 170

Catholic Church: in colonial era, xi, 11, 12, 19, 27, 90-91, 133, 161, 176, 177; anticlericalism and church-state conflict, xi, xii, 32, 48, 60-61, 76, 78, 132-133, 173-176, 178-182, 183-194; opposition to birth control, 18, 50, 51-52; Catholic Church and education, 32, 49-50, 61, 75, 76, 126, 155, 165, 175-177, 193, 194

Cedillo, Saturnino, 192

Ceniceros, José Angel, 73, 76-77, 87

Centers of Indian Education. *See Centros de Educación Indígena*

Central Agricultural Schools. *See Centrales*

Centrales (Escuelas Centrales Agrícolas), 106-109, 110, 111, 114

Centros. See Centros de Educación Indígena

Centros Coordinadores Indígenas (Indian Coordinating Centers), 153, 156, 168, 169

Centros de Educación Indígena (Centers of Indian Education), 145, 148-150, 151, 152

Cerro Hueco, Chiapas, 105

Cervantes Saavedra, Miguel de, 27

Chamber of Commerce, 24, 174

Champusco, Puebla, 107

Chamulas, 57, 145

Chávez Orozco, Luis, 54, 61, 82, 135, 144, 161, 162, 196, 201

Chiapas (state), 14, 15, 57, 105, 114, 153, 169, 198, 200, 201

Chichimecas, 10

Chiconautla, Mexico, 199

Chicontepec zone, 156

Chihuahua (state), 114, 148, 153, 154, 169

Chinantec language, 163

Church-state conflict. *See* Catholic Church: anticlericalism

Circuit-school plan, 39, 85

Civil Service Act of 1938, 119

Civil Service Act of 1941, 120

Cline, Howard, cited, 9, 10, 12, 24, 66, 210

CNC (National Confederation of Peasants), 54, 85

Coahuila (state), 35, 53, 57

Cobos, Bernardo, 213

Coeducation, 41, 50, 77, 78-79, 151, 193

Colima (state), 198

Collectivism, 45, 46, 48, 51, 118, 132, 195. *See also* Agriculture: collective farms

Collier, John, cited, 192

Comalapa, Chiapas, 200

Comaltepec, Oaxaca, 38

Communism, 60, 61, 72, 77, 119, 192

Communities of Indian Improvement, 152

Comte, Auguste, 18, 128, 131

Comunidades de Promoción Indígena, 152

Confederación Regional Obrera Mexicana (CROM), 118

Conquest, xi, xii, 11-12, 16, 29, 126, 142, 178, 179

Constitutionalists, 184

Constitution of 1857, 14, 78

Constitution of 1917: framing, scope, and application, xii, xiv, 20-21, 22, 208, 215; land reform, xii, 18, 22, 123, 182, 183; anticlericalism, 180, 183-185, 188; Article 3: 20-21, 32, 48-50, 60, 76, 77, 78-79, 119, 132, 179, 183-186, 187-188, 189, 193, 204; Article 5: 187; Article 27: 69, 186, 187, 212; Article 73: 21, 32-33; Article 123: 40, 58, 186, 210; Article 130: 187

Cook, Katherine M., cited, 96, 105, 149, 157

Coolidge, Calvin, 23

Cooperatives. *See* Agriculture: cooperatives

Cortés, Hernando, 11, 12, 128

Council of Indian Languages, 162, 165

Creel, Chihuahua, 155

Creoles, 13

Cristeros, 97, 190-191

CROM (*Confederación Regional Obrera Mexicana*), 118

CTM (Mexican Confederation of Workers), 79, 213

Cuernavaca, Morelos, 180

Cuicuilco (pyramid), 10
Cultural missions, 29, 31, 91-103, 110, 117, 139, 145, 151, 190-191
Cusarare, Chihuahua, 155

Daniels, Josephus, 60, 189
D'Annunzio, Gabriele, 33
Dante Alighieri, 27
Darío, Rubén, 74
Darwin, Charles, 7
Departamento de Asuntos Indígenas. See Department of Indian Affairs
Department of Agricultural and Normal Education, 99, 100, 110
Department of Cultural Missions, 31, 93-94, 99, 101, 139
Department of Indian Affairs, 54, 57, 139, 142, 143-145, 150, 151, 152, 153, 161, 162. *See also* Office of Indian Affairs
Department of Indian Education, 139, 145
Department of Irrigation, 54, 57, 145
Department of Labor, 58
Department of Public Health, 57, 100
Department of Rural Schools, 31, 52, 58
Depression of the 1930's, 23, 45, 46, 122, 184, 185
Dewey, John, 27, 31, 32, 37, 39, 51, 118, 138, 187, 195
Dialectical materialism, 49
Díaz, Porfirio: conditions under, 3, 4, 5, 9, 12, 14, 28, 36, 125, 178, 182; education under, 8, 36, 40, 122, 215; fall of, 18, 33; mentioned, 20, 24, 87, 121, 128, 131, 152, 216
Díaz Soto y Gama, Antonio, 131, 211
Dirección General de Asuntos Indígenas. See Office of Indian Affairs
Durango (state), 53, 57, 82

Each-one-teach-one programs, 81, 200
Education. *See* Rural education
Ejidos: pre-Columbian land system, xiii, 18, 53, 123; *ejidal* banks, xiii, 53, 54, 107, 109, 145, 155; policies and attitudes toward, 24, 53, 54, 62, 68, 69, 132; schools on, 63, 204-205, 206, 213; education for sons of *ejidatarios*, 105, 107, 110; *ejido* at Cusarare, 155; mentioned, 48, 113, 116, 151, 195, 196, 214, 215
El Mexe, Hidalgo, 114
Enlightenment, influence of the, 180
Erongarícuaro, Michoacán, 105, 164
Escobar, Gonzalo, 45

Escuela Normal Rural, Tacámbaro, Michoacán, 104
Escuelas Centrales Agrícolas, 106-109, 110, 111, 114
Escuelas Prácticas de Agricultura, 114, 115, 116
Escuelas Regionales Campesinas, 110-113, 114
Escuelas Vocacionales de Agricultura para Indígenas, 150, 151
European influence, 4, 11, 12, 13. *See also* Europeanists; Spanish influence
Europeanists, 124-126, 127-128, 129, 136

Fascism, 75, 191
Federal District, 21, 86, 107, 198, 207
Federal Institute for the Training of Teachers, 117
Federal Literacy Law of 1944, 82
Flandrau, Charles Macomb, cited, 4, 6
Flores Magón, Ricardo, 20
Foreign capital, xii, 24, 25, 47, 49, 66, 70
Franciscans, 161
Franco, Francisco, 60, 75, 85, 191
Freier, Koka, cited, 204-206
French Jacobin principles, 183
French Revolution, 184
Fuente, Julio de la, 152
Fuentes, Carlos, 68

Galarza, Ernesto, 87
Gallo Martínez, Victor, 197, 199, 207
Gamio, Manuel: "integral education," 29, 43, 56, 112, 153, 156, 203; work at San Juan de Teotihuacán, 43-44, 134, 138-139; qualifications for rural teachers, 88; Indians and *indigenismo*, 129, 136, 137, 143; views on pre-Conquest culture and religion, 133, 177, 179; dismissal from Ministry of Education, 139
Gante, Pedro de, 19
García Téllez, Ignacio, 54, 186
Garrido Canabal, Tomás, 185, 192
General Office of Literacy and Out-of-School Education, 82, 102
General Office of Primary Rural and Urban Education, 58
Gobineau, Joseph Arthur de, 7, 27
Gómez Farías, Valentín, 14, 20
Gómez Morín, Manuel, 199
González Navarro, Moisés, cited, 5, 6
González Roa, Fernando, cited, 125
Gruening, Ernest, cited, 3, 5, 7, 9, 26, 38, 41, 42, 43, 44, 59, 82, 173, 187, 189
Guachochi, Chihuahua, 153, 155

Gual Vidal, Manuel, 73, 76-77, 86, 121
Guanajuato (state), 16, 30, 107
Guerrero (state), 15, 16, 105, 149, 198, 199, 201
Gunther, John, cited, 70

Hacienda system: breaking up of, xii, 18, 53-54, 62, 182, 183; conditions on haciendas, 4-7, 22, 45; origin of, 12; policies and attitudes toward, 24, 47; schools in, 58; mentioned, 16, 159, 191, 195, 212, 216. *See also* Peonage
Hamilton, Alexander, 23
Harding, Warren G., 23, 26
Hidalgo (state), 16, 56, 91, 92, 93, 114, 145, 166, 201, 209
Hidalgo y Costilla, Miguel, 131, 178
Hitler, Adolf, 85, 191
Homer, 27
House of the Indian Student (*Casa del Estudiante Indígena*), 139, 146-148, 149
House of the People (*Casa del Pueblo*), 37, 46
Huerta, Adolfo de la, 26, 32
Huerta, Victoriano, 35, 40, 129, 178, 188
Hughes, Lloyd H., cited, 92, 102, 103
Huicholes, 146
Humboldt, Alexander von, cited, 17

Ibarra, Guillermo, 208
Illiteracy. *See* Literacy
Independence (1821), xi, 3, 12, 13, 20, 178
Indian Coordinating Centers (*Centros Coordinadores Indígenas*), 153, 156, 168, 169
Indianistas and *indianismo*, 54, 124, 129-134, 140-141, 142-144, 145, 150-151, 179, 180. *See also* Indigenistas and *indigenismo*
Indians: language problems and programs, xii, 158-172 (*see also* Literacy); colonial era and earlier, 11, 12, 13, 19; place in society, 13, 14, 30, 123, 124; programs for, 33, 34, 54, 142-157, 216; Europeanist attitude toward, 124-128, 136; *indianista* views on, 129-132, 134, 141; *indigenista* views on, 134-138, 139-140, 141; mentioned, 24, 48, 51, 53, 75, 90. *See also* names of Indian groups
Indigenistas and *indigenismo*, 134-141. *See also* Indianistas and *indianismo*
Industry and industrialization, xii, 3-4, 17, 62, 65-66, 70, 71, 87, 137, 140, 211

Infield, Henrik F., cited, 204-206
Institute for Indian Literacy (*Instituto de Alfabetización Indígena*), 166, 168-169, 170, 171
Institute for Social Action, 100. *See also* Cultural missions
Institutional Party of the Revolution (PRI), 66
Instituto de Alfabetización Indígena. *See* Institute for Indian Literacy
Instituto Nacional Indigenista. *See* National Indianist Institute
"Integral education," 43, 56, 112, 153, 156, 203
Inter-American Indianist Congress, 145
Isthmus of Tehuantepec, 15

Jalisco (state), 16
Jefferson, Thomas, 23, 130
Jesuits, 75, 155, 176, 193
Jiquilpan, Michoacán, 200
Juárez, Benito, 14, 20, 178, 214
Juaristas, 183
Juzgado de Indios, 142

Kikapoos, 145
Kirk, Betty, cited, 60, 73, 77, 192
Kneller, George F., cited, 114, 200, 203

Laguna region, 53, 63, 206, 215
Laguneros, 57
Land: ownership, xii-xiii, 5, 12, 14, 25, 45, 47, 68-69, 212; reform, xiv, 18, 23, 24-25, 53, 56, 64, 68-69, 132, 135, 145, 182, 183, 215, 216; laws of 1883 and 1894, 5; topography and water supply, 14-16, 54; mentioned, 3, 62, 101. *See also* Agriculture; *Ejidos*; Hacienda system
Languages. *See* Indians: language problems and programs; Literacy; Spanish influence: language; names of Indian languages
Las Casas, Bartolomé de, 131, 181
Lathrop, Maxwell D., 164
Law of Rudimentary Education, 33. *See also* Rudimentary-school experiment
Laws of the Indies, 12, 14, 142
Leo XIII, Pope, 193
León de la Barra, Francisco, 20, 33
Literacy: Indian languages and linguistic problems, xii, 10, 34, 83, 143, 155, 158-160, 161-165, 166, 172; illiteracy, xiv, 8, 18, 20, 34, 64, 81, 84, 170, 200-201, 216; Spanish language, 19, 33, 138, 156, 159, 166, 167; literacy programs,

76, 81-84, 155, 164-165, 167-172, 200, 215, 216; bilingual method, 154, 159-160, 161-166, 172

Lombardia region, 53

Lombardo Toledano, Vicente, 79, 197

López Mateos, Adolfo, 192, 196, 212, 216

Los Remedios, Hidalgo, 152

Lower California (state), 114

Lunacharsky, Anatol Vassilyevich, 33

Macfarland, Charles S., cited, 189

Madero, Francisco I., 18, 20, 24, 25, 26, 33, 35, 40

Magdalena, Sonora, 200

Martínez, José Luis, 207

Martínez, Luis M., 193

Marxism, 38, 49, 60, 61, 128, 132

Maximilian, emperor of Mexico, 178, 179

Mayas and Maya language, 10, 150, 158, 166, 168

Mazatecos, 153

Mendieta y Núñez, Lucio, cited, 144

Mesa Andraca, Manuel, 97-98, 99, 110, 111, 112

Mestizos, 13, 14, 125, 126-127, 129, 135, 157

Mexican Confederation of Workers (CTM), 79, 213

Mexican Institute of Linguistic Studies, 161

Mexican nationality, 12-13, 123-127, 129, 136-137

Mexico (state), 17, 83, 199

Mexico City, 10, 21, 51, 58, 60, 61, 81, 117

Mezquital region, 56, 57, 63, 145, 152, 156, 168, 170, 171, 205, 215

Michoacán (state), 15, 19, 53, 82, 92, 104, 105, 145, 162, 164, 200

Millán, Verna Carleton, cited, 27, 50, 61, 63, 189, 190

Ministry of Agriculture, 57, 100, 106, 145, 155

Ministry of Communications, 57, 100

Ministry of Public Education (also called Ministry of Education): organization and operation, xiii, 33, 35, 36, 44, 142, 189, 201-202, 204, 207, 208, 209, 216; administrators, 29, 30, 44, 73, 76, 77, 118, 139, 189, 201-202, 216; rural education, 43, 57, 58, 85, 99, 107, 139, 142, 150, 151; ideological conflict, 60-61, 73, 119, 132, 204; literacy programs, 84, 162, 168, 171, 201-202;

teachers and unions, 118-119, 121; Indians, 142, 145, 146, 150, 151; clerical conflict, 187, 188, 189, 192; mentioned, 180, 199. *See also* Calle Argentina

Ministry of Public Instruction and Justice, 8, 21

Ministry of Public Works, 145

Misión cultural. See Cultural missions

Misioneros (missionaries), 89-99, 201

Mixteca region, 98, 153

Mixtecas and Mixtec language, 150, 158, 163

Molina Enríquez, Andrés, cited, 7, 20

Montezuma II, 11, 126

Mora y del Río, José, 187

Morelia, Michoacán, 164

Morelos (state), 16, 91, 166, 193

Morelos y Pavón, José María, 131, 178

Morrow, Dwight, 24, 180-181, 190

Mosk, Sanford, cited, 65

Mújica, Francisco José, 183, 184

Mussolini, Benito, 181

Náhuatl groups and language, 150, 158, 159, 166, 168

Napoleon III, 20

National Agricultural College at Chapingo, 108

National Confederation of Indian Youth, 157

National Confederation of Parents of Families, 72

National Confederation of Peasants (CNC), 54, 85

National Indianist Institute, 140, 153, 155, 156, 157, 168, 169, 170, 216

Nationalists. *See Indianistas*

National Normal School, Mexico City, 116

National Polytechnic Institute, 62, 162

National Revolutionary Party (*Partido Nacional Revolucionario*), 46, 52, 66, 185. *See also* Six-Year Plan of the PNR

National Student Federation, 115

National Syndicate of Teachers (SNTE), 79, 83, 120-121

National University, 32, 89, 161, 162

Nayarit (state), 105

Negroes, 13

New Deal experiment, 47, 140

Normales, 94, 104-106, 107, 109, 110, 111, 113, 114-116, 117, 156

Normal schools, 89, 90, 99, 101, 102, 104, 216. *See also* Cultural missions; *Normales*

Northern Dynasty (northerners), xiv, 22-24, 26, 39, 46, 47, 52, 72, 128
Nuestra Señora de la Encarnación (convent), 35
Nuevo León (state), 105

Oaxaca (state), 15, 16, 38, 82, 98, 153, 169, 198, 201
Obregón, Alvaro: regime of, 25, 26, 29, 142; anecdote, 28; education under, 36, 40, 121-122, 139, 187; mentioned, 31, 52, 71, 87
Office of Agricultural Education, 116
Office of Higher Education and Scientific Research, 165
Office of Indian Affairs, 151, 152, 154, 155, 156-157, 216. See also Department of Indian Affairs
Office of Indian Culture and Rural Education, 142, 146
Office of In-Service Training of Teachers, 197
Office of Rudimentary Instruction, 33. See also Rudimentary-school experiment
Oil companies, expropriation of, 60, 61, 101, 145
Orozco, José Clemente, 28-29, 123
Ortega y Gasset, José, 27
Ortiz Rubio, Pascual, 26, 46, 48
Otomíes and Otomí language, 56, 145, 150, 152-153, 156, 158, 159, 163, 166, 168, 171

Padilla, Ezequiel, 46, 47
PAN (Partido de Acción Nacional), 199
Pani, Alberto, 26, 33, 34-35, 129
Papaloapan basin, 153
Paracho, Michoacán, 164
Partido de Acción Nacional (PAN), 199
Partido de la Revolución Mexicana (PRM), 61
Partido Nacional Revolucionario (National Revolutionary Party), 46, 52, 66, 185. See also Six-Year Plan of the PNR
Patrimonio Indígena del Valle del Mezquital, 156, 168
Pátzcuaro, Michoacán, 145, 164
Peonage, 5-7, 14, 17, 45, 47, 54, 182
Pérez Galdós, Benito, 27-28
Pfeffer, Leo, cited, 175, 176
Pius XI, Pope, 175

Plan de Ayala, 20
PNR (Partido Nacional Revolucionario), 46, 52, 66, 185. See also Six-Year Plan
Population: distribution, 15, 124; problems, 17, 18, 51-52, 194, 198-199, 208
Portes Gil, Emilio, 26, 182, 186, 190
Positivism, 7, 26, 28, 180
Prácticas de Agricultura (Escuelas Prácticas de Agricultura), 114, 115, 116
Preparatoria, 30, 89, 108
PRI (Institutional Party of the Revolution), 66
PRM (Partido de la Revolución Mexicana), 61
Procuraduría de Pueblos (Attorney's Office for Communities), 142, 144, 151, 155
Protestantism, 30, 175, 176, 187, 188
Puebla (state), 16, 105, 107, 166
Puig Casauranc, José Manuel, 26, 29, 119
Pulque, 7, 8-9, 38, 42, 55-56, 121

Querétaro (state), 16; (city), 20, 21, 183, 184
Quintana Roo (state), 114
Quiroga, Vasco de, 19, 29

Races. See Mexican nationality
Ramírez, Rafael: contribution to rural education, 29, 31-32, 37-38, 52, 91, 92, 93, 94, 203; career, 31, 52, 55, 94; educational philosophy, 31-32, 56, 79, 128; programs for Indians, 146, 148, 159; mentioned, 89, 97, 193, 195, 201
Rébsamen, Enrique C., 104
Redfield, Robert, cited, 128, 131, 135
Reforma, La, xi, 14, 23, 128, 131, 178, 183, 188, 191
Regionales Campesinas. See Escuelas Regionales Campesinas
Regional Peasant Schools, 99, 101
Revolution (1910-1920): ideology and reforms of, xii, 18, 19, 53, 130, 142, 180, 182, 183; implications for education, xiii, xiv, 3, 19, 57, 89, 103, 174, 185, 186, 195, 212, 213; conservatives' interpretation of, 21, 23, 25; promises unfulfilled, 45, 69, 87, 181; end of aggressive phase, 66, 71; nationalism of, 178-179; mentioned, 20, 26, 65, 70, 123, 126, 132, 140, 191
Rivera, Diego, 28, 123, 180-181
Rodman, Selden, cited, 156, 210

Rodríguez, Abelardo, 26, 46, 48, 50, 52
Rolland, Romain, 27
Romero, José Rubén, 131
Rubín de la Borbolla, Daniel F., cited, 137
Rudimentary-school experiment, 33-36, 159
Ruiz Cortines, Adolfo, 68, 70-71, 72, 77, 84, 85, 86, 122, 151, 168
Ruiz y Flores, Leopoldo, 187
Rural education: origins of rural school system, xii, 3, 20-21, 22, 25, 29, 32-37; federal vs. local support and control, xiii, 20-21, 35-36, 38-39, 40, 56, 58-60, 85, 86, 89, 96, 207, 208, 209-210; philosophies and policies, xiv, 18-19, 28-29, 30-32, 34-35, 38, 43, 45, 46, 49-50, 51, 53, 56, 61, 71-77, 78-81, 127-129, 135, 137-138, 195-196; building of schools, xiv, 48, 64, 84-86, 122, 158, 216; evaluation of, xiv, 39-43, 55, 63, 86-87, 140-141, 156-157, 196-216; before 1920, 8, 19-20, 29, 154-155; educational budgets and expenditures, 8, 38, 40, 44, 48, 59, 64, 72, 86, 122, 147, 156, 199, 206-210; experiments and programs, 33-35, 37-39, 43-44, 46-47, 48, 50, 56-58, 92-93, 134, 138-140, 146-150, 151, 152-153, 155-156; curriculum, 38, 57-58, 80-81, 137-138, 149, 151, 196; statistics about schools and schoolchildren, 40-41, 42, 63, 86, 147, 156, 197-198, 199-200, 208, 215-216; school-church issues, 49-50, 75, 76, 78, 132-133, 173-194. *See also* Cultural missions; Literacy; Teachers
Russia. *See* Soviet Union

Sáenz, Moisés: development of rural schools, 19, 37-38, 39, 55, 93, 204; career, 29-31, 44, 52, 55, 139; educational philosophy and policies, 30-31, 32, 46, 55, 78, 81, 93; programs for Indians and appreciation of their culture, 30, 38, 123, 129-130, 133, 139, 142, 146, 161, 177; views on religion, 30, 133, 177, 179, 189; death of, 74; teachers and teacher training, 104, 117, 118, 122; mentioned, 4, 50, 54, 85, 86, 97, 187, 195, 201
Samayoa, Mariano, 152
San Andrés Cuamilpa, Tlaxcala, 42
Sánchez, George I., cited, 87, 90, 94, 95, 96, 101, 108, 111-112, 146, 174
Sánchez, Graciano, 54, 144, 161
Sánchez Pontón, Luis, 72-73, 74, 75, 190, 193

San Gabrielito, Guerrero, 149, 157
San Juan de Letrán (school), 19
San Juan de Teotihuacán, Mexico, 43-44, 134, 138-139, 199
San Luis Acatlán, Guerrero, 199
San Luis Potosí (state), 16
San Pedro Arriba, Mexico, 83
Santa Anna, Antonio López de, 20, 178
Santa Justina Ecatepec, Tlaxcala, 41-42
Sapir, Edward, 162
Sarmiento, Domingo Faustino, 27
School of Action, 37-38, 42, 46, 55, 203
"School of love," 75, 78, 118
Schools. *See* Agriculture: agricultural schools; Normal schools; Rural education
Scott, Robert E., cited, 207
Secretaría de Educación Pública. See Ministry of Public Education
Sierra, Justo, 8, 21, 33, 35
Silva Herzog, Jesús, 52, 67, 71, 87, 140, 211, 212, 215
Silva y Aceves, Mariano, 161
Simpson, Eyler N., cited, 5, 39, 63, 98, 108
Simpson, Lesley Byrd, cited, 16
Sinarquistas and *sinarquismo*, 60, 85, 190, 191-193
Siqueiros, David Alfaro, 29, 123
Six-Year Plan of the PNR, 46-48, 53, 62, 64, 77, 185
Smith, F. Hopkinson, cited, 6
SNTE (National Syndicate of Teachers), 79, 83, 120-121
Social Darwinism, 7, 18
Socialism and the socialist school, 46, 47, 48-49, 50, 51, 57, 58, 60, 61, 62, 63, 77, 78, 79-80, 129, 185, 186
Sociedad Indianista Mexicana, 20
Sonora (state), 15, 56, 105, 114, 145, 150, 200
Soviet Union (Russia), xii, 33, 46, 47, 119, 140, 161, 165, 184
Spanish influence: colonial era, 11-13, 29, 159, 176; racial stock, 12-13, 124; Hispanic culture, 28-29; language, 159-160, 161-162, 163, 166-167. *See also* Europeanists
Spencer, Herbert, 7, 128, 131
STERM (Union of Workers in Education of the Mexican Republic), 119-120
Strachey, John, 51
Summer Institute of Linguistics, University of Oklahoma, 164
Swadesh, Morris, 162, 164

Tabasco (state), 15, 114
Tacámbaro, Michoacán, 104
Tamatán, Tamaulipas, 107
Tamaulipas (state), 107, 114
Tannenbaum, Frank, cited, 15, 88, 89, 212
Tarahumara region, 153
Tarahumaras, 145, 148, 150, 153-154, 155, 193
Tarascan Project, 162, 163-165, 166, 168
Tarascans and Tarascan language, 10, 158, 159, 162, 163-164, 166, 168, 171
Teachers: need for and recruitment of, xii, 36-37, 89, 116-117; qualifications and duties, 41, 88, 109, 117-118; teaching conditions, 41, 59, 90, 118; salaries, 52, 59, 116, 118, 121-122, 171, 208-209; unions, 55, 61, 118-121, 202; training of, 76, 91-103, 104-106, 110, 111, 115, 146, 168
Tenochtitlán (now Mexico City), 10
Tepoztlán, Morelos, 128, 193
Tetelcingo, Morelos, 214
Texcoco (school), 19
Tixtla, Guerrero, 105
Tlaloc (Aztec god of rain), 15
Tlaltelolco (school), 19
Tlatlauqui, Puebla, 105
Tlaxcala (state), 16, 41
Tolstoy, Leo, 27
Torres, Elena, 94
Torres Bodet, Jaime: career, 73, 76, 196; educational policies, 73-74, 76, 80, 83, 85, 196, 208-209, 216; literacy programs, 81, 82, 83, 165; teacher training, 115, 117
Torres Quintero, Gregorio, 33, 35, 127, 159
Totonac language, 158, 163
Townsend, William Cameron, cited, 214
Trique language, 158
Tula, Hidalgo, 96
Turner, John Kenneth, cited, 6, 8, 9
Tweedie, Ethel, cited, 4, 6
Tzeltales, 150
Tzeltal-Tzotzil region, 153
Tzotziles, 150

Uhl, Alexander H., cited, 65, 67
Umán, Yucatán, 200
Union of Workers in Education of the Mexican Republic (STERM), 119-120

Unions, 118-121
United States, 24, 60, 61, 67, 140, 144, 173, 176, 179, 188, 211
Universidad Nacional. See National University

Vaillant, George C., cited, 11
Vasconcelos, José: concept of Mexican culture and nationality, 13, 124, 125, 126-128; philosophy of government, 26-27; philosophy and practice of education, 27-29, 46, 118, 160, 171, 195; compared with Sáenz and Ramírez, 30-31, 38; develops plan for federal program of education, 32-33, 35-36; inaugurates rural schools, 36-37, 158; adviser to Véjar Vásquez, 74, 75-76; coeducation under, 78; sponsors literacy campaign, 81-82, 83; *misioneros* and cultural missions, 89-91, 101; attitude toward Catholic Church and church schools, 173, 187, 188, 189; mentioned, 50, 58, 73, 86, 87, 146, 180, 201, 202, 204, 206, 209, 215
Vásquez, Genaro, cited, 177
Vásquez Vela, Gonzalo, 54
Véjar Vásquez, Octavio: educational policies, 73, 74-76, 78-79, 85, 102, 165, 188; favors Catholic Church, 75, 188, 190, 193; conflict with teachers' union, 120; Europeanist views, 124-125
Vera, Oscar, 197
Veracruz (state), 15, 16, 104, 169
Vera Estañol, Jorge, 129, 178, 188, 202
Villa, Francisco "Pancho," 25
Villa Alta, Tlaxcala, 41
Vocacionales, 150, 151
Vocational Schools of Agriculture for Indians. *See Vocacionales*

Weyl, Nathaniel and Sylvia, cited, 59
Whetten, Nathan L., cited, 102, 103, 192
World War II, 65, 66, 67

Yaqui region, 56
Yaquis, 24, 145, 150
Yoquivo, Chihuahua, 148
Yucatán (state), 6, 10, 14, 15, 53, 114, 150, 166, 200, 209

Zapata, Emiliano, 20, 21, 53, 130, 214
Zapatismo, 129
Zumárraga, Juan de, 19